Basic Equality and Discrimination
Reconciling Theory and Law

NICHOLAS MARK SMITH
Massey University, New Zealand

ASHGATE

Published by
Ashgate Publishing Limited
Wey Court East
Union Road
Farnham
Surrey, GU9 7PT
England

Ashgate Publishing Company
Suite 420
101 Cherry Street
Burlington
VT 05401-4405
USA

www.ashgate.com

British Library Cataloguing in Publication Data
Smith, Nicholas, 1954-
   Basic equality and discrimination : reconciling theory and
   law. -- (Applied legal philosophy)
   1. Equality before the law. 2. Discrimination--Law and
   legislation--Philosophy.
   I. Title II. Series
   340.1'1-dc22

Library of Congress Cataloging-in-Publication Data
Smith, Nicholas, 1954-
   Basic equality and discrimination : reconciling theory and law / by Nicholas Mark Smith.
      p. cm. -- (Applied legal philosophy)
   Includes index.
   ISBN 978-1-4094-2843-5 (hbk) -- ISBN 978-1-4094-2844-2 (ebk)
   1. Discrimination--Law and legislation. 2. Equality. I. Title.
   K3242.S627 2011
   342.08'5--dc22

2011004228

ISBN 9781409428435 (hbk)
ISBN 9781409428442 (ebk)

Printed and bound in Great Britain by the
MPG Books Group, UK

Contents

Preface

This is a book, another one, about equality. My interest in the subject developed, as it happened, in the context of moral disapproval of the system of South African racial inequality, in which I grew up. Although talking about politics was discouraged in some contexts it was never far from anyone's mind and the politics of race dominated public and private social thought in South Africa. The debates, apart from some in the academic literature, were not usually very intellectually sophisticated. They did not need to be: only the fear of social rejection, or worse forms of persecution, combined with intensive indoctrination, could make the harsh regime of segregation and deprivation that constituted apartheid seem morally sensible. Apartheid in South Africa, like the terrible discrimination that black people faced in America, or that experienced by many women in patriarchal dictatorships today, was a paradigm case of failing to treat people as equals. We honour Desmond Tutu and Martin Luther King, not for their ability to state basic moral axioms, but for their moral courage and integrity.

Once all the obviously bad options are discarded – apartheid, Jim Crow, oppression of women in its various forms – moral and legal thinking, about equality for groups that have been and are discriminated against, and for those which were not discriminated against, becomes harder. If Ronald Dworkin and Michael Walzer can disagree on the morality of affirmative action, it is not because either of them is on the side of racist injustice. In my adopted country, New Zealand for example, there are quandaries for egalitarians to ponder, as there are in other multicultural and cosmopolitan democracies, about equality, that are more subtle than the acceptance or rejection of crude racist or sexist theories. These questions, in liberal democratic societies, about discrimination and the ongoing effects of past discrimination, are harder to resolve, in my view, than is commonly thought.

Many thoughtful people have responded to the challenge and have written about discrimination and equality in recent times. I alluded to the multitude of books on equality in the first sentence of this preface. It seems to me that this fact dictates that one should, when writing on the subject, discuss that literature, engage with it, and agree or disagree with it often. At any rate, that is what I intend to do. The alternative, trying to be innovative by ignoring everyone else, the writers one agrees with and those whose views one clearly contradicts, seems odd to me – and it never works. A related point about freshness: the anti-discrimination enterprise is a quite modern one and while it is, for some reason, easier to appear original, when writing books, if one relies mostly on the thoughts of deceased writers, many of the thinkers whose views I agree with or contest, are still alive. It seemed risky to wait, and churlish to wish them an imminent departure.

This book's topic is quite general in one sense, but not in the sense that it tries to provide a complete theory of justice. My focus is jurisprudential, motivated primarily by an interest in discrimination law and a concern to better understand the conundrums which arise in the interpretation and application of that law. However, because that jurisprudence is dense and conflicted I have found it helpful to first consider equality as a moral and political concept, in the hope that a clearer understanding of the nature of the value – equality – will help us to understand the difficulties, or at least the nature of those difficulties, posed by constitutional and ordinary 'equality law'.

Equality's controversies are many and they are discussed in many different sorts of academic enquiry. There are many important aspects of what it means to treat people as equals that I do not deal with at all, or only make a few passing remarks about, in this book. Because my interest is ultimately in human rights law I say little about economic or distributional equality. I do not mean to suggest that questions about social and economic inequality are quite divorced from the concerns we evince when we try to do something about discrimination. We are, in part, concerned about discrimination because of its effects on people's material welfare.

Our moral concerns about discrimination cannot, however, simply be reduced to our concerns about economic justice, and the elimination of discrimination is not all that economic justice requires. Both are important and while both may be better understood in the light of a better understanding of equality in general, they are still to some extent separate topics. Discrimination law is also not the whole story about how equality inspires legal rules, and indeed legal systems, but it is discrimination law whose interpretation and application seems most vexed.

Although my concern to understand equality is jurisprudential, I do not provide a summary or a systematic analysis of discrimination law. Works that do are amongst those which have attracted my critical attention, although I do not mean to disparage them in general. They are attempting to do what is very difficult – state and explain the law in one of its most confusing departments. Such books would be easier to write, and more satisfying to read, if the law itself, and its purposes, were less obscure.

When I do mention specific laws or cases it might seem that I have disproportionately chosen North American, particularly United States, examples. That is true, but only because that region's cases are probably more well known, in jurisdictions around the world. To the charge that I am aiding and abetting jurisprudential imperialism, I plead guilty. But there are mitigating circumstances. To the extent that so many countries have adopted trends in North American human rights law or framed their own laws as revisions of the law of that region, that law inevitably serves as the logical starting point for discussion about affirmative action, indirect discrimination and so on. I also believe that those of us who are not North American find their discussions helpful because we do, and should have, similar political and moral concerns. I do not think equality is a worthwhile value in only some cultural settings. I think it has universal importance and application though its implications, like those of any value, might be somewhat different in different contexts.

There is much useful legal and political writing about equality issues but I think, particularly in equality jurisprudence, it is a good time to go back to the conceptual drawing board and think for a while about the fundamental nature of the principle we are discussing. Much of what I want to say is in the form of a reminder rather than a discovery. Discourse on equality has become fragmented and once now isolated parts of it are reconnected both the unavoidable difficulties and the possibilities for new dialogue should be clearer. What I will attempt to do, to that end, in this book, is to bring some more general theoretical considerations to bear on the discussion of equality's law. I think doing this in a more comprehensive way than is customary in books that critique discrimination law will at least enable us to see where we are and hopefully be clearer about what to do next.

Many thoughtful colleagues and friends helped a great deal by discussing the subject matter of this book with me. I would like to thank Jim Evans, Professor Emeritus at the University of Auckland School of Law, for his guidance and encouragement. A more patient and penetrating discussant and teacher of law and the philosophical insights which underpin legal studies would be hard to find. Participants at the Annual Conference of the Australian Society of Legal Philosophy 2006 (Auckland), 2008 (Melbourne), 2009 (Melbourne) provided many useful comments on earlier drafts of various chapters in this book, as did those who attended a seminar I gave on 'Discrimination and Culture' under the auspices of the Auckland branch of the New Zealand Society for Legal and Social Philosophy in 2007.

Colleagues who attended departmental seminars over the last few years, on versions of various chapters, in the School of Accountancy, Massey University at Albany in Auckland, are also due thanks. Their fresh, insightful comments and questions always left me aware of the need to think more deeply about my subject. I also thank Massey University for granting me research leave from January to June 2010 to work on this book. Lastly, thanks are also due to the team at Ashgate, who have been efficient and friendly throughout the publication process.

'Why Do We Speak of Equality', (2005), 11(1), *Otago Law Review*, was my first attempt at the material covered in Chapters 1–3. 'A Critique of Recent Approaches to Discrimination Law', (2007), 3, *New Zealand Law Review*, 499–525, was based on an earlier version of Chapter 8 and 'The Relationship between Equality and Liberty', (2009), *New Zealand Universities Law Review*, 451–64, is an adapted form of Chapter 5. Comments that I have received on these publications assisted in the preparation of this book. The use of material contained in those articles is by kind permission of the publishers.

Chapter 1

Introduction

Equality is a core value in moral, political and legal philosophy. Morally and politically it is seen as an important part of the justification of the distribution of rights and goods, and the democratic form of government generally. It also plays important roles in other areas of moral concern. Jurisprudentially, equality has become central to modern Bills of Rights discourse and finds its most obvious role in anti-discrimination provisions in Bills of Rights and human rights legislation. The idea of equality is also used to justify or discredit a wide range of other laws, from corporate takeover codes to tax legislation. Equality is not a new idea, of course, but it does enjoy particularly high prestige in much current political and legal thought. As Louis Pojman and Robert Westmoreland, in the introduction to their anthology on the idea of equality, write:

> It is one of the basic tenets of almost all contemporary moral and political theories that humans are essentially equal, of equal worth, and should have this ideal reflected in the economic, social, and political structures of society.[1]

The editors of that compendium cite Will Kymlicka, who has suggested that all theories of justice that are taken seriously today are egalitarian in the sense that equality is their foundational value.[2] Kymlicka was, in turn, taking this idea of equality's central role in modern political philosophy from the work of Ronald Dworkin who has, over the last 30 years or so, had a great deal to say about the importance of the idea of equality.[3] The popularity of the idea, however, is not matched by agreement about what upholding that value entails in terms of the specific treatment that persons are due.

---

1   Louis P. Pojman and Robert Westmoreland (eds) *Equality* (Oxford University Press, New York, 1997) 1.

2   Will Kymlicka *Contemporary Political Philosophy* (Oxford University Press, Oxford, 1990) 4. Kymlicka is perhaps suggesting something more than Pojman and Westmoreland; a 'foundational value' might denote something more than a 'basic tenet'. See also a recent expression of the relationship between equality and a range of theories about justice in Amartya Sen *The Idea of Justice* (Harvard University Press, Cambridge, 2009) 291.

3   Ronald Dworkin *Taking Rights Seriously* (Duckworth, London, 1977); *A Matter of Principle* (Harvard University Press, Cambridge, 1985); *Sovereign Virtue* (Harvard University Press, Cambridge, 2000).

If Kymlicka is right to say that, for example, Robert Nozick's and Karl Marx's social theories both, in some sense, respect equality,[4] we cannot know all of what is to be done to achieve a just social order simply by concluding it will be one based on equality simpliciter. Naturally, Kymlicka and Dworkin, and other writers who compare and contrast different sorts of equality, understand this. They are not suggesting that we all now agree on what *kinds* of equality are required in a just society. Dworkin's own work is concerned with defending particular conceptions[5] of equality rather than the plain assertion that 'equality'[6] is what we are after. He and others have written extensively about which kind of equality produces the best theory of distributive equality, political equality, equal liberty, and so on.[7]

Although there is plenty of disagreement about which equalities we should value and employ in the creation and maintenance of a just society, the basic egalitarianism[8] identified by Kymlicka is itself a substantial value. The substance of what Kymlicka identifies as common in modern political philosophy is the requirement 'that the government treat its citizens with equal consideration; each citizen is entitled to equal concern and respect'.[9] There are theories that deny this, even if they are rare, but those who are 'egalitarians', in this broad sense, are in agreement at this abstract level at least. They may, and often do, disagree about some of the implications of that general belief in equal human worth but they are, nevertheless, constrained by it.

There is then, in modern social ethics, an abstract notion of equality, a belief in the equal worth of human beings, about which there is widespread (although sometimes implicit rather than explicit) agreement, and a large range of specific equalities about which there is much disagreement. These two senses capture the difference between, as John Rawls puts it: 'equality as it is invoked in connection with the distribution of certain goods ... and equality as it applies to the respect which is owed to persons irrespective of their social position'.[10] Noting the difference between these two meanings of 'equality' helps to explain in what sense it is meaningful to refer to a libertarian like Robert Nozick or to an apparent

---

4   Kymlicka *Contemporary Political Philosophy*, above n. 2, 4.

5   In the sense of the distinction between concepts and conceptions he uses, he tries to work out the requirements of equality. See Ronald Dworkin *Law's Empire* (Fontana Press, London, 1986) 70–71. I will argue we also need an appropriate *concept* of equality.

6   I shall be placing words (that I am not citing) in inverted commas very often. The reason for this is that I discuss the *use* of certain words a great deal. I will use single inverted commas when I do that to avoid cluttering the text too much.

7   See Dworkin *Sovereign Virtue*, above n. 3.

8   I use the words 'egalitarianism' and 'egalitarian' to denote a general belief in human equality rather than as a specific idea about economic equality. The word 'equality' itself often has a specific economic or distributional connotation but I shall not intend that meaning unless I say so.

9   Kymlicka *Contemporary Political Philosophy*, above n. 2, 4.

10   John Rawls *A Theory of Justice* (Oxford University Press, Oxford, 1971) 511.

opponent of equality like Anthony Flew as 'egalitarians', in the sense used here.[11] Libertarians are sometimes said to eschew equality in favour of freedom but it is equality in particular instances of Rawls's first sense that are usually thought to be in tension with liberty. It is at least rare in modern academic political argument to find a justification for the freedom to treat some as intrinsically less worthy of respect than others.

There is much debate, in political philosophy, about the implications of 'basic equality', to use the term Jeremy Waldron uses to refer to the abstract belief in equal human worth.[12] As Waldron says:

> A tremendous amount of energy has been devoted to ... [equality as a specific standard] ... in recent political philosophy: people ask whether equality of wealth, income, or happiness is something we should aim for; whether it is an acceptable aim in itself or code for something else, like the mitigation of poverty; whether it implies an unacceptable levelling; whether, if achieved, it could possibly be stable; how it is related to other social values such as efficiency, liberty, and the rule of law etc.[13]

The difficulty in sorting out which type or types of equality are morally supportable is also reflected in modern jurisprudential debates about the meaning of equality provisions in Bills of Rights. These provisions are concerned with discrimination on various grounds and, more recently, remedies for past discrimination. In the United States, the first country to have a Bill of Rights in the modern sense, the fundamental point of the equality provisions found in the Fifth and Fourteenth Amendments to the United States Constitution is now construed quite differently to the way it was 100 years ago and there is, still today, not complete agreement in the US Supreme Court about the meaning of the right. Equality provisions found in recently introduced Bills of Rights and various sorts of human rights legislation are, too, the source of labyrinthine expositions in which courts try to fathom what conception of equality or discrimination the legislature had in mind.[14] There is

---

11 See Anthony Flew *The Politics of Procrustes* (Temple Smith, London, 1981); Robert Nozick *Anarchy, State and Utopia* (Blackwell, Oxford, 1975).

12 Jeremy Waldron, 'Basic Equality' (2008). *New York University Public Law and Legal Theory Working Papers*. Paper 107. (Hereinafter BE.) This essay is an extremely useful guide to what has been written about the *justification* of basic equality (as opposed to its policy implications). It is a neglected topic and Waldron's contribution is seminal though tentative in nature. I have gained much from studying both it, in earlier versions and the current one, and many of the works cited therein. I will refer to the essay often in the first three chapters.

13 BE above n. 12, 1. This is only a reference to debates which would fall under the heading of economic equality but I think the point is also meant as a general one.

14 Erwin Chemerinsky *Constitutional Law* (3rd edn, Aspen Publishers, New York, 2006) Ch. 9; Cathi Albertyn and Beth Goldblatt 'Equality' in Stu Woolman et al. (eds) *Constitutional Law of South Africa* (2nd edn, Juta and Co Ltd, Cape Town, 2002) Ch. 35;

some consensus amongst political and legal philosophers about equality as a social norm, in the sense of a basic restraint. All who take the idea at all seriously now agree that treating people differently *just* because of their race or sex is wrong. And while there is a strong consensus on matters of race and sex (and some of the other 'forbidden grounds' for discrimination that are found in modern Bills of Rights, such as religion and national or ethnic origin) that agreement entails only condemnation of 'direct' discrimination.

There is widespread agreement in liberal democracies that we should not have arbitrarily treated some groups of people differently in the past. That accord does not extend, in particular, to questions of remedial action in favour of communities disadvantaged by earlier discrimination. The fight over affirmative action has been bitter and divisive.[15] The affirmative action debate is, however, only a part of, or sometimes a reflection of, a broader new set of difficulties we now have in deciding which differences between groups and individuals are morally relevant. These are various and complex.

The debate on gender and sex,[16] for example, which raises questions about equal treatment and appropriate different treatment, is now not only about whether affirmative action is permissible. There is debate about whether it is, to make up for hostile discrimination practised by men who thought, or think, that women are inherently less capable of filling demanding professional roles. But those concerned to achieve justice for women now also argue about whether women really are just the same as men in all relevant respects. Non-sexist writers do not all think that any lack of proportional gender representation in desirable roles can only be the result of discrimination.[17]

Sandra Fredman *Discrimination Law* (Oxford University Press, Oxford, 2002) Ch. 1; Hugh Collins 'Discrimination, Equality and Social Inclusion' (2003) 66 *MLR* 16; Grant Huscroft 'Freedom from Discrimination' in Rishworth et al. *The New Zealand Bill of Rights* (Oxford University Press, Melbourne, 2003) 366.

15   See Ronald Dworkin *Taking Rights Seriously*, above n. 3, Ch. 9; Ronald Dworkin *Sovereign Virtue*, above n. 3, Ch. 10 and Ch. 11; Nicolaus Mills (ed.) *Debating Affirmative Action* (Dell Publishing, New York, 1994); Robert Post and Michael Rogin (eds) *Race and Representation* (Zone Books, New York, 1998); Ch. 10 below. The literature on affirmative action is enormous for something which was only introduced around 40 years ago; mainly because we cannot agree on whether it is justified.

16   The distinction between sex and gender is sometimes used to denote the difference between biological differences and different social roles.

17   See Christine A. Littleton 'Restructuring Sexual Equality' (1987) 75 *CLR* 1279; Joan C. Williams 'Dissolving the Sameness Difference Debate: A Post-Modern Path Beyond Essentialism In Feminist and Critical Race Theory' (1991) *Duke L J* 296; Mary Joe Frug 'Sexual Equality and Sexual Difference in American Law' (1992) 26 *New Eng L Rev* 665. For a clear, though contested as ever, summary of what recent science does and does not tell us about gender differences, see Steven Pinker *The Blank Slate* (Penguin, New York, 2002) Ch. 18. Pinker includes summaries of opposing views. I consider the relevance of possible differences between the sexes, briefly, in Ch. 10 below where I discuss affirmative action.

Race and gender are difficult topics but they are at least matched by the issues and challenges which come under the rubric of 'cultural equality'. The word 'culture' can refer to entire ways of life which, while clearly different in many respects, are, according to some, all equal in some sense. This gives rise to a number of difficult ethical questions because, first, the very existence of some cultural differences is, and should be in the view of many, doubted. While there are generalisations that people make about the behaviour and attitudes of members of various groups, for example, that are reasonably accurate, some do not seem at all plausible.

'Multiculturalism' as a policy gives rise to a substantial set of questions about what should or should not be made equal. Many of these questions do not as yet have universally convincing answers. And it is not hard to see why. For one thing, if a culture is a way of life – a way of doing things – then, as a factual thesis, cultural equality runs up against the very stubborn intuition that there are always better and worse ways of doing things. It is not clear in what sense these different strategies for dealing with the problems of life in contemporary society are meant to be equal. The point for now[18] is simply, again, that with culture, as with race and gender, it is not always clear or uncontroversial what the dictates of equality and other relevant values are.

There is, despite the fact of many differences of opinion in areas such as race, sex and culture, widespread agreement that equality at a more abstract level is important. But there are some who think the difficulty in finding out what it is that equality requires is not just that one has to choose between different conceptions of equality, to decide what or which equality or equalities are fundamental and which incidental. There are those who think the problem is a more basic one: 'equality' is not a useful concept at all. Professor Peter Westen has proposed that we recognise the 'emptiness' of the idea of equality[19] or at least the 'derivative' nature of statements about normative equality.[20] Professor Westen argues that not only are calls for equality often elliptical but also that when the desired metric, in terms of which equality is required, is identified, the rule of distribution that is being commended can be expressed without any reference to 'equality'. Talk of equality is not only often confusing and misleading, it is redundant. Westen is not alone in thinking that equality is a worthless concept. Other legal philosophers, including the renowned British scholar Joseph Raz, have expressed similar views.[21]

---

18 See Ch. 7 below. The policy implications of multiculturalism are usually expressed in the language of rights. But the question of whether such rights should be granted to cultural minorities must also be answered, in part, by asking whether having special minority rights is fair to others, including the majority and other minorities.

19 Peter Westen 'The Empty Idea of Equality' (1982) 95 *Harv L Rev* 537.

20 Peter Westen *Speaking of Equality* (Princeton University Press, Princeton, 1990) xx.

21 Joseph Raz *The Morality of Freedom* (Clarendon Press, Oxford, 1986) Ch. 9; see also more recent expressions of the idea by Christopher J. Peters 'Equality Revisited'

If one takes this criticism of the usefulness of 'equality' seriously, one's starting point, in any treatment of the point and value of equality, must be its refutation. I will accordingly, in Chapter 2, first set out Westen's thesis and then turn to a promising exploration of the point of talk about equality which was a direct response to his redundancy thesis. This is the response to Westen's suggestion, that talk about equality is pointless and misleading, made by Jeremy Waldron, first expressed in his review of Westen's book *Speaking of Equality*.[22] I will agree with Waldron's analysis and offer an expanded argument, which I think is consistent with his. While Westen has helped to identify the sources of much confusing talk about equality, his work has failed to make the distinction, made by Rawls and others, between the role played by 'equality' in claims for treatment made in terms of other standards, and the abstract equality expressed as the idea that we should treat people with equal concern and respect.

Demands for equality in specific contexts are often inchoate because they do not specify the measure by which they want people to be equal. Westen shows that when we know what the desired standard is, we are able to express the claim without reference to 'equality'. But when we ask what justifies the principles Westen has liberated from their egalitarian baggage, part of the answer is, very often: equality. Equality in the sense of the 'basic equality' which dictates that the interests of all persons concerned must be taken into account when deciding how society is to be ordered or administered, and in morally relevant decision making generally.

Westen usefully stresses the confusing nature of much talk about equality, and while he is right to point out the manipulative uses that the vague positive connotations of the word may allow, he has not shown that 'equality' as a basic constraint on all rule and policy making is redundant. That notion of 'basic equality' is clear and has substance. There is no good reason to stop speaking of equality. Westen thinks there is because he has forgotten about half of the idea of equality – the most fundamental part of it.

The core idea of basic equality is well known, at least intuitively; we should treat people as equals. Its justification and role in social policy making are not particularly well understood. It is a very abstract idea and that has tempted some to replace it with various conceptions of equality. But conceptions of some broad notion must come from the same concept, and a clear concept of equality is missing in much recent jurisprudential writing. That concept, the idea of equal human worth, is not another conception amongst many; it is, I will argue, *the* concept of equality which will in turn require equal treatment or equal outcomes sometimes and permit unequal treatment or unequal outcomes at other times.

(1997) 110 *Harv L Rev* 1211; Anton Fagan 'Dignity and Unfair Discrimination: A Value Misplaced and a Right Misunderstood' (1998) 14 *SAJHR* 220.

22   Jeremy Waldron 'The Substance of Equality' (1991) 89 *Mich L Rev* 1350; see also BE, above n. 12, 3.

I think remembering this will help us to think more clearly about the moral importance of equality. But accepting that it cannot be reduced to a simpler, more concrete, idea that could be applied like a rule does mean admitting that equality's conundrums will be with us for some time. It is hard to know, for example, whether treating people as equals justifies treating some differently, beneficially, when what their forbears asked for was equal treatment; and simply choosing a conception of equality which determines the matter one way or the other by semantic fiat does not solve the moral problem.

Equality as a basic constraint on policy goals is quite abstract and its implications still have to be argued about, as they of course are. A more neglected task has been the justification of the commitment to basic equality itself. I will address this issue in Chapter 3. The idea of equal human worth is of course the rallying point of our intellectual resistance to, and political struggles against, racism and sexism and the like; it is the point of a large part of the twentieth century's political philosophising. But what supports that belief? There is an important sense in which individual humans are in fact equal. We share what John Rawls calls 'range properties'. Human characteristics like rationality, capacity for moral judgment and our specifically human needs are properties that we share even if we do not share them in equal 'amounts'. It makes sense then to think of each other *as equals* in a way that we are not the equals of cats or trees.

In part, particularly at the level of group conflicts, we have been largely engaged in factual disputes with those who contend that some races, or women in general, do not share these properties to a significant extent. When arguing with advocates of discrimination we have tried to point out that group differences they pointed to were either imaginary or irrelevant. We may feel that those factual arguments have, to a large extent, been won, but things may seem more difficult when we consider individual differences. Some of these are ineliminable; however we might improve our social structures: some types of factual inequalities are, for better or worse, a part of the human condition.

I will argue that this gives us no reason to reject basic equality. The racist's (or sexist's or whatever) crude elitism is not improved by a social order based on privileging every conceivable superiority. Such a system would be unworkable, unsaleable and cruel. Moreover, the focus on facts about our individual differences can make us forget another important fact about who we are; we are social creatures. The fact of our interdependence is not socially constructed. Better forms of cooperation can make our lives go better but without some cooperation we cannot live at all. Although it is ultimately a matter of choice, it makes sense to respond to the sameness we share with other humans by embracing them as equals.

After offering a justification of our commitment to basic equality, I will consider the nature of this value more closely in Chapter 4. The idea of an equal concern for others comes close to a general idea of morality itself but I will argue that it is not an essential part of morality. We may think any moral outlook that does not include a commitment to basic equality is deficient for that reason but that does not mean that it is not a moral outlook. Basic equality also entails more than the idea that our moral judgments be 'universalisable'. That requirement is consistent with the denial of basic equality because universalisability only requires that we 'treat like cases alike' and that understanding of what 'equality' means in modern political philosophy and human rights theory does not, in itself, take us very far.

The general nature of basic equality lies, rather, in its relevance to so much of our ethical thought. If we do value it, we always have to consider the interests and concerns of others, and resist the temptation to ignore the interests of those whose strangeness tempts us to ignore their needs. While it does have a role in the decision making of individuals, and not just communities, I will argue that a special concern for those closest to us need not be inconsistent with a commitment to basic equality. That commitment will mean, though, that we may not put the interests of our families or friends above the requirements of justice. And this limited justifiable partiality is not easily extended to wider groupings such as ethnic groups.

Even if we think commitment to basic equality is a sine qua non of good political philosophy we have to ask how that affects the implementation of other values or if that commitment is even consistent with some political ideals that are currently thought worthwhile. I will focus, in Chapter 5, on an aspect of the relationship between equality and liberty. Talk about these two values dominates much of modern political philosophy and there is much to say about how they relate to each other. I will limit my efforts to arguing, first, that the fundamental freedoms that are typically found in a Bill of Rights are compatible with basic equality. Indeed a commitment to it provides one reason for upholding these freedoms though that does not mean that these basic freedoms are *only* entailments of basic equality.

There is, on the other hand, a choice to be made at times between freedom and the various equalities we may pursue as a matter of social policy. I note, though, that these clashes are not between *basic* equality and liberty. We have a duty, as individual moral agents and through our governmental structures, to uphold the values we believe in, but the desire to institute policies compelling others to live according to basic equality's dictates has to be weighed against considerations of freedom.

Finally, also in Chapter 5, by way of application of what I will say about equality's relationship with important freedoms, I note and suggest a riposte to a tendency in contemporary political debate to underestimate the importance of certain liberties; freedom of speech in particular. Attacks on freedom of speech often rely on equality for their justification and it is always important to remember, when evaluating them, that basic equality itself is a reason to protect freedom of speech to the extent that it is upheld in liberal democracies.

In Chapter 6, I consider the scope of basic equality further by reflecting on what it means to deny it. My remarks in this regard will not be intended as attempts to resolve all (or, in most cases, any) of the important issues concerning the types of discrimination that I discuss. My purpose will mainly be to indicate something of the range and perplexity of these. Because basic equality is quite an abstract value it is not possible to reduce to a simple formula all the considerations one should take into account when deciding whether it has been disregarded in a particular case. Racism and sexism, for example, are alike in some respects but differ in others and they both differ from religious or cultural discrimination in important ways. In every case there are specific questions to ask which might not always, or ever, apply in other types of disrespect for the equality of persons.

The question of culture, as I have already noted, looms large in contemporary discussions about equality. I argue in Chapter 7 that those discussions will go better once we have agreed not to rely on any of the dubious conclusions of cultural relativism. Ethical criticism must not acknowledge any no go areas: morality is a jealous god. Cultural accommodation which respects this, on the other hand, seems worthy of consideration. I will argue that while exemptions from the application of general laws of universal application, on cultural grounds, seem intuitively acceptable, we still have some way to go in finding a complete justification for them. This is only one of many unresolved issues in the area of cultural equality.

The remaining chapters address aspects of the application of basic equality which are of central concern to human rights law. Having argued that basic equality is a substantive value which is worth upholding, and after outlining something of the basic nature and demands of this value, in itself and in the context of other values, I turn, in Chapter 8, to the troubled discourse of the interpretation of current 'equality jurisprudence'. Equality is not just a moral and political idea. It is also enshrined in contemporary law. In the last decades of the twentieth century, in particular, liberal democracies in North America and elsewhere have tried to give effect to their commitment to basic equality by enacting 'equality laws'. The laws address important issues and their authors are well meaning, but the interpretation of this human rights legislation and that of older (and recent) constitutional provisions dealing with discrimination has proved difficult. Much recent legal theorising about discrimination is characterised by seemingly endless debate about what 'equality' means. It has either forgotten that it simply means treating people as equals or is reluctant to state the obvious because that abstract idea is not amenable to straightforward application in difficult cases.

Unfortunately that is also true of the various conceptions of equality that are offered as alternatives. Nor do these resolve any of our most important debates about what a commitment to basic equality demands. While there are some things that basic equality clearly rules out, the abstractness of basic equality means that we cannot read off its general formulation a solution to our questions about many matters that concern us.

What basic equality, together with other considerations, requires will not be discovered by simply choosing a conception of 'equality' which determines that our intuitions about these matters are justified. A lot of recent equality jurisprudence expresses that unjustified optimism. I will illustrate this by discussing some current, in the end unsatisfactory, ways of talking about the underlying purpose of discrimination law. I will argue that talk about 'substantive equality' does not offer much help, though it purports to, in understanding what is morally important about equality. The idea of 'dignity' as it is used in recent equality jurisprudence is suggestive of something important. But the denial of basic equality does not consist, as some recent jurisprudence sometimes suggests it does, simply in the subjective injury to an individual's sense of his own dignity. We might say that the dignity which is the inherent worth of every person inspires our commitment to basic equality. But that sense of 'dignity' is even more abstract than the idea of basic equality itself. It will not serve as a concretisation of the latter.

The failure of recent attempts in discrimination law theory to recognise that equality is an abstract value, not empty but also not very specific, will lead some to think of replacing it as the rationale for discrimination law. Hugh Collins's idea that discrimination law is really about 'social inclusion' is negatively inspired by the failure of various interpretations of that law in terms of equality. But 'social inclusion' is itself a quite abstract notion. In particular its own relationship with the great Enlightenment values of equality, liberty and community needs to be clarified.

In general I think more jurisprudence should come before future legislative drafting here. The law is probably just incurably abstract. Basic equality will not stop being an abstract idea; however we dress it up in terms of new theories or 'conceptions' of equality. It will not be possible, then, to solve any of the complicated issues that we discuss under the rubric of equality by coming up with a better or more specific idea that is easier to apply. The solution to equality's puzzles requires sophisticated moral analysis and some issues will just be very difficult to resolve at all in the foreseeable future.

In Chapter 9, I note that recently a set of intractable issues has occupied us concerning the propriety of differential treatment on grounds once thought to be only useful for those who had discriminatory purposes. Our commitment to basic equality will make us want to respond to the disadvantage caused by discrimination. When we do this by trying to prevent 'indirect discrimination' by private persons we do not have to only contend with clashes between our goal of achieving more equal outcomes for disadvantaged groups and concerns about freedom and efficiency. We also have to consider the right of all affected parties, including the members of other groups, to be treated as equals. The idea of indirect discrimination is a prominent one in discrimination law theory. I think the morally important essence of its 'indirectness' is that it is not done intentionally. That does mean, as some have noted, that the idea extends the usual meaning of 'discrimination'.

There is a tension between wanting to prevent the effects of unintentional 'discrimination' and not wanting to impose burdens on employers and others, who have not deliberately discriminated against anyone, which are not imposed on other members of society. Any response to inadvertent indirect discrimination must not impose all the costs of dealing with the effects of past discrimination on one group of social actors alone.

In Chapter 10, I discuss the role of equality in assessing the justice of affirmative action. Affirmative action is perhaps the most intractable 'equality issue'. Its relationship to our commitment to basic equality is not straightforward. It is plausible, however, to see affirmative action as a well-intentioned response to the effects of earlier denials of basic equality. On the other hand, not all of the elements of a full argument to justify this form of preferential treatment are convincing. I will suggest that a forward looking justification for affirmative action, which stresses the need to improve the present circumstances of a currently disadvantaged target group, is the most promising candidate for our moral approval, although the issue of its fairness to some members of other groups is not quite resolved. The problem in broad terms is the same as the obstacle facing the justification of current remedies for indirect discrimination.

Respect for the basic equality of those concerned is a crucial requirement for any justified preferential treatment of certain groups. We also do not seem to be clear enough about the positive effects and costs of such policies to be able to prosecute them with much confidence. I make some suggestions about how, if we are to practise affirmative action at all, we may practise it in ways which match our best rationale for doing it. The debate about affirmative action is not over. It may be that the role basic equality plays in its justification will only become clearer once we understand better the role it plays in justifying ways of distributing goods generally.

Chapter 2
Why Should We Speak of Equality?

Why Westen Thinks 'Equality' is Empty

Professor Westen's thesis about equality is not just that there are many different views about how we should or should not be treated equally, although that is an obvious problem posed by the use of the concept. 'Equality' is also a vacuous concept because *any* rule we might choose to live by achieves equality in that everyone to whom the rule applies is treated equally, simply by being subject to the same rule. This follows, says Westen, from the very meaning of the word. By 'equality' he 'mean[s] the proposition in law and morals that "people who are alike should be treated alike" and its correlative, that "people who are unalike should be treated unalike"'.[1] In order to say anything about equality that is morally interesting, Westen argues, we will have to say which similarities or differences are morally relevant or, in the jurisprudential terms he uses, which rights people (or a certain group of people) should have. Once we know that, he says, we know that 'equality' is otiose, and this is why Westen wants us to stop talking about it.[2]

After a thorough and lengthy analysis of the idea of equality in general, in his book on the subject, Westen provides another definition of prescriptive equality, now in terms of the relevant differences: '[equality is] the comparative relationship that obtains among persons who are completely identical in relevant prescriptive respects'.[3] As with his earlier definition, what is morally relevant is always another matter. Normative equality is just the formal aspect of having any moral or legal rule, Westen says. In itself it does not help us to decide what is to be done. Westen does not simply want to save us from pointless discussion using redundant terms. He also thinks rhetoric on equality can at times be misleading and manipulative when people fail to provide a full argument for a moral view or a particular policy, relying instead on the positive associations of the word 'equality'. We can see this happening in the debate over affirmative action.

We are familiar with the argument made by opponents of that policy that there is a plain contradiction in holding that discrimination is wrong when black people or women, for example, are discriminated against but not wrong when white males are discriminated against. Advocates of affirmative action also often expound their justifications of that response to earlier negative discrimination in egalitarian terms.

---

1   Peter Westen 'The Empty Idea of Equality' (1982) 95 *Harv L Rev* 537, 539–40.
2   Ibid. 542.
3   Peter Westen *Speaking of Equality* (Princeton University Press, Princeton, 1990) 63.

They argue that affirmative action provides 'real equality of opportunity', or, more optimistically, that it is a means of achieving 'equality of outcomes' between the different groups.

Professor Westen illustrates the elliptical use of 'equality' in affirmative action debates in the context of the dispute over whether affirmative action programmes are valid under the Equal Protection clause of the Fourteenth Amendment to the United States Constitution.[4] Westen argues that different conclusions about that follow from premises containing different views about *what* should be equal. He thinks the civil rights cases of the 1950s and 1960s, which were decided on the basis that blacks and whites are equal in some sense, did not have to decide in exactly what sense a black person was (prescriptively) equal to a white person, and that the controversy over affirmative action forced egalitarians to confront this issue.

The advent of preferential policies forced Americans to consider whether racial equality under the Constitution meant that no person, white or black, should ever be disadvantaged on grounds of race, or that no black person (and no person from any other community already disadvantaged by discrimination) should be disadvantaged on the grounds of race.[5] Of course it is, as a matter of US Supreme Court jurisprudence, still not really clear what the US Constitution means for affirmative action.[6] Westen's point is that just being in favour of 'equality' will not in itself determine how we should think about remedial group preferences.

Westen thinks that this problem and others posed in terms of the, seemingly, contradictory or competing demands of equality, should be solved without reference to 'equality', which is really a quite unnecessary idea. His first (in the book length version of the thesis) of many illustrations of the redundancy of 'equality' is the wording of the proposed Equal Rights Amendment to the US Constitution which read as follows:

> Equality of Rights under the law shall not be denied or abridged by the national government or by the states on account of sex.[7]

Westen thinks the word 'equality' in this formulation is superfluous because the authors may have made their point more concisely without it:

> Rights under the law shall not be denied or abridged by the national government or by the states on account of sex.[8]

---

4   Ibid. 269–70.

5   Ibid.

6   See *Grutter* v *Bollinger* 539 US 306 (2003). This is the US Supreme Court's latest attempt. The judgment was as divided as ever.

7   Westen *Speaking of Equality*, above n. 3, xiii.

8   Ibid.

Just as he thinks that removing references to equality takes nothing away from statements about what is or is not morally relevant, Westen's thesis is also that reliance on the language of egalitarianism will not, in itself, solve anything, morally speaking. His conclusion, that equality as a moral, legal and political idea is sometimes worse than ineffective, is disconcerting because many programmes for social reform have been proposed and undertaken in the name of equality. Discrimination on the grounds of race and gender, for example, have been and still are, high on the agenda of those seeking a more just society. It seems axiomatic to many that eradicating racism and sexism is something worth doing because we value equality.

But even anti-discrimination rights, whose very purpose is to achieve equality in certain respects, and so, as Westen puts it 'stand in a special relationship to equality'[9] are not the whole of what equality is about and that whole is the much less interesting fact that all rights result in prescriptive equality. It is central to Westen's thesis that all rights, including anti-discrimination rights can be expressed without any reference to equality. In his discussion of anti-discrimination rights Westen notes two forms they can take:

> F1: If persons in class X receive benefit B, then persons in class Y shall also receive benefit B.

> F2: If any persons in class X receive benefit B, then all persons in class X shall receive benefit B.[10]

As these examples show, we can express the essence of anti-discrimination rules in either of these formulations without any use of the term 'equality': 'simply by specifying *who* the X's are, *who* the Y's are, and *what* the benefits B are'.[11] If the concept is not even needed here, it may seem difficult to see where it is required. If its use can only lead to confusion about which standards are being recommended why refer to equality at all?

Waldron's Defence of Equality

Jeremy Waldron expresses the essence of Westen's view, in his review of *Speaking of Equality*, as follows:

> The language of equality is a rhetorical cover under which political claims are advanced and contested; but it very seldom captures the substance of those political claims in any clear or interesting way.[12]

---

9   Ibid. 142.
10   Ibid. 145.
11   Ibid.
12   Jeremy Waldron 'The Substance of Equality' (1991) 89 *Mich L Rev* 1350 at 1351.

Professor Waldron agrees with the lexicological point that 'equality' is strictly redundant in the formulation of many rights. If we believe, for example, that all people should have votes of equal weight because all people are rational, rather than votes of unequal weight, weighted in accordance with their various formal educational achievements, we can just say 'weight should be assigned to people's votes on the basis of their rationality'.[13] I think we would need to make it clear that by saying all people are rational we are not suggesting that all people are *equally* intelligent or wise, just that rationality itself is something we all (or almost all of us) share. But this is also not a point about equality; it is just a generalisation that we know is true.

In the same way Waldron notes that in a situation where the law allows public demonstrations but, *de facto*, only one racial group is allowed to protest, one does not have to talk about equality to explain what is wrong. The moral problem can be expressed simply by saying that the other group ought to be allowed freedom of expression and association.[14] Waldron also accepts that Westen is right to say that his point is equally valid whether applied to discourse on 'non-comparative standards' or talk about 'comparative standards'. Waldron explains these terms:

> A noncomparative standard is one that entitles each person to some good or liberty by virtue of possessing some feature or characteristic: 'Anyone who is a citizen has the right to demonstrate peacefully'. If P and Q are both citizens, then P has the right to demonstrate (because P is a citizen) and Q has the right to demonstrate (because Q is a citizen). Although they both end up with a similar liberty, the equality or similarity is incidental. Q has a right to a liberty which is similar to that afforded P because Q, like P, is a citizen, not because it is important for Q and P to be treated the same. With comparative principles, by contrast, what matters for a given person is the relation between what she gets and what others get. We usually think about voting this way. Since the value of someone's vote is the difference it makes in an election in which other people also cast their vote, anyone concerned to get a vote will be deeply interested in whether her vote has the same weight. The idea of a comparison matters here in a way that it does not matter in the case of the right to demonstrate. For the latter case, universalizability really does all the work that equality appears to do.[15]

Waldron accepts that even comparative principles do not necessarily involve a reference to equality. In terms of one of his examples I have mentioned, if we believe weight should be assigned to people's votes on the basis of their (common) rationality rather than on their various educational qualifications, we can express that, as I just have, without reference to 'equality'.[16] Waldron also agrees that

---

13   Ibid. 1355.
14   Ibid. 1356.
15   Waldron 'The Substance of Equality', above n. 12, 1356.
16   Ibid. 1356.

Westen's point is a good one even in relation to anti-discrimination laws, whether one is thinking of direct discrimination or indirect discrimination. Waldron discusses the example of height requirements in police force recruitment.

Where height requirements are used they will have a 'disparate impact' on women because women are, on average, shorter than men. The result is an inequality in the treatment of women as compared to men just as it would be if a law directly discriminated against women by not allowing any woman to become a police officer. But that is not the end of the matter as a question of justice. We still have to ask whether there *should* be a height restriction policy for entry into the police force despite the consequent disadvantage suffered by female applicants. Is there a good reason for having this requirement which will result in proportionately fewer women in the police force of a jurisdiction that adopts it? Waldron appreciates that Westen has made this clear. But he bemoans the fact that Westen provides little help in ascertaining *what* the right and wrong principles of distribution are.[17]

In his discussion of what these might be Waldron finds a role for equality as a necessary, if not sufficient, condition for the appropriate principles. Here Waldron means the abstract egalitarian ideal identified above. Some principles of distribution do not show concern for everyone's interests and it is therefore natural to criticise these in terms of that 'basic' equality. In a later, expanded, version of this illustration Waldron[18] notes that if we want tall police officers so they can be seen in a crowd or because they are more intimidating, it cannot be objected that these concerns are sexist – that they do not take the needs of women into account. But if we wanted to have the height requirement because it supported macho values that would be a motivation that ignored the interests of women and would thus not be consistent with fidelity to basic equality.

Waldron illustrates the point again by discussing the failure of the Israeli government, during then recent attacks by Iraqi forces during the Gulf War, to distribute gas masks to those living in the Occupied Territories. Because gas masks were scarce the government gave priority to citizens. They might, of course, have employed other principles of priority. They could have, for example, given priority to emergency workers or to those most at risk. These two alternatives, unlike the decision to favour citizens over non-citizens, take everyone's interests into account. If emergency workers are given priority in the distribution of gas masks it will not be because they are seen as more important, the point will rather be that they will be better able to help those affected by the attacks. Again if the most vulnerable are given the masks in a situation of scarcity the motivation is to give protection to those who need it most rather than to unfairly discriminate against other groups potentially affected.

---

17   Ibid. 1358.

18   Jeremy Waldron 'Basic Equality' (2008) *New York University Public Law and Legal Theory Working Papers.* Paper 107 (hereinafter BE) 4.

Which of the alternatives to favouring citizens over non-citizens that Waldron suggests, is the best, is an open question. Waldron's point is that equality of concern favours either of them over an option (such as giving the masks to citizens only) that does not take the interests of some people under threat seriously.[19] Equality as a moral concept can thus be seen, Waldron argues, to play an important role in arguments about just distributions, at least to the extent that it rules out options that do not take every affected person's right to be treated as an equal into account. Equality thus conceived is not a simple rule to apply to the sorts of social moral problems Westen and Waldron discuss; it is a 'deep principle' which it seems natural to use when referring to the rejection of social attitudes and policies based on racism and sexism or any other denial of equal human worth.[20]

The Point of Talk about Equality

I think Waldron is right to say that Westen has overlooked this aspect of talk about equality. Westen's analysis does not reach the abstract egalitarianism identified above as the principle that the interests of all affected persons must be taken into account when distributing social goods. There are, as we have seen, three strands to Westen's thesis. First, although the word in itself does not mean different things in different contexts, equality is a *relational* concept. Unless it is obvious from the context we have to ask: equality of what? 'Equality' is like 'freedom' in that regard. We need to know in what respect a person or a group is free or wishes to be free before we can understand, or judge from a moral point of view, their freedom. We all approve of some equalities and freedoms and disapprove of others. This characteristic of the term 'equality' is particularly likely to produce semantic confusion because equality is a 'virtue' word.[21] It does not look good to be against it.

The second aspect of Westen's thesis flows from this and is that unscrupulous or careless advocates of controversial distribution claims may realise that by justifying their positions in terms of equality *per se*, instead of identifying clearly what equality they want to achieve, they can put their opponents on the defensive.[22] But this strategy is a sleight of hand as it ignores the fact that each equality produces its own inequality. If, for example, we approve of affirmative action because of equality (to achieve a more equal representation of certain groups in a particular prized social position) we must approve of the unequal treatment of all similarly qualified applicants who are not members of a currently targeted group. That inequality may be justified but we cannot have it both ways. So just being in favour of equality, in this sense, does not tell us what to do.

---

19   Waldron 'The Substance of Equality', above n. 12, 1360–61.

20   Waldron 'The Substance of Equality', above n. 12, 1363.

21   J. Roland Pennock 'Introduction' in J. Roland Pennock and John W. Chapman (eds) *Nomos* IX *Equality* (Atherton Press, New York, 1967) ix.

22   Westen *Speaking of Equality*, above n. 3, Ch. 11.

Westen's analysis is right to stress this. We often have to choose between the different actual distributional equalities that result from different choices about what people deserve. Waldron's critique does not deny this but suggests that equality, in the sense of a belief in equal human worth, can help us to decide which specific equalities we wish to achieve. The *result* achieved thereby can, as Westen says, be expressed without reference to equality, but its *justification* may be, without redundancy, expressed in the language of equality.

If the fact that equality is a relational term, coupled with its positive connotations, was all that Westen could say in favour of abandoning the idea we should also have reason to stop talking about *other* concepts which are vague when expressed at an abstract level and which are also at times applied in controversial ways and supported by incomplete practical reasoning. Talk about the idea of 'freedom', for example, is also, as already noted, vague if we do not specify who is to be free, from what and so on. 'Freedom' is a relational concept. That word also has positive connotations: people value freedom for themselves and others, but we do not always know what it is they want until we know which conception of freedom they are using and how they are applying it. And we do not always want people to have the freedom they desire any more than we want people who are not really equal in morally relevant respects to be treated equally. Westen himself makes this point:

> Of course, equality is not the only form of normative discourse that lends itself to ambiguity. Claims of rights and freedoms can also be stated ambiguously … [t]hus, one cannot meaningfully assert a 'right' without specifying more or less precisely *who* is entitled to *what* from *whom*. No one can meaningfully assert a prescriptive 'freedom' without specifying more or less who ought to be unconstrained by what to do what.[23]

Many of the points Westen makes about equality are indeed also true of the general term 'freedom'. The latter term enjoys positive connotations although it is not always, morally speaking, a good thing. 'Freedom' is not, strictly speaking, an evaluative term, any more than 'equality' is. And yet it is sometimes used as if it is and in ways that do not literally specify who is to be free from what. That use is elliptical of course. If someone says, for example: 'In 2002 the East Timorese finally won their freedom', we will likely conclude the speaker means to applaud the fact that those people now have something like Isaiah Berlin's 'positive freedom'.[24] That is to say, the speaker means that the East Timorese since 2002 have, as she thinks they should have had previously, the freedom to govern themselves as an autonomous people. Berlin compares and contrasts the notion of

---

23   Ibid. 268–9.
24   Isaiah Berlin 'Two Concepts of Liberty' in Isaiah Berlin *Four Essays on Liberty* (Oxford University Press, Oxford, 1969) 121.

positive freedom with that of 'negative freedom',[25] by which he means the civil liberties people enjoy in a liberal state. If someone says: 'Citizens of America are free to criticise their political leaders', we will assume it is Berlin's negative conception of freedom she is employing. In this example, too, the speaker will be taken to be saying that the freedom under discussion is a good thing. But some may disagree. And these two notions of freedom may be confused (as Berlin was at pains to point out) and used in misleading or manipulative ways.

Moreover we sometimes have to choose between them, which we do, for example, when we decide whether to respect the sovereignty of a state which does not grant its citizens civil rights, and of course that choice cannot be made by resorting to the value of, an unspecified, 'freedom' itself. We see then, limiting the discussion to the two types of freedom one author discusses in one essay, that at least some of the problems that Westen has identified in his analysis of talk about equality are not peculiar to that concept.

But Westen makes a third claim about equality. It is not just a tricky concept that we must use more carefully: it is an entirely unnecessary idea. We can clear up a lot of confusion and avoid obfuscation by saying what, or who, we want to make equal, and in what respect. But when we do, we will find we have no need for the word 'equality'. Claims to rights, even the right not to be discriminated against, can be made without reference to equality. Westen compares the wording of the Equal Rights Amendment (referred to above) which does include the word 'equality' with that of the Nineteenth Amendment to the US Constitution which reads:

> The right to vote shall not be abridged or denied by the national government or by the states on account of sex.[26]

Referring to this right as the 'equal right to vote', would be semantically redundant says Westen.[27] But when we ask, again, what the *moral point* of the Nineteenth Amendment is, the most obvious answer is that it expresses a commitment to the equal human worth of women and men. That is why rules of the sort expressed in the Nineteenth Amendment are thought to be, quite naturally, as much about equality as the particular right they express. Not just in the sense that they, like all rules, treat all people affected by them equally in terms of their content, but also in the prescriptive sense that they give effect to equality as a value, the value referred to by the term 'basic equality'.

The question remains, however, whether the essence of this abstract right to equality can itself be expressed without reference to 'equality'. If Westen's thesis passes this hurdle it might seem to have won the day. But that will only be so if the resulting formulation of the idea captures the essence of the value more

---

25   Ibid. 122.
26   Westen *Speaking of Equality*, above n. 3, 145.
27   Ibid.

naturally than the expression 'basic equality' or its other specifically egalitarian formulations. I think Westen can do the reduction but only trivially. The result is not a more efficient, clear or natural way of stating the value to which we are referring. Westen can say, by means of reduction, in response to the idea that the concerns or interests of affected persons should be taken into account equally in decisions of social distribution, that when making such distributions the only relevant criterion is personhood. The reduction is possible but pointless. The word 'personhood' in that formulation of the idea of basic equality suggests the very universality that 'equality' does.

It is, then, in no way redundant to use the word 'equality' to refer to the idea that everyone's interests must be taken into account when distributing social goods. Indeed, it is the alternative which is strained. Westen's point was supposed to be that the idea of equality was redundant, not that he could find technically adequate synonyms for the word. For the most part, as Waldron notes, Westen's account says very little about equality in this more abstract sense.[28] Westen comes closest to discussing the abstract notion of equal worth in a brief discussion of Ronald Dworkin's well-known distinction between 'equal treatment' and 'treatment as an equal'.[29]

Dworkin used the example of a parent who has two children suffering from the same disease but to different degrees. One is dying from the disease while the other is merely uncomfortable. Equal treatment would be meted out if the one remaining dose of the required medicine were allocated by the flip of a coin. But this arbitrary method of deciding who gets the medicine would not treat the children as equals; as worthy of equal concern. As Waldron concedes here, rightly, Westen is syntactically correct to say that Dworkin *could* just talk about a right to concern and respect owed to humanity as such, rather than a right to *equal* concern and respect. But the word 'equal' seems a natural one to use in our world where unfair distinctions between groups of people are so often made and where so many political causes are concerned with fighting policies and practices of discrimination.[30] And the concern and respect is owed to all humans *because* they are equals.

If equality is, as I think it is, a useful concept, then Dworkin's distinction between equal treatment and 'treatment as an equal' is also useful because it helps us to get a sense of what is normatively important in talk about equality. In his example of the two sick children we see at once the unfairness, in this case, of equal treatment. To be fair, to do the right thing in this situation, requires not giving the children equal treatment. Giving the medicine to the child that needs it

---

28   Waldron 'The Substance of Equality', above n. 12, 1361.

29   Ronald Dworkin *Taking Rights Seriously* (Duckworth, London, 1977) 226–9; cited by Waldron in 'The Substance of Equality', above n. 12, 1361; see also Westen *Speaking of Equality* above n. 3, 102–8.

30   Waldron 'The Substance of Equality', above n. 12, 1362.

most treats the children as equals because it takes both their interests (which are different) seriously. That is what is normatively important. As Dworkin says:

> This example shows that the right to treatment as an equal is fundamental, and the right to equal treatment, derivative. In some cases the right to treatment as an equal will entail a right to equal treatment, but not, by any means, in all circumstances.[31]

Westen is correct to say that 'as equals' can, again, just mean treating people as those who happen to be governed by a certain rule.[32] Dworkin's formulation, however, is meant to be normative in a sense that 'as equals' need not always be. The children in his example should be, we think, treated unequally, not equally, and Westen is right to say that this is partly because they are not equals (in terms of their need for medicine and under any rule which pays proper attention to those needs). It is clear from the context in *Taking Rights Seriously*, however, that Dworkin is arguing for *equal concern and respect* and not for equality in the sense of the open formula of treating likes alike. I have argued that because this concern and respect is to be accorded on the basis of undifferentiated personhood it is not inappropriate and is indeed apposite to refer to it as 'equal' concern and respect and to acknowledge that this is what basic egalitarianism is, fundamentally.

Our commitment to basic equality gives us a moral *reason* to have a rule that human need should prevail in deciding which of the children in Dworkin's example should get the medicine. Westen cites the following passage from H.L.A. Hart as 'the argument that the word "equal" does not add anything to what Dworkin means by "concern and respect"':

> When it is argued that the denial to some of a certain freedom, say to some form of religious worship or to some form of sexual relations, is essentially a denial of equal concern and respect, the word 'equal' is playing an empty but misleading role. The vice of the denial of such freedom is not its inequality or unequal impact: if that *were* the vice the prohibition by a tyrant of all forms of religious worship or sexual activity would not increase the scale of the evil as in fact it surely would, and the evil would vanish if all were converted to the banned faith or to the prohibited form of sexual relationship. The evil is the denial of liberty or respect; not *equal* liberty or *equal* respect: and what is deplorable is the ill-treatment of the victims and not the relational matter of the unfairness of their treatment compared with others.[33]

---

31   Dworkin *Taking Rights Seriously*, above n. 29, 227.

32   Westen *Speaking of Equality*, above n. 3, 103.

33   H.L.A. Hart 'Between Utility and Rights' (1979) 79 *Colum Law Rev* 828, 845; cited in Westen *Speaking of Equality*, above n. 3, 102.

This is a very interesting passage, worthy of study for what it suggests about the relationship between two important political values,[34] but it should be noted that Hart is not here arguing to establish the redundancy of 'equality'; he merely wants to distinguish it from liberty (and perhaps other values, like respect). He is worried by Dworkin's imperial claims for 'equality', not the idea that equality, properly defined and limited, is a useful one. Hart does not believe equality is redundant: he simply wants to tame its ambition to be the political value from which all else flows. What he says next makes this apparent:

> This becomes clear if we contrast with this spurious invocation of equality a genuine case of failure to treat men as equals in the literal sense of these words: namely literal double counting, giving the Brahmin or the white man two votes to the Untouchable's or the black man's single vote. Here the single vote given to the latter is indeed bad just because the others are given two; it is, unlike the denial of a religious or sexual freedom, a genuine denial of *equality* of concern and respect, and this evil *would* vanish and *not* increase if the restriction to a single vote were made universal.[35]

So Hart's point is not Westen's. Westen would not want us to complain about the racism of the constitutional arrangements in Hart's examples by talking about 'equality'. Hart is quite happy to do that and his phrase 'to treat men as equals' seems quite clearly to denote basic equality. We do not respect this fundamental and abstract equality; we fail to take all affected person's interests into account, if we deny people the right to an equal vote on account of the colour of their skin.

Hart does not want to abandon the idea of equality: he is applying it. He is merely taking a position on the relationship between equality and other political values. His comment that 'equality' is playing an 'empty and misleading role' must be understood in its context; that of Hart's argument against understanding infringements of liberty as breaches of equality. Hart also thinks that 'respect' is a separate value – '[t]he evil is the denial of liberty or respect; not *equal* liberty or *equal* respect'. It is of course, at some level, but what Dworkin means by 'concern and respect' in the phrase 'equal concern and respect' appears to be quite abstract. The whole notion seems to be one of equality in the abstract sense whose usefulness I have endorsed.

Westen's focus has been the accurate observation that calls for equal treatment often beg the question. Equal treatment is not always justified. But the requirement that people should be treated as equals helps to determine whether it is or is not in a particular instance. The scope of Westen's analysis will not generate this insight. The belief that all people count, and matter equally, is not empty or tautological. But that belief cannot be derived, without more, from the idea that equals should

---

34   See below, Ch. 6.
35   Hart 'Between Utility and Rights', above n. 33, 845.

be treated equally and unequals should be treated unequally. The Aristotelian idea of equality that Westen works with does not entail modern egalitarianism.

Aristotle did not think that we are all equal or that we should all be treated with equal concern and respect. And his 'likes should be treated alike' formula does not force him to think that. It does not compel him to accept any specific judgment about who should or should not be treated equally, and it was not intended to compel any such conclusion. His response to the query he phrased about the equality that should be assigned to equals – 'equals and unequals – yes; but equals and unequals in what?' [36] – is not the modern egalitarian one.

The idea of the fundamental equality of all persons, implicit in modern political philosophy, is, on the other hand, a clear affirmation that everyone's interests and concerns must be taken into account because of their equal human worth. It would be wrong to conclude, therefore, that because the use of the idea of equality can be vague or elliptical it is unnecessary and has no useful role in jurisprudential discourse or moral and political philosophy. The meaning of equality as a fundamental commitment to equal human worth is clear, though abstract. It is an abstract principle that can be used to justify the allocation of rights and goods in society. Its application will at times be controversial and sometimes relatively straightforward.

In deciding which policies and practices are consistent with that value, it is true, however, that questions will have to be answered about what should, in another sense of the word, be equal and what should not be equal. Questions like: if we respect the fundamental equality of all persons does that entail the equalisation of income? Or the rejection of all policies that take race into account, directly or indirectly? And so on. These questions still need to be answered and they are questions about equality, though, as I said, they are questions about a different application of that word; its use in Rawls's first category of equality: 'as it is invoked in connection with the distribution of certain goods'.[37]

Specific prescriptions of equality or inequality of treatment are often discussed in confusing and misleading ways because, as Westen says, even at this level 'equality' has positive connotations and 'inequality' negative ones. But equal treatment and different treatment both require justification. Neither is automatically warranted. That 'equality' in the abstract sense of 'basic equality' can supply part of that justification is surely part of the reason why things so often get muddled when we speak of equality – we do not always identify which sense of the word we mean. But that is a solution, as Waldron points out, to the puzzles that Westen identifies, that he fails to recognise and that is because he does not recognise the meaning of 'equality' suggested here.[38] Basic equality, or in Rawls's terms 'equality as it applies to the respect which is owed to persons irrespective of their

---

36   Aristotle *The Politics* (Oxford World Classics, Oxford, 1995) Book III Ch. 12 1282b14.

37   John Rawls *A Theory of Justice* (Oxford University Press, Oxford, 1971) 511.

38   Waldron 'The Substance of Equality', above n. 12, 1368.

social position',[39] is not empty. It has a content: the respect which is owed to all by virtue of their personhood, the consideration, in the realm of policy making, of the interests of all affected persons.

Equality in this sense is not just the requirement of consistency. It is not satisfied by a policy or practice that is equally harsh to all concerned. Consistency is a requirement of good moral thinking of course. But it cannot on its own justify the requirement that everyone's interests should be taken into account. An elite might consistently not do that. Basic equality does require that and the fundamental role it plays in modern political philosophy should make us wonder why more has not been written about why we accord it such pride of place in our social and legal theory.

Jeremy Waldron asks this question when he notes that while a lot has been written about equality as an aim very little has been written about basic equality.[40] Similarly Louis Pojman thinks that recent justifications for equality as a sine qua non of political philosophy that have been offered are not convincing and leave basic equality unjustified despite widespread, almost universal, reliance on it as an axiom of modern political philosophy.[41] Waldron and Pojman's point should give us pause I think. We should have some idea at least why what we take to be axiomatic in political theory is valuable. I will argue that we can justify embracing basic equality as part of the adopting of a coherent set of ethical commitments, chosen by us, the purpose of which is to enhance our communal life in the circumstances in which we find ourselves. I agree with the non-cognitivist school of metaethics that no argument will show that equality's rejection is wrong in the way a mistaken view about some scientific fact might be shown to be wrong, but that does not mean we should choose our moral systems (including our commitment to basic equality) arbitrarily; we should choose them for the purpose just noted, and our arguments about their respective merits are therefore quite sensible.

In discussions of equality's merits it is often asked why we take to be equal, creatures, human beings, who are so different from each other in so many respects. I think it is true that for basic equality to make sense we must think that humans are alike in some fundamental way or ways. Even if, however, we do believe that people are basically alike, so that a commitment to basic equality is not peculiar, we must accept that this does not make it 'right' in the sense that we are right to believe the earth is not flat. This is because ethics is a practical matter. Knowledge of right and wrong is 'a matter of knowing how to act, when to withdraw, whom to admire, more than knowing *that* anything is the case'.[42] Basic equality is not unique in this respect. We cannot point to any facts or sequence of reasoning which demonstrate that its rejection is necessarily irrational. Morality does have a purpose however,

---

39   Rawls *A Theory of Justice*, above n. 37, 511.

40   BE, above n. 18, 3.

41   Louis P. Pojman, 'Are Human Rights Based on Equal Human Worth?' (1992) 53 *Philosophy and Phenomenological Research* 605.

42   Simon Blackburn *Ruling Passions* (Oxford University Press, Oxford, 1998) 1.

and its point allows us to assess the respective merits of different ethical attitudes. Our ethical views must make sense as attempts to improve our circumstances in a less than perfect world. Basic equality makes sense, first, because its rejection in the form of group prejudices is grounded on differences which are often imaginary or misunderstood.

Human beings, as individuals, also share important characteristics and the recognition of this makes sense of our commitment to basic equality. If we tried to implement a more objectively based elitism than racism or sexism, grounded in our individual differences, we would not only find it to be impractical, we would also be hard pressed to justify the harshness and exclusiveness of a system that did not even pretend to be devoted to the common good. It makes more sense to note the ways in which humans are equal, the important fact of our interdependence, and the opportunities for a richer communal life made possible by a commitment to basic equality.

Chapter 3
Why Do We Value Basic Equality?

Introduction

The 'basic equality' identified in the last chapter and found not to be redundant, is an important value in modern political and legal philosophy. I began Chapter 1 by citing just some of the contemporary writers who stress this. But what establishes its importance? It is true, as Will Kymlicka puts it, that:

> If a theory claimed that some people were not entitled to equal consideration from the government, if it claimed that certain kinds of people just do not matter as much as others, then most people in the modern world would reject that theory immediately.[1]

That the equal consideration of the interests of persons acts as a constraint on our political ends is widely accepted. There are of course modern political programmes that are clearly not egalitarian. The policies of Nazism or apartheid, the lack of concern for non-citizens shown by the Israeli government during the Gulf War discussed by Waldron,[2] and the ongoing restriction of civil, political and socio-economic rights of women in some countries are examples of policies that fail this test. Although basic equality does not, of itself, tell us everything about what should replace Nazism or apartheid or patriarchy, it does rule out every policy option, and so these too, that treats some people as less worthy of consideration than others, as all these policies do.

But what *justifies* the rejection of political theories that deny the right to concern and respect to all persons? Why must all political ends, including each *equality of* end, respect basic equality as a constraint? We may think we can dispense with the views of those who lived in very different times and had very different worldviews. And we may just choose not to take modern racists and other contemporary inegalitarian thinkers seriously. But that would be to leave something that we take to be axiomatic in our political philosophy unjustified.

As Jeremy Waldron reminds us, in context, philosophy does not rest just because of unanimous consent to some conclusion:

---

1 Will Kymlicka *Contemporary Political Philosophy* (Oxford University Press, Oxford, 1990) 4–5.

2 Jeremy Waldron 'The Substance of Equality' *Michigan Law Review* May 1991 1350–59. See Ch. 2.

> We are all agreed that the sun will rise tomorrow in the east, but that is not
> a reason to stop discussing problems like induction, causation, the regularity
> of nature, and the reality of the external world. Indeed it is one of the marks
> of philosophy to continue investigation into an issue long after everyone else
> has reached agreement about it for practical purposes and gone home to play
> backgammon.[3]

Many political and legal philosophers *do* just make the assumption of basic equality
and then move on to work out the implications of a commitment to that value. And
they might do that just because basic equality is taken to be so fundamental to our
social thinking, but of course it need not be and that means there is justificatory
work to be done.

Basic equality is a prescriptive belief; it is not in itself a description of how
humans are, in fact, the same; although it might be thought to depend on such a
belief. It is often noted that we maintain a belief in basic equality despite enormous
factual differences between individual human beings. Pojman and Westmoreland,
for example, put the matter well:

> It is an empirical fact that human beings are unequal in almost every way. They
> are of different shapes, sizes, and sexes, different genetic endowments, and
> different abilities. From the earliest age, some children manifest gregariousness,
> others pugnacity, some pleasant dispositions, others dullness and apathy. Take
> any characteristic you like: whether it be health, longevity, strength, athletic
> prowess, sense of humour, ear for music, intelligence, social sensitivity, ability
> to deliberate or do abstract thinking, sense of responsibility, self discipline or
> hormonal endowment (e.g. levels of testosterone and endorphins) and you will
> find vast differences between humans, ranging from very high amounts of these
> traits to very low amounts.[4]

These factual differences, which I assume most people would accept are real
enough at least when understood as individual differences (and not as, for example,
biological differences between racial groups), can be seen as an embarrassment for
both basic equality and for equality as a policy aim or goal. Egalitarian policies
designed to get around or even mitigate these factual human differences may
provoke charges of hubris. The accusation may be fair or unfair and that will partly
depend on what basic equality dictates.

Differences among humans also make us think about justifications for basic
equality though. If we had, as humans, nothing or little in common with each other
it would be odd to think of ourselves as one another's equals. Odd in the way it

---

3   Jeremy Waldron 'Basic Equality' (2008) *New York University Public Law and Legal
Theory Working Papers.* Paper 107. (Hereinafter BE) 7.

4   Louis P. Pojman and Robert Westmoreland (eds) *Equality* (Oxford University Press,
New York, 1997) 1.

would be strange to think of ourselves as the equals of trees. Of course it does not follow from the variation in the human range that we have nothing in common. What people who do not believe in basic equality usually do, however, is rely on real or supposed differences. A clear expression of this sort of view, held by the early twentieth-century philosopher Hastings Rashdall, is cited by Waldron in his essay on basic equality. Rashdall wrote:

> Individuals, or races, with higher capacities (i.e. capacities for a higher sort of Well-being) have a right to more than merely equal consideration as compared to those of lower capacities. [5]

Rashdall's view is not, as Waldron notes, utilitarian. Rashdall does not justify giving more consideration to 'individuals or races with higher capacities' because he thinks that will benefit everyone, including 'lesser' human beings: he just does not think that those he designates lesser beings count, or at least not as much. Rashdall's view denies that everyone interests are important while basic equality entails that '[m]oral argument (including argument purporting to justify discrimination) ranges over the good of all human beings, and that range does not admit of any further fundamental divisions'.[6] Rashdall clearly wanted to exclude certain groups from equality's protection.

We reject Rashdall's views on race just as we reject the similar views of apartheid's apologists and those of Nazi theorists; we think they are just wrong about this. There are no races (whatever 'race' might mean after a thorough critique of the idea)[7] with 'higher capacities' in some intrinsic sense, that we know of, although history does of course leave some groups worse off on the whole, including their preparedness for certain tasks.[8] We also now reject the view that one sex is in some sense or senses a higher or even fundamentally different form of life than the other. Whatever the differences between the sexes may be they are not, in our view, of the kind that make one a more valuable sort of human being than the other. Differences between the sexes like (average) physical strength, the ability to give birth to offspring and the biological and psychological differences related to these are all things we may sometimes need to take into account, when deciding how to treat people, but they are not rational grounds for placing on women all the draconian limitations they were subject to almost universally until

---

5   Hastings Rashdall *The Theory of Good and Evil* (2nd edn, Oxford University Press, Oxford, 1924) vol. 1, 237–8, cited in BE, above n. 3, 7.

6   BE n. 3, 9. My use of 'basic equality' is looser than this formulation. My use of it as an alternative to 'equal concern and respect' or Rawls's expression of the concept is not, exactly, mandated by Waldron's use or definition of 'basic equality'.

7   See K. Anthony Appiah and Amy Gutmann *Color Consciousness* (Princeton University Press, Princeton, 1996); Philip Kitcher 'Does Race have a future?' (2007) (35) *Philosophy and Public Affairs* 293.

8   See Jared Diamond *Guns, Germs and Steel* (Vintage, London, 1998) for an interesting account of how this happens.

fairly recently. We are, though, still left with the issue of *individual* differences between people.

The differences between individual humans are significant as the nice collection of examples given by Pojman and Westmoreland cited above reminds us. They are not all of the same kind and that fact will be relevant at the level of deciding policy. Some were unfairly caused by our social structures and some of these in turn (though not all) may be corrected by new ones or better applications of old policies. Some of the differences again are just a matter of genetic or social luck, but we might want to argue that that should not influence an individual's chance to have a good life[9] or, more cautiously, at least commit ourselves to avoid discriminating against the less fortunate.

Some of the differences between us that might be relevant when thinking about the appropriate way to treat people, for example things like physical and mental well being, are even chosen in the sense that often we might have taken better care of ourselves. In this last case we also want to avoid discriminating against people who are, to some extent at least, authors of their own misfortune and we might still want to do more than that to ameliorate their circumstances. Our moral response to all three kinds of differences will not be unanimous. There are of course different views about how to respond to each of these factual inequalities. But those I have just mentioned are all *prima facie* consistent with a commitment to basic equality.

Is that commitment justified if we, as individuals, are so different? While it is possible to refute the racist and to demonstrate that he or she is at least often guilty of bad faith, it is not possible to explain away all of our individual differences. Why then do we choose to think of each other as equals? Why do we think it is right to say: 'I am as good as anybody else; I may not be as clever or hardworking as you are, but I am as good as you are'.[10]

Range Properties

We are different in many ways of course but we also have much in common. What we have in common we may not, though, have in equal amounts. It is useful to think of the thing or things that make us like other people as 'range properties'. Jeremy Waldron defines this idea, which he takes from John Rawls:

> RP: R is a range property if it is a binary or non-scalar property (one either has
> it or one does not) which applies to a class of items that may also be understood

---

9   See R. Dworkin *Sovereign Virtue* (Harvard University Press, Cambridge, 2000) Ch. 2.

10   J.C. Davies *Human Nature in Politics* (New York, 1963) 45, cited in Stanley I. Benn 'Egalitarianism and the Equal Consideration of Interests' in J. Roland Pennock and John W. Chapman (eds) *Nomos* IX *Equality* (Atherton Press, New York, 1967) 69.

in a scalar way, i.e. in terms of a scale measuring the degree to which an item possesses the associated scalar property S.[11]

We recognise a common 'moral capacity', for example, or we may focus on our nature as rational beings. (These two are related of course.) We may all have these range properties but because they are *range* properties we do not all have them, or need to have them, to the same degree. We have them in the way that a particular city may be just as much in a certain state in America as another city is, although the first is near the border and the second in the middle of the state.[12]

Cases like those of the infant or the cognitively disabled person do not have to be seen as extremes on an artificially extended range.[13] Some people have little of what we usually take to be characteristic of humans. Infancy is a notorious topic in this regard. But children have the potential to become fully human: of course we never say they are *not* human. One can, therefore, agree with the suggestion Waldron takes from John Locke, that very young children will become our equals because they will, all being well, become like us more fully as they mature. I think Waldron rightly rejects, therefore, Peter Singer's worry that we cannot find the relevant difference between a human infant and an adult non-human primate.[14] And we can think of the severely disabled as victims of a tragic loss of their capacities, as we of course do, rather than as a different sort of being. As Stanley Benn says in the context of cognitive impairment:

> For if someone is deficient in this way, he is falling short of what, in some sense, he *ought* to have been, given the species to which by nature he belongs; it is, indeed, to be deprived of the possibility of fully realising his nature. So where the mental limitations of the dog can be amusing, without lapse of taste, those of an imbecile are tragic and appalling.[15]

I do not mean to suggest that these special cases do not raise particular, and very complex, issues of their own. They do require separate, special, treatment but I do not engage in that here. I do think, though, that the points made by Locke and Benn, that I have cited, suggest a way to understand why we feel that children and cognitively disabled people share a common humanity with us. But Rawls did not think that the idea of a range property *per se* covered such cases.[16]

---

11   BE, above n. 3, 32.

12   Ibid.

13   Ibid. 35.

14   Ibid. 36; see Peter Singer *Animal Liberation* (3rd edn, Jonathan Cape, London, 2002) Ch. 1.

15   Stanley Benn 'Egalitarianism and Equal Consideration of Interests' in J. Roland Pennock and John W. Chapman (eds) *Nomos* IX *Equality*, above n. 10, 71.

16   John Rawls *A Theory of Justice* (Oxford University Press, Oxford, 1971) 509–10.

For the usual range of human condition, philosophers have relied on different aspects of our shared humanity as the appropriate range property which makes us deserving of equal concern. Rawls himself, whose *Theory of Justice* is premised on basic equality, takes it to be the common human capacity for moral personality.[17] Moral persons are capable of having a conception of their good and of having a sense of justice. This is what makes us moral equals, in Rawls's view. But why choose this capacity? Waldron suggests that from a moral point of view we may be more inclined to focus on common *needs*.[18]

It might seem odd to think that our capacity to be moral is what entitles us to consideration when moral calculations are done.[19] It is true, on the other hand, that morality is a joint enterprise and those beings with whom we share the range property of moral capacity are also those with whom we can have common moral understandings and commitments, enabling us to form a moral community. That does not justify moral concern being exclusively for other humans but there are some moral concerns that are peculiarly human, just because of our capacity for moral personality.

We often deny basic equality by limiting the exercise of peculiarly human capacities. In particular we often impose our conception of the good on others in ways that cannot be justified as expressions of genuine concern for them or others. This denies their status as equals. We deny basic equality in this way when we do not uphold the kind of rights usually included in a modern Bill of Rights.[20] I am thinking here of the rights which guarantee our freedom to express our moral concerns and views. Rights to freedom of speech, religion or association, for example, are rights that only humans can be entitled to, because only they are capable of enjoying them.

That does not mean we have no moral duties with respect to non-human animals, but they will mostly be different from our duties in respect of humans. We should, in some suitable way, which will differ sometimes in the case of different animals, care about the wellbeing of non-human animals but our moral concern for them need not extend to considerations about capacities or interests they do not have.[21] The nomination of the range property 'moral capacity' as a candidate for explaining why we think of our ourselves as equals need not imply a lack of moral concern for other animals then; it can instead be a recognition of a distinctive and

---

17   Ibid. 505–10.

18   See BE, above n. 3, 40.

19   Ibid.

20   See Ch. 5 below.

21   See Roger Scruton *Animal Rights and Wrongs* (Metro Books, London, 2000) for a view of the moral status of animals which is, to my mind, eminently sensible: because our decisions about our behaviour towards non-human animals can cause them pain or pleasure, we have to accept that those decisions are moral ones. Creatures that have sensations of pain are worthy of our sympathy, but not in many of the ways that persons are. Even the experience of pain differs as between humans and other animals because of our mental differences. Morality requires us to care, in suitable ways, about animals, but not as *our* equals.

very broad human capacity, the suppression of which is an injury to anyone who is denied the right to develop and express it. Humans may suffer from the denial of their moral personality by measures that limit its expression, so that capacity is worthy of moral solicitude.

Rawls's suggested range property to account for equality can, however, I think, be broadened to include all specifically human interests. The usefulness of the range property 'moral capacity' is that it reminds us of some very important and, as far as we know, for now at least, exclusively human capacities,[22] which, if disrespected, may cause persons much frustration. It is a useful reminder of that, but we have other interests and needs too. Even these more typical animal needs of ours are structured differently, however, because of our capacity for moral personality and our unique mental life generally. Because of this sophistication a simple utilitarian calculus in terms of pain and pleasure should not be applied when considering our response to human needs, though it would often be suitable in the case of animals – for example, when deciding whether to put an injured animal out of its misery.[23]

The range property idea is controversial, however, and although Waldron discusses it sympathetically, and much more thoroughly than Rawls himself does, he does raise sceptical questions about the strategy. It is hard to find a range property which is important enough to explain our commitment to equality and whose existence is uncontroversial. I have suggested that the importance of the range property 'moral personality' is that it points to a justification for a large part of our political morality. We have other morally relevant interests too and the fact that we share them, including the way we share them (in part, at least, by being creatures with a capacity for moral personality) is also reason to favour basic equality. But the idea of moral personality is not an uncontested one, and, if we have such a capacity, it is not something we are all equally endowed with. I will discuss the first of these difficulties now and the second after discussing how we may proceed from the identification of morally relevant human characteristics to our moral conviction about basic equality.

Jeremy Waldron shows, in his book *God Locke and Equality*, that John Locke's argument for basic equality relies ultimately on theological premises about our equality in the eyes of God. Children of God are equally God's children. Locke starts with corporeal rationality as what we might call his range property. We qualify by having the power of abstract reasoning. The importance of that is all above a minimum threshold can reason to the belief of the existence of God and come in different ways to understand his Law and in particular the nature and moral importance of other creatures with this ability.[24] Bernard Williams notes

---

22   Ibid. Ch. 7.

23   Roger Scruton *Animal Rights and Wrongs*, above n. 21, 46.

24   Jeremy Waldron *God Locke and Equality* (Cambridge University Press, Cambridge, 2002) Ch. 3. The adequacy of this argument, of Locke's, is a moot point. See Cecile Fabre 'Book review of *God Locke and Equality*' *Modern Law Review* May 2003 470–73.

how Kant relies on a similarly transcendent, albeit 'secular', property that all humans share, equally.[25] Williams notes that Kant's account of our status as moral, rational, agents is not an empirical one (like Rawls's is) and does not differ as between persons. Kant thinks being a 'free and rational will' is something we all are, equally.[26]

If neither of these transcendental options is available, which is to say, acceptable, to the modern humanist then she must, in Waldron's view, come up with another and it must be uncontroversial if, like Rawls, we are trying to find a foundation for a theory of justice that all reasonable people can assent to regardless of how much they might differ in their detailed conception of what a good life consists in. Waldron notes – this is the problem – that there are people who deny that what we call our 'moral personality' denotes anything real.

There are those who think all our talk about moral decisions and opinions is just a matter of rationalisations and drives.[27] If we think Locke's theological argument is far-fetched and would rather keep religion out of it so that our commitment to basic equality can be 'non-sectarian' – well – there are those who think 'all this [Rawlsian] moralistic talk of agency and moral personality ... [is] redundant and reducible nonsense'.[28] Waldron does concede the correctness of Rawls's view that without some notion of moral personality theorising about justice is on shaky ground. We need to believe that people have the 'capacity for a conception of the good, and the capacity for a sense of justice'[29] if we are going to appeal to that ability when discussing justice.[30] This comes close to saying that if we are to do moral and political philosophy sensibly we must be talking about something which is potentially realisable. (If this sounds blindingly obvious, and it should, we might remind ourselves that in talking about basic equality we are in the realm of fundamental moral theory.) The controversial nature of the idea of moral personality is a problem for Rawls, however, if he wants us to think that his starting point for thinking about justice is something that no one can reasonably object to. Perhaps the Nietzscheans and Freudians (who Waldron identifies as likely sceptics in this matter of moral personality)[31] will have reason to object, and will offer interesting reasons that cannot just be shrugged off.

Only if the sceptics about the existence of real moral agency can be convinced otherwise will we have complete agreement that it is sensible to think about what is just; but that ongoing – we may call it – metaphysical – project does not mean

---

25   Bernard Williams 'The Idea of Equality' in Peter Laslett and W.G. Runciman (eds) *Philosophy, Politics and Society* (Basil Blackwell, Oxford, 1972) 110 114–8.

26   Ibid.

27   Jeremy Waldron *God Locke and Equality*, above n. 24, 239.

28   Ibid.

29   Ibid.

30   Ibid.

31   Ibid.

those who are not sceptical about the existence of moral personality should call a halt to moral and political philosophy in the meantime.

We must be guided by our own light in this matter just as we are at many points in moral theorising. The extreme relativist's view, to take another example, makes moral judgments seem senseless, but if we are not extreme relativists it is perfectly sensible for us to continue making judgments. It is true then that the way we distinguish human beings, as self-conscious moral beings, is to some extent controversial, but then so is the whole project of normative moralising. We are not quite finished with the role of range properties in the argument for basic equality but I want to turn for a while to the point of identifying range properties or identifying similarities, which play some role in justifying basic equality, between humans.

Metaethical Considerations

Even if we think we can show that humans are equal in this more complex sense, though, the question still remains: what moral conclusion can we draw from this? Despite the plain evidence of differences between individual human beings we may think that there are indeed appropriate range properties which make us equal in at least that sense. I think in this we are on the right track at least. But what can we infer from that, ethically speaking? Can we simply argue that because we are alike we should be treated alike, in the general sense of having our interests taken into account along with everyone else's? If we do, are we not proceeding from an 'is' to an 'ought', inferring values from facts, without providing a reason for doing this?[32]

The idea expressed in the slogan 'no ought from an is' is that nothing about how things should be follows from facts about the way things are. At least they do not as a matter of logical necessity. It does not follow, for example, from the fact that kicking a dog causes the dog to suffer pain that we should not kick it. What is missing is our moral opinion that causing pain to dogs in this way is wrong. We are, of course, normally quite happy just to say 'don't do that, you are hurting the dog', but that expression is elliptic. What is missing is a moral proposition to the effect that causing pain to animals in this way is wrong.

I think it is not easy to avoid metaethical questions here precisely because basic equality is such a fundamental part of our social morality. It is not an application of a more general ethical theory (whose own ultimate justification we might postpone). So it cannot be read off our prior commitment to a yet more fundamental ethical idea. Jeremy Waldron makes this point in terms of the connection between basic equality and utilitarianism. He chides Isaiah Berlin for thinking that basic equality

---

32   The most famous source of the distinction between 'is' and 'ought' in moral philosophy is L.A. Selby Bigge (ed.) David Hume *A Treatise of Human Nature* (Oxford University Press, Oxford, 1888) III i 1.

might be defended on utilitarian grounds. This is confused, Waldron notes, because the maxim 'every man to count for one, nobody for more than one' which Berlin thinks could be defended on utilitarian grounds, is itself one of *utilitarianism's* axioms.[33]

Indeed one of the many current critiques of that system of social ethics is the charge that utilitarianism does not treat people as equals.[34] Equality is thus used both to argue for, and against, utilitarianism: it cannot be the product of that ethical system.[35] The most celebrated political theory of the twentieth century is in the same boat. John Rawls's theory of justice, 'justice as fairness', is premised on basic equality – hence the need to justify that belief in his book after setting out the basic theory.[36] Contractarian theories in general obey basic equality's injunction to include the concerns of all affected persons in ethical decision making. The contract is meant to be one made by equals.

Asking what basic equality is itself based on is, therefore, a large part of asking what modern political philosophy is based on. And the answer to that question is, for some: nothing really. It might just be a commitment we choose to have. Margaret McDonald has written:

> Value utterances are more like records of *decisions* than propositions. To assert that 'Freedom is better than slavery' or 'All men are of equal worth' is not to state a fact but to *choose* a side. It announces *This is where I stand.*[37]

This non-cognitivist approach which originated, in modern moral philosophy, in David Hume's thesis, just mentioned, that no 'ought' can be deduced from an 'is' threatens to leave us where we started; with no reason for believing in equality, although equality would then be no worse off than liberty, or kindness or any other moral commitment.

We do give reasons, though, when we argue for or against basic equality. Our arguments are usually about the facts concerning the ways in which human beings differ and are the same. The observation that these debates are usually about the facts of the matter would not surprise a non-cognitivist like Alfred Ayer. He wrote that moral argument *could* only really be about the facts of the matter or the logic

---

33   Jeremy Waldron *God Locke and Equality*, above n. 24, 14.

34   See, for example, Will Kymlicka *Contemporary Political Philosophy* (2nd edn, Oxford University Press, Oxford, 2002) 37.

35   We should be clear here that we are talking about *basic* equality. Equality as a policy aim in various areas could be inspired by utilitarianism. One might think, as some have, that income disparity should not be too great because the notion of marginal utility tells us that increases in income produce more welfare (or satisfy more preferences) at the lower end of the socio-economic scale.

36   John Rawls *A Theory of Justice*, above n. 16, 504.

37   Margaret McDonald 'Natural Rights' (1947) reprinted in Jeremy Waldron (ed.) *Theories of Rights* (Oxford University Press, Oxford, 1984) 35, cited in BE, above n. 3, 27.

of applying principles consistently. We could only have a 'moral' debate if we were already in agreement about the *moral* issue concerning which itself there could be no real discussion; since moral statements are not propositions but expressions of approval.[38]

It is not quite true, however, that our moral commitments are lined up in advance of any factual discussion. Our attitudes, including our moral attitudes, change during discussions about the facts. But I agree they are not to be *inferred* from the facts. So how could we respond, then, to someone who agreed that we are alike in the way or ways we agree matter but who refuses nonetheless to embrace basic equality? Such an opponent would not be the usual anti-equality advocate of course. The usual sort, like Hastings Rashdall, the racist thinker referred to just now, do not agree, *as a matter of fact*, that we are each other's equals. They usually do agree with the human rights advocate about what is important (rationality, moral capacity, structure of needs etc.) but disagree with us about whether people of colour or women or some other group of people have those attributes. As Bernard Williams notes, the racist does not usually rest his case with 'but they are black': 'black' is normally a proxy for a deficiency of attributes the racist agrees with us are important.[39] And racists are not done with finding differences of course.[40] But they are not usually arguing with us about whether, if we were equal in the ways they think we are not, we should treat each other as equals.

The non-cognitivist position stresses, though, that whether or not we agree about descriptive equality, the facts of the matter will never be enough to show that basic equality is a good thing. In the end it is something we have to choose. Bernard Williams may want to say:

> The principle that men should be differentially treated in respect of welfare merely on grounds of their colour is not a special sort of moral principle, but (if anything) a purely arbitrary assertion of will ...[41]

But it is a norm racists can adopt if they so choose.[42] The reasoning they may use to justify their position may be so bad, though, that we do not need to take it seriously.

I think that non-cognitivism is right to insist we have to choose our norms. Here it is right to insist that the rightness of our commitment to basic equality cannot be inferred from any descriptive equality. But that does not mean we cannot have *reasons* for our commitment to basic equality. We can, though not the kind of

---

38   A.J. Ayer *Language, Truth and Logic* (Pelican Books, Harmondsworth, 1971) 148.

39   Bernard Williams 'The Idea of Equality', above n. 25, 113.

40   Jeremy Waldron 'Whose Nuremburg Laws?' review of Patricia Williams S*eeing a Colourblind Future* 19 March 1998 *London Review of Books*, 12.

41   Williams 'The Idea of Equality', above n. 25, 113.

42   Although it is a senseless one, which is perhaps Professor Williams' point.

reasons that we want in order to see if something is the case as a matter of fact. I do not think accepting non-cognitivism means that we cannot give *any* reasons for our value commitments. Even Ayer, the arch non-cognitivist I referred to just now, agreed, in later work, that our moral views were not simply a matter of taste, like a love of ice-cream:

> This [his emotivist theory of ethics] does not mean that we have to regard every moral standpoint as equally correct. In holding a moral principle, one regards it as valid for others besides oneself, whether they think so or not. In cases where they do not think so, it will depend on their circumstances whether one judges that they are unenlightened or morally at fault. What has to be admitted is that there is no way of proving that they are mistaken. The most that one can do is argue *ad hominem.* One may be able to show that their principles are inconsistent, or that they are based on factual assumptions which are false, or that they are the product of bad reasoning, or that they lead to consequences which their advocates are not prepared to stand by [hence all the ethical argumentation which proceeds *reductio ad absurdum*].[43]

The fact that we do reason about ethical matters and that that reasoning can make, or not make, sense explains why we do not have to accept just any old moral conclusion and are suspicious of moral opinions that just announce themselves *ex cathedra*. I think that is something like the point just referred to that Bernard Williams is making about the strange racists who would base their views on colour alone. They have no reasons that *make any sense*. They are a bit like the person in G.E.M. Anscombe's example of someone who gathered together all the green books in his house and laid them out on the roof and explained his action by saying he had no special reason to behave like this. He just felt like it.[44] Some ends that humans might adopt just do not make any sense in our world.

We do give reasons for our practical conclusions, including our moral conclusions when pressed. 'This is just the way we do it' sounds more like a confession of laziness than a thoughtful contribution to moral thinking. To be taken seriously our reasons must make sense but that of course leaves room for much disagreement. There is no uncontroversial bedrock on which all our ethical reasoning rests even if our ethical commitments are usually not invented arbitrarily.

At least much modern political theorising, and practical ethicising about equality and other social ideals, seems to proceed on these non-cognitivist assumptions. It does this by weighing up various intuitions or accepted principles and teasing out their consequences and the assumptions behind them. We ask whether if we believe in liberty we can believe in equality as well. And what sense of 'equality'

---

43   A.J. Ayer *The Central Questions of Philosophy* (Penguin Books, Harmondsworth, 1976) 226–7.

44   G.E.M. Anscombe *Intention* (2nd edn, Basil Blackwell, Oxford, 1963), s 18, 26.

might conflict with which sense of 'liberty'? And whether these ideals enhance 'community' or are compatible with the efficiency needed to exploit and preserve our environment. There is not much in the way of providing proofs for basic axioms.

It might be that, instead, a coherentist approach is at least implied in much modern political thought. We, as Ayer suggests we might, examine each other's positions for internal consistency. Assuming the importance of a cluster of values we ask: does this theory, which implies a commitment to equality of some sort, pay enough attention to the needs of women or disabled people or poor nations? Does that approach, which stresses the rights of peoples to determine their destinies, place enough stress on the protection of the autonomy of individuals?

But coherence by itself is not enough to ensure that our moral thinking is the best it can be. Louis Pojman, after dismissing some recent attempts to justify basic equality, opines: '[i]f an egalitarianism [sic] rights theory is to succeed, my guess is that it will be a coherentist theory ...'.[45] But after rejecting an example of that approach, that of the Marxist egalitarian Kai Nielsen, Pojman qualifies his confidence in coherence by noting two problems. No convincing coherentist account has been produced yet. The second objection is seemingly more damning:

> Coherentist justifications in general are subject to the criticism of not tying into reality. A Nazi world view, a religious fundamentalist theology, and Nielson's Marxist egalitarianism, not to mention fairy tales, are all coherent and internally consistent, but no more than one of these mutually incompatible world views can be correct.[46]

One can entertain serious doubts about the coherence or internal consistency of some of these world views, I would have thought. Be that as it may. The consequences of living by these different world views will differ. And that will help us choose between them. But only because of other values we want to uphold, so the point is taken: coherence is not enough. Coherence is important, but as Simon Blackburn notes:

> It [coherence] should not blind us to other virtues. As well as coherence, there are maturity, imagination, sympathy, and culture. An immature, unimaginative, unsympathetic, and uncultivated ethic might be quite coherent ...[47]

---

45   Louis P. Pojman, 'Are Human Rights Based on Equal Human Worth?' (1992) 53 *Philosophy and Phenomenological Research* 605, 615.

46   Ibid. 615.

47   Simon Blackburn *Ruling Passions* (Oxford University, Oxford, 1998) 310. This book is a major non-cognitivist treatise which also provides a very useful grounding in modern moral theory. The alternatives to 'expressivism', the term Professor Blackburn uses in place of the older term 'non-cognitivism', are very well expounded and analysed.

We might focus too much on a too narrow range of values, as fundamentalists of all sorts often do, which is internally coherent but ignores important concerns of others. Coherence is important. An ethic which used the other ingredients Blackburn mentions well would still have to be coherent – as any good theory must. But even when they are, and all these other things are respected, ethical assessments still do not seem grounded in the way that natural science is. This is a feature of all moral thought, though, not just our ideas about equality.

But though it does not follow, as a matter of logic, from the fact that we are equal in some way or ways that we should treat one another as equals, there is, I think, some kind of connection between the 'is' and the 'ought' here. Even if we cannot *prove* that everyone should join our egalitarian consensus we can argue that it makes sense. It is a bit odd, although not *logically* incorrect, for one to agree that humans are alike in some fundamental non-scalar sense or senses, and then turn one's back on prescriptive equality, if one wants to be moral at all. It may be an open question, as G.E. Moore famously put it,[48] whether the facts about anything authorise our adopting, as a matter of logic, any view about what is good. But we probably need our notion of descriptive equality, expressed here in terms of the Rawlsian idea of range properties, to make sense of prescriptive equality – possibly because one *supervenes* on the other.[49]

In *God Locke and Equality* Jeremy Waldron discusses, in the context of John Locke's theologically based theory of human equality, the difference between prescriptive equality *supervening* on descriptive equality and the former being an implication of the latter. Locke himself did not believe, Waldron explains, that one could argue from the relevant factual similarity to the value of normative equality. Locke just realised, as we usually do, that there clearly seems to be some connection between the fact that there are beings who are alike in an important way and the commitment to treating them all as equals.[50]

The idea of *supervenience* in ethical theory means: 'the requirement that moral judgments supervene, or are consequential upon natural facts'.[51] The supervenience thesis holds that two states of affairs could not be identical in their natural aspects but differ morally. But that is consistent with accepting that the moral evaluation itself is not determined by the natural state of affairs. Different evaluators will, of course, sometimes assess the same situation differently.

---

48   George Edward Moore *Principia Ethica* (Cambridge University Press, Cambridge, 1959) 15, cited in Luther J. Binkley *Conflict of Ideals* (D. Van Nostrand Co, New York, 1969) 288–9.

49   See Waldron, *God Locke and Equality*, above n. 24, 69.

50   Ibid.

51   Simon Blackburn *Spreading the Word* (Oxford University Press, Oxford, 1984) 220. 'Natural' here is not the opposite of 'supernatural'. The theory of supervenience is not metaphysically fussy. The 'natural fact' that inspires a commitment to basic equality, for example, could, for the purposes of the supervenience requirement, be that we are all made in the image of God, although that would make the argument a lot more complicated.

Getting the 'ought' of basic equality from the 'is' of some specified factual human equality makes sense but the former is not implied by the latter.

The, at least plausible, connection between descriptive and prescriptive equality which we can think of in terms of the supervenience idea, explains why most of the debates we have and have had about equality are about how we are, or are not, the same in what we think are morally relevant ways. We often assume that if we can show that the purported difference is imaginary our opponents will agree, if they are in good faith, that the treatment we are concerned about was discriminatory. Political movements seeking greater equality have generally argued in this way. And their racist, sexist or homophobic opponents usually respond by justifying their unfair practices and policies by reference to alleged significant differences which make one group, in their view, inferior to others. The facts, in terms of these types of groupings, are on the side of the basic egalitarian here, though of course one rarely wins a moral argument with prejudiced people simply by pointing to the facts.

In terms of individuals we can justify our commitment to basic equality by relying on the range property idea though there is no strict logical connection between our sameness (or our differences) and adopting any value. The plausibility of doing that lies in the fact that we all, or at least all normal adults do, have the appropriate range properties. But there is a further riposte to be made to all this. This is the last point of contention about range properties, to which I said I would return: we must allow that others might prefer to focus on the individual differences themselves – the different points we occupy on the scale of a range property. In terms of these we are not equal. Why should our social ethics not supervene on *that* fact?

The Ethics of Superiority

Louis Pojman thinks 'the empirical and theoretical data we have count against the notion of equal worth'.[52] Pojman means these individual differences between human beings. He appears to suggest focussing on these makes more sense than relying on the factual equality of humans Rawls points to in his range property idea. But why should these individual differences make us think there is no reason to adopt basic equality as a norm? Why should our differences in physical strength, intelligence, wisdom or foresight lead us to think it would be better not to adopt that principle? Pojman says: '[e]mpirically, it looks like Churchill, Gandhi, and Mother Teresa have more value than Jack-the-Ripper or Adolf Hitler'.[53] They do in a way, but only in the sense that they made a more positive contribution to our moral environment. The other two belonged in jail because of the threat they represented to others. But why does it follow from that that moral argument should

---

52 Pojman 'Are Human Rights Based on Equal Worth?', above n. 45, 621.

53 Ibid.

not have to consider their good? Moral argument may have even justified killing Hitler during the war but it could have done that while still not discounting his interests (to not be tortured if caught alive for example) entirely. Even more so it is not clear why moral argument should not equally consider the good of Einstein and someone else not as clever as he was.

Larry Alexander notes that it is controversial whether all biases, against persons, are wrong:

> Many believe that all persons deserve equal concern and respect, but many others believe that the morally virtuous deserve more concern and respect than the morally vicious. For this group, a bias in favour of the virtuous and against the vicious is not only morally permissible but morally required.[54]

But I do not see how a bias in favour of anyone, in the sense that we could see some as intrinsically more worthy than others, could be justified simply because they are more virtuous. That of course is not to say that we should not be biased in favour of their virtue itself and against the viciousness of others. And that bias will require us to treat people differently. As I said it may even require us to imprison them, or take their lives in defence of others. What more could be required from those who think the virtuous deserve more than equal concern and respect? Should we discriminate between the morally superior and the morally less accomplished in the same way that some have discriminated in favour of whites and against blacks?

To turn the question around: if we are convinced of the similarity of our human condition, which Rawls expresses in terms of the range property idea, why do *individual* differences justify the denial of basic equality? I think they do not. Such a denial makes no sense; first, because it is not practical. Historical examples of elitism based on groups had one advantage over a more careful rejection of basic equality, one based on the different estimation of the worth of *individuals*. They were much more practical. A society which accorded rights on a differential basis according to individual differences would be completely unworkable. Of course racial classification under apartheid, for example, was ultimately incoherent, but it worked, more or less, at least for a while.[55] It worked because the groups were more or less identifiable and not so many as to necessitate the countless bureaucratic distinctions that would be necessary if almost everyone (or everyone at the same point on a continuum of, say, intelligence scores or virtue scores, or some sort of aggregate score combining these two and perhaps other capacities) constituted her own category of citizen. To work at all, elitist systems have to conflate many distinctions that could be

---

54   Larry Alexander 'What Makes Wrongful Discrimination Wrong? Biases, Preferences, Stereotypes, and Proxies' (1992) 141 *U Pa L Rev* 149, 159.

55   See S.D. Girvin 'Race and Race Classification' in A.J. Rycroft (ed.) *Race and the Law in South Africa* (Juta and Co Ltd, Johannesburg, 1987) 1.

made, thus undermining their own rationale. It may seem odd to accuse those who reject basic equality of being too idealistic but not all ideals are pleasant ones and those that we dislike can be criticised for being impractical just as much as those we favour.

An accurate elitist morality would also not convince enough people for it to serve as a tie that binds. A moral idea that is to serve its purpose as an alternative to the war of all against all must appeal to at least a good number of people. Strict elitism would be its own bar to any sort of solidarity and therefore unworkable on that count as well. The rejection of basic equality which relies on the fact of our individual differences is also just not decent. We cannot all build rockets or cure intransigent diseases but that is not a worthy reason to deny any of us access to as much education as we may benefit from.

The crude rejection of basic equality found in its racist or sexist variety often involved that particular inequality of course: separate schools for blacks in South Africa and the United States and exclusion from tertiary education of women in many countries. The obvious cruelty of those policies, which were based on group favouritism rather than on the real ability of individuals, is matched by one that would divert all or most resources to a small elite, more objectively determined than the taxonomy of the racist or sexist allows, that might achieve marginally more learning for a few at the expense of what the rest might learn with a more even sharing of resources.[56] A strict elitism values only excellence. And it employs a limited vision of excellence at that. It is one that counteracts human sympathy and the possibility of rich community that a commitment to basic equality makes possible. My argument here is not simply that a commitment to basic equality will do a better job of keeping the peace. That can be achieved in a number of ways, some of them quite unsavoury. I mean a community of equals that respect each other as such can be a friendlier, more cooperative, community which recognises more eagerly what we all have in common.

Given the existence of equality, of both peculiarly human range properties, and the fact of our individual differences, it makes sense to choose to value a basic equality which entails a commitment to equal consideration to the interests of each person. That is if we do not want the awful consequences I have suggested issue from the moral elitism which takes its cue from our individual differences. We cannot ignore the individual differences. We do have to respond to them when, for example, choosing between medical school applicants, aspirant national sports players, or who to vote for. But we do not have to think these differences justify denying a fair share of resources to some or that these variations might be used to determine anyone's intrinsic worth.

---

56 This is quite different, of course, from allowing distinction to count in the allocation of scarce educational resources such as university places. That can, all other things being equal, be consistent with basic equality. This reminds us once again that basic equality does not always require equal treatment.

Equality is a central value in modern political theory. Even those who do not think it is our 'sovereign virtue'[57] take it seriously. When commentators rail against it they commonly have some kind of policy aim in mind (equal wealth or income is a popular target) rather than the basic equality discussed here. That fundamental commitment to take everyone into account in our moral calculations is not immune to attack nor is it always honoured but it is, now, seldom dismissed as wrongheaded. Equality's popularity may make it difficult to be against but that does not justify our acceptance of this way of deciding the range of moral argument. That, the justification of basic equality, I have tried to do by noting the unattractiveness of the alternative. To ignore what we, and only we, as human beings, have in common, albeit in different degrees, seems arbitrary. Responding to individual differences in ways which respect our unique, shared, human existence makes more sense. Neither approach entirely ignores important facts. We do have to choose. I think the choice in favour of basic equality is the better one, for the reasons I have offered.

So far I have argued that equality is not an empty idea. The moral requirement to treat people as equals has substance, even if alternative ways of expressing that requirement can be found. The reason why its application may sometimes appear indeterminate is because it is a very abstract idea. Like 'liberty' or 'community' its application often has to be argued. Because of the abstractness of basic equality, I have argued therefore that we should value basic equality, without expecting that its application will often be uncontroversial. So this is perhaps a good time to see where basic equality might fit into the architecture of moral thought in general.

---

57   The title of Ronald Dworkin's recent book, above n. 9.

Chapter 4
The Scope of Basic Equality

Introduction

I have tried to defend from the charge of vacuity, and justify our acceptance of, a fundamental commitment to basic equality. Basic equality is a large notion and its implications will not always be apparent. There will be different views about what commitment to it entails and there are no shortcuts to the resolution of many controversial policy issues. On the other hand we do know what equality is, its meaning is not literally elusive: it is a commitment to treating persons as equals. But more must be said about basic equality's role and status in political ethics and moral thinking generally.

In my justification of basic equality I have relied on a bare sketch of what that value entails and I will now say something more about its scope. The entailments of basic equality are many of course and my remarks in this chapter will only try to add, to the basic notion I have introduced above, a rudimentary understanding of basic equality's place in our ethical thinking. I will suggest that the very general nature of basic equality does not mean that there can be no moral thinking which does not respect it. Equality is, however, general in the sense that it has (implicit usually) application in every moral assessment for those who are committed to it. Basic equality requires impartiality as between persons in the construction and application of other values and that we act impartially in general.

Although my main concern throughout this work is with the political and legal dimensions of basic equality, I will say something here about how commitment to basic equality implicates all of our moral thinking including both the personal and political levels. We want our governments to uphold equality because we think that it is a fundamental part of our moral obligation to others generally. Equality is not only a political concept; though our personal and political obligations to treat each other as equals are not symmetrical in all aspects.

Basic Equality and Morality

I have been talking about basic equality as a 'value'. This is right in the sense that it is something that we do value. We think it is a good thing to observe. But basic equality can also be a part of our whole moral structure, as in modern moral thought it typically is, in the sense that commitment to it means there is no moral argument of which it does not form a (usually implied) part. If one agrees to be bound by its dictates one cannot, on pain of inconsistency, simply ignore the interests of some affected parties in deciding what should be done. This is true, although sometimes in different ways, at the level of both personal and political ethics.

We cannot, though, despite the fundamental role played by basic equality for those who maintain its importance, claim there can be no real moral system which does not include a commitment to basic equality. It is perfectly possible for racists, for example, to have moral views and commitments, and they typically do. A commitment to basic equality is not an essential component of a moral system, however deficient we might think a set of moral values is without it. The fact that *we* think it is a sine qua non of ethical decision making does not make it one as a matter of logic.

It might seem too generous to say that the racist has a moral 'system'. But by that I do not mean that his[1] views are well ordered. Clearly they are not. Although other implications of basic equality may be justifiably controversial, the requirement not to discriminate against people on the ground of race is not. For the racist's views to make sense at all they must rely on some relevant difference between racial groups, and there is none that would make any moral sense of the various forms of discrimination that less favoured races have suffered and continue to suffer. This is what our best information today tells us and that has been the case for some time.[2]

What should we think, then, of the morality of a person who, like the racist, clearly does not believe in basic equality? We surely cannot demand that every morality must be coherent and consistent with our best understanding of the human situation, including our understanding of humans as the equals of one another. Very few people are educated to the extent of having that level of understanding. We cannot, in the case of racism again, assume everyone understands the factual basis of non-racism. But that is no reason to think someone who does not has no truly moral views. It is simply good reason to think his moral views are seriously limited. If we were today presented with someone with a pre-Copernican cosmology we would not deny that she had *a* cosmology.

The problem with this line of argument though, one might think, is that it seems to have forgotten the very point of morality: to get along with others in a cooperative way in the 'circumstances of justice' we share.[3] Our very survival depends on the enterprise, although we also think our existence is *better* if it is in the context of a caring community. We disagree about the content of morality of course, but when we do so, thoughtfully, we disagree in familiar ways. Moral argument is a particular form of arguing. An important aspect of this type of reasoning is the demand that we ask ourselves to consider whether we would wish our suggestions about how others should be treated to be applied to us. It is not

---

1   I have tried to use 'his' and 'hers' and their cognates evenly, hopefully not making either the villain on too many occasions.

2   See Steven Pinker *The Blank Slate* (Penguin Books, New York, 2002) 144.

3   See J.L. Mackie *Ethics: Inventing Right and Wrong* (Pelican Books, Harmondsworth, 1977) Ch. 5.

surprising that something like the Golden Rule is a recurring theme in the history of moral thought.

We must think there are worse and better ways to conduct moral argument, unless we embrace a crude relativism; which we should not. One argument against that sort of relativism is that it allows us to believe that all sorts of contradictory conclusions can be good answers to a moral question as long as they are being asked by different people or different groups of people: no relevant difference is required; only difference itself. The racist might rely on that sort of thinking but only at the cost of plausibility. If we reject crude relativism we will require moral conclusions to be justified in ways that show how they are good for all of us and respect us all, regardless of what is acceptable in a particular community.

Proceeding in this way, it does not seem difficult to show that the racist is wrong. He either appeals to differences we can show him do not exist or do not have the significance he thinks they do, or he appeals to race *per se*, which, as we noted Bernard Williams has said, makes little sense. Even though the racist does not give up the argument so easily, assuming any further points he makes will be as unconvincing as the ones he has made already, we may feel justified in saying there is no *good* moral defence of racism.

Of course, apart from racism and other group prejudice, there is still the argument from individual differences to deal with. I have argued that there is a good response to be made to that argument but it cannot be knocked down simply by stipulating that it is not a moral viewpoint at all. Many people are adherents of one or other partial morality or holders of a jumbled set of inconsistent or partly incoherent ethical views. They, including racists, and elitists of whatever ilk, still have moral views although they are vulnerable to attack on normative first order grounds if not metaethical ones. Not all people who have moral values think about them in a careful way. When faced with someone whose moral sentiments do not extend to the concern for everyone that basic equality requires, we will feel justified in pointing out to her that her moral opinions are incomplete. We do not have to think that it is possible to show her that her partial moral views are wrong in the same way that we can show her it is wrong to think the earth is flat. But we think we can ask her to think more clearly about why it is that she bothers to have moral views at all. We think it is worth pointing out that we all have similar needs and concerns to the ones that the members of her group have. But if we do not convince her she simply retains her deficient moral outlook. We need not claim she does not *have* one; even though she is, in our view, obtuse when it comes to improving it.

If this is right then basic equality is more than just the requirement of 'universalisability' – at least in a modest sense of that idea. Universalisability is, in the basic sense of that term, the requirement that we make the same moral judgment in situations that share relevant features: it is implied by the idea that moral qualities supervene on natural ones.[4] As J.L. Mackie puts it:

4   See Ch. 3.

Anyone who says, meaning it, that a certain action (or person, or state of affairs, etc.) is morally right or wrong, good or bad, ought or ought not to be done (or imitated, or pursued, etc.) is thereby committed to taking the same view about any other relevantly similar action (etc.).[5]

As Mackie notes, this all depends on what is relevantly similar.[6] No situation is exactly the same but some differences are not important. We want to take into account only qualitative differences. If adultery is wrong it is just as wrong whether it takes place on Friday or Saturday and whether Peter commits it with Susan, or Angela with Michael. If someone maintained that adultery was only wrong if committed by persons other than himself that would not be universalisable because it is not likely that he will be able to point to something about himself which is different in a plausibly relevant way. A more limited proscription which forbade adultery except in certain circumstances might, on the other hand, be universalisable.[7]

This much universalisation does not rule out much apart from extreme egoism although it is, Mackie argues, a bit substantive. It does require a certain degree of fairness. It does make us treat like cases alike.[8] But as we have seen, accepting that formula does not commit us to basic equality.[9] As Mackie says:

It is unfair in almost all circumstances to discriminate between people on grounds of colour; it is unfair to discriminate in the provision of educational opportunities on grounds of sex; it is unfair to discriminate in the allocation of council houses on grounds of religious affiliation; but none of these is excluded by our first stage of universalizability.[10]

Universalisability is claimed by some to be a formal requirement of moral logic and a source of moral values.[11] These claims become less plausible when the idea is given more content. Whether or not simple (what Mackie calls 'first stage') universalisability is a part of the logic of moral terms,[12] it does occupy an even more *structural* role in ethics than basic equality does. If it is substantive it is less so than basic equality. It is possible to moralise, within the fetters of universalisability, unconstrained by basic equality, even if this is now unusual in public discourse. Basic equality is still, however, a very general requirement.

---

5   Mackie *Ethics: Inventing Right and Wrong*, above n. 3, 83.

6   Ibid.

7   These are not Mackie's examples.

8   Mackie *Ethics: Inventing Right and Wrong*, above n. 3, 88.

9   See Ch. 2.

10   Mackie *Ethics: Inventing Right and Wrong*, above n. 3, 89.

11   R.M. Hare *Moral Thinking* (Clarendon Press, Oxford, 1981).

12   See Bernard Williams *Ethics and the Limits of Philosophy* (Fontana Press, London, 1985) 85. Williams does not accept Hare's claims for universalisability.

The generality of basic equality is due to its relevance to the process of any moral evaluation, once it is accepted. That relevance is a matter of logic once we have accepted basic equality because it tells us *whose* needs or interests, or concerns generally, we need to take into account in the construction and application of our ethical standards – those of all persons affected by our decision. It indicates the range across which moral argument applies. Commitment to basic equality does not rule out concern for other creatures but it is a humanist commitment in the sense that it rejects ethical systems that deem some humans more important than others.

When we construct ethical standards they are for the benefit of all if we respect basic equality. Ethical decisions based on values other than basic equality itself, then, have a dual nature if we think all people are equals: they are implicitly about basic equality, and whatever else they are about. It is (usually) wrong to steal and it is wrong to think stealing is acceptable just because the victims are people we do not care about. It is (usually) wrong to kill people, and it is wrong to think killing people is permissible simply because the victims belong to a group whose members' right to life we do not take seriously. The argument that this dualism is metaphysically extravagant is, as I have argued, not convincing. It is true that it is just wrong to steal from or kill people, generally. But it is a separate wrong to think stealing and killing is acceptable just because we do not think the victims are our equals. The wrong consists in the way the racist, for example, defines his moral responsibility generally.[13] In this way basic equality has something to say in the construction and application of all our values.

Do we not know cases, though, where the only moral issue is basic equality? Are there not some wrongs which consist only in ignoring basic equality? This would seem to be the case where we have no moral duty to do or not do something but do it, or neglect to do it, in a partial way. At the level of personal morality: I have no duty to play bridge, or refrain from playing it, in my free time. It is of course permitted, morally speaking, to eschew bridge altogether in favour of reading books or going to the movies. But if I decide to play bridge and start a club, *choosing the members using only or partly racist criteria*, then I have breached my duty to treat people as equals (which would not be the case of course if all the available people just happened to be members of one race group). While it would be absurd to have laws about whom I may invite to my bridge club, that does not mean I would not be denying the basic equality of someone I thought of, but specifically did not invite, because of his race.

---

13   It is not the case, of course, that all racists think it is acceptable to steal from or kill members of less favoured racial groups, although history and current affairs provide examples of those who do. On a related matter: how my thoughts here relate to the moral justification for laws which punish so-called 'hate crimes' is not something I consider in this book. I would just note that that justification does not follow in any obvious way from what I have said. With a 'hate-crime', if you take away the action itself all you are left with is the bad attitude, and it is quite plausible to argue that bad attitudes should not be criminalised.

At the political level, a state may have no duty, founded in justice, to fund any particular sort of cultural activity, say dance or music, but does so in a clearly partial (as between the affected persons) way, not respecting the legitimate expectations of all affected parties. If there is no value other than basic equality which is being offended here then the dualism referred to a moment ago is not complete. Basic equality monitors the application of other values but also applies, again, independently in some cases.

Although basic equality can be an independent concern in this way, there is no duty, flowing from basic equality, to do morally impermissible things, to everyone in equal measure. The fact that we have treated some people badly, or some too well, is not a sufficient reason, in itself, to equalise the treatment. Only if equality is limited to the 'treat like cases alike' formulation is it a matter of *equality* that an apparent comparative unfairness of that nature should always be corrected by equal treatment. A child should not be allowed to stay up late *just* because his brother was wrongly allowed to the night before. An errant driver should not be let off his fine *simply* because an offending driver just ahead of him was not fined. There is, in these examples, a certain unfairness. But the urge to correct that unfairness must compete with, in these examples, other values – the need for children to have a good night's rest and our concern to be safe on the road.

Basic equality, which I have suggested does not compete with other considerations, thus does not require mindless consistency with past moral error. Christopher Peters (the examples in the previous paragraph are his) notes equality might be thought to recommend equal treatment in these cases.[14] By 'equality' he means a 'non-tautological' application of the treat likes alike formula[15] – 'Identically situated people are entitled to be treated identically merely because they are identically situated'.[16] In his debate with Kent Greenawalt about cases like these, he and Greenawalt may indeed have discovered a substantive idea in the treat likes alike formula.[17] But it amounts to something like: if you have made a moral mistake you should stick to it in the future, as a matter of consistency; that idea is not basic equality.

Professor Peters, when he wrote about these matters, feared that he would be accused of attacking a straw man,[18] of missing the true meaning of equality. In a sense I am suggesting that but I think the conception of equality he is discussing is widely used and worth debunking. That conception focuses too much on comparisons between two parties and prescribes solutions which do not necessarily

---

14   Christopher J. Peters 'Equality Revisited' (1997) 110 *Harv L Rev* 1211.

15   Ibid. 1212.

16   Ibid. 1223.

17   See K. Greenawalt '"Prescriptive Equality": Two Steps Forward' (1997) 110 *Harv L Rev* 1265, 1266–8. Although I think Greenawalt, as I note below, may have been more concerned with a *perception* of fairness, which can have its own impact sometimes and thereby introduce a morally relevant difference between two otherwise similar situations.

18   Peters 'Equality Revisited', above n. 14, 1214.

respect basic equality because they do not take *all* affected parties into account or even the *whole* good of the parties whose interests are considered. A caveat should be inserted here. Sometimes the perception of unfair treatment might only be assuaged by an otherwise, all-things-considered, unwise application of equal treatment. This can involve an important interest of others; their need to believe in the 'system'. In cases like that this concern is one, amongst others of course, which must be taken into account too. [19]

There are some situations where the law too might be applied in a discriminatory fashion, where the inequality itself is an issue that should be addressed. Basic equality requires a response to such situations as they do constitute failures to treat people as equals. But the morally correct response is not necessarily to 'treat everyone the same'. It might be instead that the rule itself, or the way it is applied in the future, needs to be reconsidered. Or some other measure may be required, depending on an assessment of the whole situation. Basic equality provides no uniform solution to these legal situations either, though a partial, biased application of rules and principles, good ones or bad, is a distinct moral problem.

It is therefore not necessary to think that adherence to basic equality merely requires, or even necessarily requires, that any particular inequality of treatment by the state should be eliminated in a perfunctory fashion.[20] If, for example, a police force shows racial bias in enforcing a particular (uncontroversial in itself) rule of criminal law so that more black offenders than white offenders are convicted, that is better dealt with by a review and training intervention than by, say, pardoning every third black offender until the racial statistics are proportionate. And the first solution is consistent with basic equality because it does take the interests of all affected parties into account. We would prefer, in general, no crime to go unpunished. Full enforcement of the law usually not being possible, we would rather there was no bias in its application. The important thing then is to remove the bias, not to arbitrarily remove some of its effects, regardless of the consequences of that – in this case allowing some offenders who could be dealt with to proceed unhindered. Basic equality does not commit us to a meaningless mathematical equality, although the treat likes alike formula might sometimes.

Basic equality's generality lies then, first, in its application to all our moral decisions. Say, for various reasons, we believe in adult suffrage. If no one is allowed to vote or if the constitutional arrangements for voting are not really democratic we think that is wrong. We also think it is wrong if only some are denied suffrage; that is a breach of basic equality. I have also suggested that it has application in its own right, so to speak. That second kind of lack of respect for basic equality

---

19   See Kent Greenawalt '"Prescriptive Equality": Two Steps Forward' above n. 17, 1265. Professor Greenawalt thought he had to send his younger child to violin lessons although he suspected it would be as futile as sending his older child had turned out to be. He would not, of course, simply for the sake of consistency, have sent his younger child to a doctor who had previously treated his older child negligently.

20   I agree with Professor Peters on that score.

is found in situations where morally optional – in themselves – behaviours or policies are partial because some are included or excluded in an arbitrary fashion. A third role for equality might be that it is a source of other values.

Perhaps it is better to say that belief in equality might be a *reason* to hold other values rather than that it is a source of those values. To suggest that equality is a source of those other values might seem to rule out the possibility that there could be other reasons for having them. One reason for allowing people to express thoughts we disapprove of is that our status as equal moral persons demands that, but that does not mean there are no other justifications for free speech.[21]

To return to the voting example: apart from anything else we might think that people should have the vote *because they are equals*. At each stage of reform towards universal suffrage previously excluded groups were included and basic equality was only fully respected, in the matter of political representation, at the end of the process. Even when no one had a vote as such, however, someone had the power to decide policy; a monarch's council or whatever. There is always political power and the question 'who has it?' is always as important as the issue of how it is used. The right to vote is valuable for various consequentialist reasons but it is also required in a society of equals because basic equality is not respected when some are ruled without their consent. I will defer further discussion of this point until my more focussed treatment of the relationship between equality and other values. It is an aspect of that topic and the topic itself is complex.[22]

When are We Bound by Basic Equality?

Because basic equality is a very general requirement it applies in all spheres of life. By that general remark I mean here that the principle binds us as individual moral agents in our personal lives as well as in the political realm. Even if we think we sometimes have to pay special attention to the needs of those who are related to us in some intimate way, we can still honour basic equality by recognising that we cannot put the needs of, say, our families above the demands of justice itself.[23] Assuming we can decide what a just distribution of wealth or resources and liberties is, we cannot, as individual moral agents, be committed to basic equality while demanding more than that for our charges or kin.

Part of the justification for allowing this limited sort of partiality is, as Larry Alexander says, because favouring a small group, because of positive personal affection and loyalty, has a different moral quality from disfavouring a small group, which is more likely to be motivated by an ideology that claims that group is less

---

21   See Ronald Dworkin *Freedom's Law* (Oxford University Press, Oxford, 1996) Ch. 8.

22   See Ch. 6.

23   Jeremy Waldron, 'Basic Equality' (2008). *New York University Public Law and Legal Theory Working Papers*. Paper 107. (Hereinafter BE) 6 n. 13.

morally worthy.[24] But the consequences of any favouritism are also important to bear in mind as they may also indicate that some are being treated as less worthy.

Within the limits that distributive justice does allow, we might think we should be free, without moral restraint, to favour those we are more closely or intimately related to if we allow that everyone should be entitled to do so. The freedom to plan and live our own lives with a just share of resources reasonably includes the freedom to do that in a group such as a family which inevitably involves giving preference to that grouping in some ways. It is at least arguable that having such ties is a universal good. Friendship outside of intimate biological groupings could also not exist if we rigidly distributed our attention amongst everyone. But that does not mean the individual moral agent who believes in basic equality only has the moral duty to support a political arrangement that upholds it.

We must decide, as a matter of justice, how much the law should constrain *us* because the *state* wants to uphold equality. We always have to decide, in general, to what extent people should be free to do wrong. But the moral responsibility of the individual *per se* is another matter. At the personal (as opposed to the political) level basic equality does not only constrain us as much as the law does. The moral right to use our just share of resources in partial ways that favour an intimate grouping such as the family or a circle of friends is arguably consistent with an equal right for others to do that. But there is no similar justification available for a general social bias on the part of the individual.

The law may or may not, for example, proscribe the offering of goods or services for sale, on a racial or some other discriminatory basis but whether or not it does we have, as individuals, a moral duty not to do that because we must honour basic equality in our dealings with others. Likewise it would be impossible outside a totalitarian state to ensure that we did not discriminate when seeking out services from private persons or in our role as consumers generally but our loyalty to basic equality would require that we did so desist. A state bound by, or just committed to, basic equality may not differentiate unfairly between groups of people. Neither may an individual who is so committed, even in those circumstances where that individual is not constrained by the law.

I am not discussing here the question of whether such discrimination *should* be proscribed by law, even in the less intrusive context where we limit the freedom of suppliers (or employers) but not consumers.[25] I am talking about the individual's personal moral responsibility. But if it is acceptable, in the personal sphere, to favour, in certain respects at least, one's family or friends, why is it not morally acceptable to favour one's ethnic or racial group as well? If we allow that it is morally permissible for *anyone* to favour his ethnic group does that not show equal consideration? In a society with a just distribution of resources why should it matter if people exercised their freedom to deal with others on ethnic lines?

---

24 Larry Alexander 'What Makes Wrongful Discrimination Wrong? Biases, Preferences, Stereotypes, and Proxies' (1992) 141 *U Pa L Rev* 149, 160.

25 See Ch. 6.

Three, rather disparate, considerations present themselves. First, it is unlikely that in our world there will be a perfectly just distribution of resources and more particularly it is unlikely that there will be a just distribution between the groupings that we notice or want to identify with. Further partiality will only make things worse. That response does not really address the question though: what if there *was* a just distribution, including between ethnic groups? Would group favouritism then be acceptable? In any society it would not be efficient if carried out to any great extent of course. It might also be thought that no one would want to behave like that in such a society.

A second consideration is that we might want to say that someone who behaves in this clannish way just has the wrong moral attitude towards diversity. Why do people want to favour their own if not because of a plain preference for certain *sorts* of people? The third consideration is that they might sometimes claim that they have a good *moral* reason to favour their own group as there is not, because of discrimination, a just distribution at present. Someone may argue that their ethnic group or, perhaps, women in general, deserve preferential treatment – not just from the state but also by private individuals. Here the considerations that apply to preferential treatment which is motivated by a desire to uplift a disadvantaged group, generally, apply. But if this preferential treatment is justified it will be consistent with basic equality. It must, in other words, not infringe the requirement to treat us all as equals.

That requirement may not be easy to satisfy here. Even disadvantaged minorities must be sensitive to the fact that there are other disadvantaged minorities and it is easy to confuse mutual support, which is needed and not forthcoming from society, in general, with exclusive practices motivated by prejudice. One of the issues that frequently arises in affirmative action debates is the question of how long such preferential treatment should last. That question is relevant here. It is hard to think of a reason why we would approve, morally, of permanent social exclusivity on an ethnic, or gender, basis in our public dealings with people.

There are different ways of 'favouring an ethnic group' and I do not mean to suggest that they are all morally equivalent. Getting together, as immigrants often do, with people who have a common background need not imply any attitude of superiority or exclusiveness. Someone's preference for marrying someone with a similar background to their own may also not involve the kind of prejudice we usually assume accompanies a decision never to patronise the business of an 'outsider'. But there is the danger here that bad motives can creep in: old-fashioned prejudice; revenge; a desire that certain groups do not prosper too much. Solidarity is not an absolute good.[26]

Although the value of basic equality has application in both the personal and political spheres, the way that it does is not entirely symmetrical, then. I shall

---

26   I should stress, in case it is not quite clear, that I am talking about the individual's conscience here. It would not be at all appropriate to police, formally or informally, anyone's prejudices *per se*.

argue below that basic equality requires more than just refraining from the types of discrimination that are typically covered in human rights laws. It requires impartiality as between persons in general unless we can justify a particular impartiality on the grounds that allowing it to everyone generally advantages all of us. Nepotism in government affairs, for example, is a breach of basic equality just as much as racial policies are, because it offends against a rule we have because of a commitment to partiality between persons. Nepotism is also a starker example, than the ones suggested by what I have said thus far, of what I think is an important asymmetry between the moral duties of the state and the individual moral actor.

While racist or sexist dealings, for example, are wrong for both, the evil of nepotism has no parallel in the personal sphere. By 'personal' here I do not mean 'private' in the sense of 'non-state'. Of course nepotism can be objectionable in the business context. What I mean is there is a narrower (than 'private') sphere where it is not wrong to give a friend or family member custom or some sort of valuable opportunity just because of those ties. This is an example of the asymmetry I am trying to get at. If the Minister of Education gives a government contract to a family member she does not act with a proper concern for all affected persons. But does she commit the same wrong if she contracts a family member to provide a service for herself in her private capacity? Surely she does not. There might of course be prudential reasons for not using one's relatives to get the job done! But it does not seem unfair to others to do so, as it would at the political level.

How can we explain these different judgments? One relevant difference is the government uses public money when it hires. It seems wrong that that money should be spent according to private considerations. It is not just that a lack of objectivity might mean the best person for the job is not hired although that will often be a problem. There is also the benefit to the contractor, which is not available to others, to consider. And there is, perhaps most importantly, the 'message' such favouritism sends to the populace; that some are favoured and some are not. We have a rule against nepotism in government because taking all these considerations into account we cannot honour impartiality, in the sense that it is required by basic equality, if we allow nepotism in state affairs.

In the personal context, on the other hand, there might even be a duty to favour a family member or friend. The asymmetry is explained by the first point made above on this topic. Favouring a family member or friend when procuring supplies or services, in our personal capacities, is acceptable because it is an example of the special treatment which is in part constitutive of that sort of relationship. It is consistent with respect and concern for all. This is only one subtlety to take into account. The moral obligations of individuals and governments to uphold basic equality are of course different in many ways, some of which I have suggested. My main point here is that basic equality plays an important role in each.[27]

---

27   The relationship between the two is complex of course. For a recent discussion of various takes on it see Kwame Anthony Appiah *The Ethics of Identity* (Princeton University

I have argued that basic equality is a part of the background of modern moral thinking. It is not, however, impossible to moralise if one is not committed to it. Racists and sexists may hold all sorts of (even sound) moral views without being disposed to give women or people of a different race the full benefit of their application. They are not even necessarily inconsistent in their moral views because of this, as long as they believe that those whose basic equality they are denying *deserve* to be excluded because of something that makes them relevantly different. Basic equality means extending all our moral concerns to persons without discrimination. It also requires that we, as a community or as individuals – in different ways – not be partial in general.

Basic equality can also be a source of other important social and political values. Or perhaps it is better to say that our belief in basic equality gives us a reason to uphold other values. This is what I will argue in the next chapter. I will limit my discussion to the relationship between equality and liberty and suggest that seeing other persons as equals entails allowing them the liberty to develop, in a way consistent with the rights of others, their own morality and understanding of what a good life consists in.

At the level of basic equality there is no need to choose, if my argument is correct, between equality and liberty but equality as an aim of a social policy might indeed clash with certain liberties. In assessing those conflicts it should be remembered that one reason for upholding liberty, even liberty to do wrong, is our belief in basic equality. It is not sufficient when arguing for the limitation of important liberties, just to suggest that a particular freedom must be curtailed for the sake of equality.

Press, Princeton, 2005) Ch. 6. Appiah separates the realm of the personal and the political more rigidly than I have.

Chapter 5
Basic Equality and Other Values

Introduction

In this chapter I argue that basic equality itself requires a strong commitment to certain important liberties – those typically found in a Bill of Rights. The second meaning of 'equality', as a policy goal, may clash with particular important liberties and then a balancing process must be entered into. If we bear in mind that fundamental liberties should themselves be protected because of our commitment to basic equality we will be less likely to accept, uncritically, arguments for the suppression of basic freedoms couched in terms of 'equality'.

There are two intuitions that we have about equality which are in tension with each other. On the one hand we think there is some sense in which equality is a moral absolute; it cannot be overridden by some other moral consideration. This sense of equality is expressed in different ways; the idea that we deserve to be 'treated as equals' is one familiar way of putting it. On the other hand we also intuitively feel that equality does clash with other moral values; most notoriously with liberty, and we sometimes have to decide for or against it.

Neither of these intuitions is easy to dismiss. Our intuition, which I have argued is supported by good reasons, that we all deserve, in abstract terms, to be treated as if we mattered equally, in every conceivable situation is hard to ignore. But it is also hard to ignore the apparent conflict between equality and liberty in discussions like those on economic rights or hate speech.

The tension can be partly resolved by noticing that we are using the two quite different senses of 'equality' that we have identified: basic equality and equality as an aim. It will be helpful, in ways which will become apparent, if we keep this distinction in mind when discussing the general topic of the relationship between equality and liberty.

I have noted our sense that basic equality is an absolute requirement. Equal concern and respect must be afforded, always, in the choice of public policy.[1] Basic equality does not bow to other concerns when the situation seems to call for the application of some other principle that is incompatible with it. If basic equality is a moral filter, no social policy or practice which does not take seriously the concerns of all affected persons is justified and no such policy or practice is exempted from this test simply because it serves some other social value that we think is a good one.

---

1   I do not mean it is irrelevant to an individual's moral choices.

But we do have other political ideals; liberty and community amongst others. Clearly then, the idea of equality as a basic constraint has implications for the relationship between equality, in that sense, and other political values. These implications need to be elucidated so that, in particular, the relationship between basic equality and liberty, and the relationship between liberty and the sorts of equality that we might aim for in society, can be understood.

My discussion will make particular reference to some of the debates and controversies generated by Ronald Dworkin in this area. I will argue, in Dworkinian fashion, that basic equality is compatible with fundamental liberties such as freedom of speech and freedom of religion. I will show that that is most clearly so because basic equality requires that we respect those liberties. We do not acknowledge the equal worth of others if we allow them no freedom to develop their own ideas or, without good reason, refuse them permission to express their own thoughts; or unfairly restrict their cultural or religious practices.

Unlike Dworkin, however, I am not concerned with the question of whether rights to certain liberties should be protected by special legislation which can be applied to strike down or limit the application of other laws.[2] I will refer often to the type of liberties 'found in a Bill of Rights' but this usage is my, stipulated, ellipsis of 'found ... or in ordinary legislation; or in the exercise of legislative restraint'. I am also not concerned with defending a more specific equality such as Dworkin's equality of resources[3] or with the project of fitting a specific conception of equality into an overall moral scheme or theory of justice.

Equality and specific liberties are in tension at times when a policy goal aims at some greater equality of welfare or opportunity. Here we are talking about equality in Rawls's first sense concerning the distribution of goods.[4] ('Goods' can be interpreted broadly here to include things like a racially equitable workplace.) While equalisation policies can be motivated, in part, by a belief in basic equality they are also constrained by it to the extent to which they might damage the liberties inspired by our commitment to basic equality.

In particular I note that if treating people as equals is one reason to support and protect fundamental liberties then these freedoms are not as vulnerable as they otherwise would be to careless arguments that they should be restricted in the name of 'equality'. Such arguments may arise in relation to various types of liberty. I shall mention the ongoing critique of the liberal notion of freedom of expression, in particular, towards the end of this chapter, after making the general argument with reference to that freedom and others. Because it is important to understand what is wrong with such critiques of freedom of expression, most of the chapter deals with the general argument that credible concern for equality includes a concern for that freedom and other important liberties.

---

2   See Ronald Dworkin *Freedom's Law* (Oxford University Press, Oxford, 1996).

3   See Ronald Dworkin *Sovereign Virtue* (Harvard University Press, London, 2000) Ch. 2.

4   John Rawls *A Theory of Justice* (Oxford University Press, Oxford, 1971) 511.

Basic Equality and Fundamental Freedoms

One way to defend the claim that a state which upholds the equal worth of persons will protect basic freedoms is to show that it is possible to find an argument, for the basic freedoms we value in the modern liberal state, which flows from our commitment to basic equality. If granting people certain freedoms is part of what it means to treat others as equals, and if these are the usual freedoms that make up the standard list of civil and political liberties, then we do not have to choose between basic equality and the usual freedoms found in a Bill of Rights.

The argument that the endorsement of basic equality entails approval of those liberties is not made just by noting that we want people to enjoy an *equal set* of freedoms. It might be considered a good thing for a community to allow its members an equal say in questions of governance, an equal right to express opinions on other matters, an equal right to choose who to associate with and so on. But from that we cannot infer that basic equality itself motivates any entitlement to liberty. We might just believe that whatever rights we think people should have, if any, we want them all to have.

It can indeed be argued, however, that a commitment to basic equality entails the right to be free from the domination of others in important ways. We should be in charge of our own lives, it can be argued, because we are equals – not being in charge of our own lives necessitates someone else's control, which implies they are more worthy than we are to decide how our lives should be led. The freedom we are talking about is the freedom not to be interfered with by others, in certain important aspects of our lives.[5] One reason why they should not interfere is that such intervention suggests that some people are better placed, in general, than we are, to decide how our lives should be lived.

I do not mean it is reasonable to complain that one has been discriminated against simply because some have the power to limit liberty while others are merely subject to that power.[6] A properly constituted government will have to limit its citizens' liberty in certain ways including, at times, ways that impinge, at least to some extent, on their core civil liberties. In that respect government officials will have powers that ordinary citizens do not have. But that is compatible with basic equality if it is carried out in a manner that respects everyone and weighs their concerns in an even-handed manner. It is only unwarranted intrusion on our liberty that we can argue fails to pay us the respect due to equals. A government may properly prohibit the sacrifice of humans to assuage the anger of a god, but it

---

5   Something like 'negative liberty' in Isaiah Berlin's taxonomy of freedom. See Isaiah Berlin 'Two Concepts of Liberty' in Isaiah Berlin *Four Essays on Liberty* (Oxford University Press, Oxford, 1969) 121. But see Ronald Dworkin 'Do Liberty and Equality Conflict?' in Paul Barker (ed.) *Living as Equals* (Oxford University Press, Oxford, 1996) 39 for a different characterisation of what is important about the freedoms under discussion.

6   See Bernard Williams, 'From Freedom to Liberty: The Construction of a Political Value' (2001) 30 *Philosophy and Public Affairs* 3, 12.

may not properly forbid religious activity or expression simply because it deems it irrational or frivolous.

It is at least easy to talk, as I am now, about basic equality, and the liberty of human rights and constitutional law discourse, as if they were parts of a whole. Such talk does not seem strained. It sounds reasonable to say that if someone's speech is censored because she expresses, say, communist views that are not approved of by the majority, or those in power, she has been discriminated against on the ground of her political beliefs. We see this clearly, to take another example, in the modern Bill of Rights which typically includes a provision to protect freedom of religion as well as a clause which proscribes discrimination on that ground.[7] These provisions clearly overlap.[8] Suppression of one religion has typically favoured another, or other, religions. That is usually the effect, and usually the point, of restrictions on religious liberty.

Again, we naturally do not think we should allow all religious activity. The denial of medical treatment to children is justifiably forbidden by the law against murder just as some limits on freedom of speech are acceptable. The idea that any practice or expression should not be prohibited *just* because someone values it, no matter how harmful it is, is absurd. But this understanding of the sorts of liberties that are protected in Bills of Rights is consistent with a plausible account of the denial of religious equality which would recognise that it is not necessary to allow all sincerely held beliefs to be acted on.[9] Religious discrimination is constituted by the unjust limitation of some forms of religious expression; not all censure or restriction of religion is unfair. The basic liberties themselves are not moral absolutes, they must be protected in a way that respects the rights of others; this is also, of course, an implication of our commitment to basic equality.

It is not necessary to suggest that a belief in basic equality is the only good reason to favour typical Bill of Rights liberties. I am suggesting that one moral justification for the freedoms protected in a liberal state is that a commitment to upholding them is required if we believe in basic equality. This does not exclude other reasons for protecting certain liberties. But are unjustified restrictions of these liberties always a denial of basic equality? Historically the liberties of certain oppressed groups have been denied in an uneven way which does constitute

---

7   See, for example, the New Zealand Bill of Rights Act 1990, ss. 13, 15, 19; Constitution of the Republic of South Africa Act 1996, ss. 9, 15.

8   No substantial comment on the meaning or application of either of these provisions is offered here; nor am I arguing for any specific legislative reform. I think a commitment to basic equality requires, amongst other things, something like the usual commitment to freedom of religion but 'basic equality' is far too abstract a notion to serve as a legal rule even in the notoriously abstract context of Bills of Rights provisions.

9   I do not discuss the issue of which limitations are justified but they would also have to be decided in a way which treats us equals and, accordingly, takes our rights into consideration. For a useful discussion of the problem see Denise Meyerson *Rights Limited* (Juta and Co Ltd, Cape Town, 1997).

discrimination. Restricting, for example, freedom of religion for Protestants and, at different times, Catholics in England, or denying black people in South Africa freedom of movement, were denials of basic equality; whatever other descriptions may serve. So a restriction of liberty can be (or accompany) a denial of basic equality, but does it have to be? May the two not just sometimes overlap?

To show that it does not have to be the case that the authoritarian curtailment of basic freedoms is a denial of basic equality it would seem we just need one counter-example. That is H.L.A. Hart's strategy in his debate with Ronald Dworkin on the matter. An infringement of liberty, for Hart, is just that. Equality has nothing to do with it. Hart says:[10]

> When it is argued that the denial to some of a certain freedom, say to some form of religious worship or to some form of sexual relations, is essentially a denial of equal concern and respect, the word 'equal' is playing an empty but misleading role. The vice of the denial of such freedom is not its inequality or unequal impact: if that *were* the vice the prohibition by a tyrant of all forms of religious worship or sexual activity would not increase the scale of the evil as in fact it surely would, and the evil would vanish if all were converted to the banned faith or to the prohibited form of sexual relationship. The evil is the denial of liberty or respect; not *equal* liberty or *equal* respect: and what is deplorable is the ill-treatment of the victims and not the relational matter of the unfairness of their treatment compared with others.

Hart's argument was meant to counter Dworkin's idea that infringements of the kind of liberties that we find in Bills of Rights are wrong because they offend 'that [liberal] fundamental conception of equality'.[11] Hart's counter-examples are quite extreme and bring to mind a citation of Peter Westen's in his book *Speaking of Equality*. William Frankena said: 'If a ruler were to boil his subjects in oil, jumping in afterward himself, it would be an injustice, but there would be no inequality of treatment'.[12]

Westen himself doubts whether this is correct: 'Frankena's example is not the example of equal treatment Frankena thinks it is, because while the ruler *kills* [murders] all his subjects, he merely *commits suicide* himself".[13] I think Westen means the ruler would be getting his way and everyone else would not be; so there *is* unequal treatment though it is not, strictly speaking, the treatment which is unequal in Frankena's example: they all get cooked. There

---

10   H.L.A. Hart, 'Between Utility and Rights' (1979) 79 *Colum Law Rev* 828, 845.

11   Ronald Dworkin *Taking Rights Seriously* (Duckworth, London, 1977) 274.

12   William Frankena 'The Concept of Social Justice' in R. Brandt (ed.) *Social Justice* 17 (Prentice-Hall, Englewood Cliffs, 1962) 17, cited in Peter Westen *Speaking of Equality* (Princeton University Press, Princeton, 1990) 90.

13   Westen attributes this insight to Brian Simpson. See Westen *Speaking of Equality*, above n. 12, 90 n. 45.

is an inequality in the situation though. The inequality lies in the constitutional arrangement which gives the ruler the power to make this sort of decision. A better political system, which was itself constrained by the value of basic equality, would not allow such an awful policy. Frankena is right, on the other hand, in the sense that the policy would ultimately affect, in terms of their longevity at least, everyone equally. I will return to the significance of this difference between the polity and the policy after considering Hart's scenarios and Dworkin's response to them.

Hart's counter-examples are like Frankena's. Taking his second one first, the evil of the prohibitions would indeed not vanish if all converted to the prohibited religion or sexual practice, partly because, as Hart implies, the restriction of liberty would still be a wrong. It is difficult to make a case that anyone, for the time being, would be being treated differently in this situation because all are equally restricted. We might note that even if Hart's tyrant applied the proscription to himself he would merely be abstaining whereas everyone else would be being oppressed though that is, once again, a critique of the political system and not of the policy *per se*. Under it, all are, as Hart implies, treated equally.

Turning to Hart's other counter-example: if all religious devotions and all sexual practices are banned there is again the difference between the one who makes this decision and the others who just have to live with it, but here again the policy itself applies equally and is of course still unjustifiable because of the infringement of liberty.

Hart's and Frankena's examples are of the same type. They both describe a totalitarian situation of a very extreme nature and Dworkin notes, in his riposte to Hart, that in that kind of situation there is not much to say about rights of any sort.[14] Dworkin says, in response to Hart's examples:[15]

> Suppose some tyrant (an Angelo gone even more mad) did forbid sex altogether on penalty of death, or banned all religious practice in a community whose members were all devout. We should say that what he did (or tried to do) was insane or wicked or that he was wholly lacking in the concern for his subjects which is the most basic requirement that political morality imposes on those who govern. Perhaps we do not need the idea of equality to explain that last requirement. (I am deliberately cautious here.) But neither do we need the idea of rights.

14   Ronald Dworkin 'Is There a Right to Pornography?' (1981) 1 (2) *Oxford Journal of Legal Studies* 177, 211.

15   Dworkin 'Is There a Right to Pornography?', above n. 14, 211. We may note how Dworkin improves Hart's example with the words 'in a community whose members were all devout'. Without that tightening up, Hart is exposed to the objection that in his counter-example atheists are privileged. 'Angelo' is, presumably, the character of that name in Shakespeare's *Measure for Measure* who enforces an old law, which carries the death penalty, prohibiting sex out of wedlock.

Dworkin's point seems to be that since the debate is about the relationship between equality and rights to liberty, it is not affected by Hart's counter-example which is a hypothetical in which neither have a place. The suggestion is that Hart should be looking for a counter-example in a context more like the one in which we talk about rights and how they relate to each other.

Even in the totalitarian extremes of the twentieth century it is not easy to find such a counter-example. Another suggested case of equal misery is one produced by Gregory Vlastos. This example differs from the ones already discussed here, in one respect. Vlastos wrote:[16]

> Would any of us feel that no injustice was suffered by Soviet citizens by the suppression of *Doctor Zhivago* if we were reliably informed that no one, not even Khrushchev, was exempted, and that the censors themselves had been foreign mercenaries?

Inequality is still present, in that some have the right to ban books and others do not, but not in the policy itself. Or so it seems. There is an inequality (of decision making powers) here between the censors and the citizenry but at first glance everyone in the political system being considered is treated equally. But are they really? The policy, apart from restricting freedom of speech, also discriminates against authors of 'undesirable' literature. In the example only one book is banned. In the real Soviet Union many, but not all, were. This is typical in the modern world. Hart's view would presumably be that what is at stake in Vlastos' example is freedom of expression. It is of course, literally, an infringement of freedom of expression when one book is banned, however many others are, or are not, banned. But one could also argue that basic equality had been denied.

If a book by Boris Pasternak is banned for expressing anti-communist sentiments while another is allowed to flourish because it tows the party line, Boris Pasternak and his would-be readers are not being treated as equals. Is it possible then that two rights are being infringed, or rather that there are two legitimate ways of talking about the wrong that has been committed by imposing the ban? It infringes, morally speaking, both the right to freedom of expression and the right to be treated as an equal.[17] This way of understanding the wrong the ban causes seems plausible. Vlastos's example is from a more familiar world and it does not exclude equality from the story as Hart's cases might seem to.

I am not quite convinced by Hart's counter-examples anyway. Their force depends on the distinction I made between inequality in policies and inequality in constitutional arrangements. It is a real distinction but both constitute a denial

---

16 Gregory Vlastos 'Justice and Equality' in R. Brandt (ed.) *Social Justice* 17 (Prentice-Hall, Englewood Cliffs, 1962) 31, 62, cited in Westen *Speaking of Equality*, above n. 12, 90 n. 45.

17 No doubt, as noted, the latter is too abstract to be a 'right' in the way that, say, freedom of speech may be.

of basic equality. One of the reasons why certain liberties should be upheld is that basic equality itself implies that no one should have unfettered power to decide for others what it is appropriate to think, or say, or worship.

Because unjustified censorship fails to treat us as moral equals it does not matter if we can produce examples of total censorship. They too have to be decided on and implemented by someone. Thus making the treatment equal does not mean that all were treated as equals. There is no more equality here than there is, as Westen noted, in Frankena's murder/suicide scenario.

Hart clearly thinks it is wrong to think the restriction of liberty, in his counter-examples and generally, is not just an issue of freedom. We certainly are used to discussing curtailments of liberty under the topic of how much government should be permitted to interfere with our liberty and that discussion takes the protection of certain freedoms itself to be a value that should be treasured and protected. Hart is thus against Dworkin's more imperial claims for equality.

Dworkin has at least shown, however, that where rights to liberty are not entirely extinguished, for everyone, their partial extinction (which is much more common) shows a lack of equal concern and respect and thus constitutes a denial of basic equality, as well as a disregard for a particular liberty. Even totalitarian government typically requires loyal supporters and these are afforded rights that others are not, and that is discrimination; an offence against basic equality: whatever else it might be. But I think, as I said, the point is more general. One reason why unjustified curtailment of the basic liberties is wrong, however evenly it is applied, is that it fails to treat us as persons who have the capacity to develop our own conceptions of the good life and to act on these, subject only to limitations which take into account the interests of all.

Is there not perhaps an argument that Hart could make from the other end of the political spectrum? In a democracy, with a fairly elected government, could the people not themselves just decide to forgo certain basic liberties? Widespread agreement in a society that certain offensive thoughts should not be expressed or that some doctrines ought never to be advocated will not do if we think minority views should be respected. Unanimous support for certain restrictions of liberty seems a more plausible counter-example for Hart to rely on.

Suppose a government, democratically elected in a free and fair election, holds a binding referendum in which electors are invited to vote for or against some restriction of liberty; where the restriction cannot be justified on any ground other than that it satisfies the sheer will of the people. If every elector votes in favour of the restriction they will be bound by it, but voluntarily. Each elector would have chosen to forgo the freedom she no longer had. Does this scenario give Hart a counter-example to the idea that any restriction of fundamental liberty involves a failure to treat people as equals?

There is no restriction of liberty when someone gives something up of her own accord, as long as she is allowed to change her mind. In this hypothetical, however, people are bound; they have made a law, not just a group decision to give up a particular freedom. As soon as one of them changes her mind, her freedom is limited: by the decisions of others (who have not changed their minds). In fact all the members of this society are limited, after the agreement was made binding, by the decisions of others. That they chose to be does not alter the fact that they cannot now exercise their freedom to change their minds about the restriction of liberty, even though they can be said to have contributed to their own predicament.[18]

The referendum hypothetical, where all the members of the affected community once approved the limitation of freedom, is thus no different in this respect to the normal situation where some will oppose the infringement of liberty from the outset, though it is different to a situation where a group of people voluntarily give up a right to do something but are free to start doing it again if they, or any one of them, wishes to. In the latter case their liberty was never really restricted.[19] It seems we may conclude then that all curtailments of liberty, in the sense that we are concerned with in human rights discourse, involve coercion by others and thus raise the question of whether they can be justified without ignoring basic equality.

Enforcing Basic Equality

People often think there is a tension between particular sorts of equality programmes and specific liberties and that is undeniably the case even if, as some argue, these tensions can be resolved.[20] Those moral arguments are often about what we should allow others to do; not what we, as moral agents who are committed to basic equality, should feel at liberty to do. As people who are committed to treating others as equals we are not morally permitted to indulge in 'hate speech', hire on a discriminatory basis, or commit other acts of discrimination. The only liberty we give up because of our commitment to basic equality is the freedom to ignore our own moral axioms. But what we should allow others to do is another matter.

If we, as a community, through the mechanism of the state, do not prohibit discrimination we may be failing to promote some goal of equality but we are not denying anyone basic equality. We do sometimes make the state responsible for what private parties do. We have done that to some extent in human rights legislation, throughout much of the democratic world, but it is important to be clear about what we have done, morally speaking, in this regard.

---

18   As can anyone who does not encourage the maintenance of important freedoms and then finds these to be eroded.

19   We do not say of someone who has given up smoking that her freedom to smoke has been taken away or, that those who take a vow of silence have been censored.

20   See Williams 'From Freedom to Liberty: The Construction of a Political Value', above n. 6, 13. His point here, that the desire people have, for liberty, must be taken seriously, applies, in the liberty versus equality debate, to equality as an aim rather than basic equality.

Those of us who are liberal democrats do not believe the law should enforce every aspect of morality. Sometimes it is carelessly said the law should not enforce morality at all, but what is meant is we should be free to decide for ourselves, at least to a certain extent, what is permissible and what is not. There is only some agreement on how free we should be. In those countries where discrimination in employment and in the provision of certain services is prohibited, liberty is restricted in ways that are relatively new and still sometimes controversial.[21] And that liberty is restricted in the name of another value – equality.

If we do interfere with the individual's freedom to deny others basic equality our concern for promoting equality will clash with some people's concerns about liberty. The equality at stake here, though, is not basic equality but the goal of achieving some particular equality,[22] although the goal may be laudable and may not in itself be inconsistent with basic equality – it will often be inspired by it. The goal of achieving a more equal representation of races in the workforce, for example, may be hindered by allowing freedom of association, in the employment context, to racist or ethnocentric employers. The clash here is between the goal of racial equality – specifically a more proportionate representation in the workplace and freedom of association, or the right of employers to conduct their businesses in the way they see fit.

Because interfering with others' freedom sometimes runs counter to liberties we hold dear, we need to consider when this is justified, even when our motivation for restricting freedom is laudable. We do not have to justify, for example, our practice in liberal democracies of allowing patriarchal churches to refuse to ordain women by saying this practice is not discriminatory. It clearly is and thus is a denial, by those churches, of basic equality. We just think the values of freedom of religion and association outweigh our desire to make others uphold basic equality in this case. Apart from liberty our equality policy goals also have to be assessed in terms of other values as well, such as efficiency,[23] and even other equality policy goals. A policy that aims to achieve a particular equality might offend any of these.

It might restrict liberty too much. Just to establish the principle: imagine a very strict piece of 'hate speech' legislation that proscribed any public speech that was in any way critical of the views or practices of certain groups. Or a policy might

---

21   See, for example, Richard Epstein *Forbidden Grounds* (Harvard University Press, Cambridge, 1992).

22   See Grant Huscroft 'Freedom of Expression' in Paul Rishworth et al. (eds) *The New Zealand Bill of Rights* (Oxford University Press, Melbourne, 1993) 308, 323 n. 98 citing James Weinstein, 'An American's View of the Canadian Hate Speech Decisions' in W.J. Waluchow (ed.), *Free Expression* (Clarendon Press, Oxford, 1994) 175. Huscroft notes Weinstein's view that the clash is between a particular liberty and a communal commitment to promoting equality.

23   Efficiency is not a moral value but a good thing to do is sometimes a better thing to do if it is done efficiently, and the consequences of doing it inefficiently may make it a morally bad thing to do. The devil frequently lurks in the detail with matters concerning the promotion of equality.

cause unwarranted inefficiency: imagine one that imposed excessive reporting duties as part of an equal opportunities accountability exercise. Or advancing some sort of equality might deny a purported right to another form of equality. This is the charge often levelled against affirmative action in general but one can think of a less controversial example. An extreme affirmative action plan will do, for example one requiring all tenders for a certain sort of government contract to come from one race or sex for a period of 20 years. I am purposely using outlandish examples[24] to establish the point that laws and policies that promote equality of some particular outcome are not immune to moral evaluation and that moral evaluation is not done in advance simply by justifying basic equality itself. In other words they cannot rely on the absolute status of that ideal.

It is not enough, therefore, to justify such policies, to point out that they are motivated by a concern for 'equality'. That in itself may or may not be a good thing but it is only one consideration in the moral analysis of such policies. Even a plain anti-discrimination law, prohibiting the denial of basic equality by private persons in respect of certain categories such as race or sex is not automatically justified simply because its promoters believe in 'equality'. Such laws characteristically only forbid the denial of basic equality indirectly by forbidding 'discrimination', on those sorts of grounds in certain, not all, areas of our communal life.

Laws that forbid discrimination in the workplace or in the provision of services are much less controversial than the regulation of our personal choices about who to associate with in our leisure time would be (or even, say, our choices about with whom to start a business). Even the goal of promoting the adoption of basic equality is only a good thing after all relevant consideration of other factors. We may look forward to a world where basic equality is universally valued, and applied, but our desire for such a world does not justify using totalitarian methods to bring it about.

Each method that we do use will have to face moral scrutiny but that is not moral scrutiny of basic equality itself. That is what I mean when I say that, in this sense, basic equality is not implicated in the conflict between equality and liberty. Its absolute status means that it is not just a good thing all else being equal. It is not something that is, in constitutional law parlance, 'subject to reasonable limitations'. The pursuit of particular equalities is.[25] Indeed, because the liberties implicated can themselves be justified by our commitment to basic equality, infringing them will not be justifiable by reference to that value *tout court*.

If that is correct, then the compatibility of fundamental Bill of Rights liberties like freedom of speech and religion with basic equality is not threatened by potential conflicts between some freedoms and some equalities people strive for.

---

24   Although one does not have to *imagine* outlandish examples.

25   Which is why the law *upholds* basic equality when it binds the state, and *promotes* it when it binds private persons. The latter type of regulation should be subject to reasonable limitations. The mysteries of a common type of the former sort of legal protection, discrimination provisions in Bills of Rights, are considered below, in Ch. 8.

It is true of course that my exercise of free speech or freedom of religion may be discriminatory. The views that I express may be racist and my religion may irrationally consign others to damnation in an afterlife and contempt in this one. I cannot be racist or a religious bigot and believe in basic equality. But while at the communal level a state should not express or imply such views in its policies or practices, what we do, as a community, about others is a different matter. If we do too much we may limit autonomy in ways that deny the very basic equality we claim we want to uphold.

Other Types of Liberty

It is true then that 'equality' may clash with 'liberty'. But I have argued that does not mean basic equality clashes with the sorts of liberty we try to protect, to a certain, quite great extent, in a Bill of Rights or in other ways. It is rather that equality, as an aim, will sometimes clash with other values, which may themselves (or their application in some cases) be justified by basic equality, and then a balancing exercise must be carried out. In restricting my comments, for the most part, to this one aspect of the relationship between 'liberty' and 'equality' I may seem to have sidestepped an important debate – the one that deals with the tension between economic freedom and equality. In a sense that is true but that debate is also really only about one aspect of that relationship. It is just that it has received a lot of attention because the relationship between economic freedom and a concern for decent living standards for all is an important and difficult topic.

It is often, though not always,[26] to debates about that matter which we refer when we note that in recent times the perceived tension between equality and liberty has been the subject of much debate. Much modern political philosophy consists of attempts to reconcile these two values in a harmonious liberalism.[27] There are also recent theorists who deny that such a reconciliation is possible.[28] There are not, of course, just two points of view in these debates. They are important and, although I do not discuss them here, I think it is worth noting that they might be clearer if they distinguished different uses of 'equality'.[29]

Basic equality will have something to say about which economic system best treats people as equals but, because basic equality itself justifies certain liberties,

---

26   Often the tension is between freedom of expression and some equalising project. See, for example, Catherine Mackinnon *Only Worlds* (Harper Collins, London, 1994).

27   See, for example, Rawls *A Theory of Justice, above* n. 4; Ronald Dworkin *Sovereign Virtue* (Harvard University Press, Cambridge, 2000).

28   See Berlin 'Two Concepts of Liberty', above n. 5; Bernard Williams 'From Freedom to Liberty: The Construction of a Political Value', above n. 6.

29   See, for example, the exchanges between Dworkin and Bernard Williams in Mark Lilla, Ronald Dworkin and Robert B. Silvers (eds) *The Legacy of Isaiah Berlin* (*The New York Review of Books*, New York, 2001).

it will suggest a distributive system which respects those liberties. Of course the substantive issues remain and are far from being resolved,[30] but that does not mean some conceptual clarification is not helpful. Every conversation or debate on this topic which does not specify what the participants mean by 'equality' begs the question[31] – and as the discourse grows the question becomes more pertinent. Here, as with questions of discrimination and freedom of association, the right to economic freedom must be weighed against the need to ensure that all enjoy a real opportunity to live a worthwhile life. What that entails, in detail, is another matter, but it is not the equal worth of persons in general that is weighed in the balance. That is our starting point – the provenance of our concern for socio-economic welfare and a reason for our respect for individual autonomy. But each application of basic equality requires, of necessity, a separate discussion. Even the freedoms discussed here and particular instances of each of them can and must be defended in specific terms.

Equal Values?

It might be objected that by affording an absolute status to the principle of basic equality, while denying that status to even the fundamental liberties, I have biased the whole discussion in favour of equality. On the other hand some might think that because I have said basic equality justifies the fundamental freedoms prized in a liberal state I have undermined projects to equalise important outcomes.

My loosely Dworkinian approach is guilty on both counts. My excuse is that I think this is the right approach. There is of course nothing novel in saying that freedom cannot be absolute. Nor do I think there is anything peculiar in saying that our right to be regarded as equals is absolute. A complete answer to these objections, however, would require an exposition of the value of liberty, including whether there is a general value in liberty itself. Dworkin's own position on this, incidentally, is not quite clear to me.[32]

---

30   For a sampling see Dworkin *Sovereign Virtue*, above n. 27 Ch. 2; Samuel Scheffler 'What is Egalitarianism?' (2003) 31 *Philosophy and Public Affairs* 5, criticising Dworkin's approach to the issue of distributional equality; Elizabeth Anderson 'What is the Point of Equality?' (1999) 109 *Ethics* 287, in similar vein to Scheffler but also developing an alternative theory.

31   Though, as I have argued, this is not a reason to give up on the word 'equality' altogether. See Ch. 2.

32   Dworkin originally argued there was no such thing as a right to liberty in general. His argument was a principled one and so he must be saying there is no corresponding moral value, not just that the United States Constitution does not provide one. In later work he does talk about a special responsibility to live our lives according to our conception of what makes them successful and worthwhile and the need for a social environment that supports that enterprise. Liberty, like equality, might seem to have its own abstract background idea in this scheme. But in fact Dworkin still defines liberty, and distinguishes it from Berlin's

The scheme presented here is coherent however, although it appears too neat to some critics – who think a political philosophy this tidy must be overlooking something.[33] Although coherence is not all we require from an ethical system it is surely a point in its favour.[34] The point of talking about ethical values and how they complement or compete with other values must, however, at least eventually, be a practical one. Tidy or not the scheme must ultimately be judged, in the case of political morality, in terms of whether it is useful to people who care about social justice.

I think the practical value of the exposition of the relationship between liberty and equality given here is that, while a less coordinated view of the connection between these two values would leave room for more extreme views to be taken seriously, the advantage of this one is that it insists that liberty and equality must be taken seriously, together, at the same time. We are in danger of losing sight of something important, not when we fail to take seriously proposals which promote a certain equality or liberty and which are justified without reference to countervailing concerns. We are, rather, at peril when we do pursue liberty without thought for equality, or some procrustean equalising project without regard for the autonomy of persons.

A Case in Point

Although a concern for fundamental liberties is widely accepted in contemporary political thought and reasonably well protected in liberal egalitarian democracies,[35] there are illiberal attacks, even within respectable political philosophy, in the name of equality, on the freedoms which people who believe in basic equality should be anxious to uphold. The freedoms I refer to here are, again, of the Bill of Rights sort; this is why, apart from their central role in the general argument, I have focussed on them in this chapter. Freedom of speech, in particular, is currently under attack in ways that should concern liberals.[36] The offending expression is often now that which criticises religious or 'cultural' perspectives which are thought to need special protection from 'mainstream' society. If it can be shown, as this chapter

---

'negative' liberty by, in part, making it subject to his conception of 'equality of resources'. See Ronald Dworkin *Taking Rights Seriously*, above n. 11, Ch. 12; 'Do Liberty and Equality Conflict?' in Paul Barker (ed.) *Living as Equals* (Oxford University Press, New York, 1996) 39, 42–4.

33   See Williams 'From Freedom to Liberty: The Construction of a Political Value', above n. 6.

34   See Simon Blackburn *Ruling Passions* (Clarendon Press, Oxford, 1998) 309.

35   Although it must be said that such countries are a minority in the world.

36   See, for example, the discussion of careless attacks on freedom of speech in Brian Barry *Culture and Equality* (Harvard University Press, Cambridge, 2001) 30. By 'liberals' I mean those of an egalitarian ilk who, while they believe that people's socio-economic needs are important, are also convinced that certain liberties are essential for human flourishing.

argues it can, that freedom of speech, amongst other basic liberties, is justified in part because of our basic egalitarianism, then it will be less conceptually vulnerable to the charge that it must often be sacrificed for the sake of 'equality'. Many of the recent attacks on freedom of speech are motivated by a commitment to some notion of 'equality', often expressed as a commitment to 'equality of outcomes'. The speech which ought to be suppressed, on this view, is the speech of those who are thought to be privileged in some way. The type of speech we are encouraged to censor is often that which causes offence to those who are less privileged or who form some sort of a minority, although status and size do not always count.

Words, or pictures, or other types of expression, can of course be deeply offensive and hurtful. And defending a right to certain types of expression can make one deeply unpopular. This is partly because liberals feel obliged to protect the right to say certain things that they themselves would not choose to say, the right to view or read things, for example, they do not particularly care to. As Dworkin noted some time ago,[37] in countries which now, by and large, do protect freedom of expression, the arguments have often been about inherently undesirable expression, such as racist speech or expression of dubious value such as pornography.

One reason why Dworkin has defended the right to indulge in even the two types of speech mentioned in the last paragraph is because he thinks we owe to others their right to define for themselves their conception of the good. That liberty is the freedom equals should enjoy unless it can be clearly shown, not just assumed, that exercising those freedoms in a particular way or form does cause a much greater harm than giving offence.[38]

Much has been written about whether freedom to publish pornography or hate speech should be limited because it interferes with rights that all should enjoy. I only note here that objections to each of these freedoms, which usually have something to do with 'equality', must be weighed against a right to liberty which is itself justified by our commitment to basic equality. These two issues, offensive expression of sexual matters and racist speech, are still with us but we have now also moved on to areas where freedom of speech is contested in more troubling ways.

More recently, offence to religious or cultural sensibility is the target of incautious attacks on freedom of speech. The argument here is much weaker than in the case of pornography or racist hate speech, which can hardly be said to express anything interesting. Those who want to cast scornful criticism of a religion or religious or cultural practices as denials of equal human worth will have to do much more, to be convincing, than point to instances of people being upset by the irreverent expressions of cartoonists or television writers. The attack on free speech here is clearly one on ideas about ways of life and patterns of belief. This

---

37 Ronald Dworkin, 'Women and Pornography' (1993) 40 (17) *New York Review of Books* 38.

38 See, for example, Ronald Dworkin *Freedom's Law*, above n. 2.

goes to the core of the importance of freedom of speech. Calls for such criticism to be 'responsible' or even 'respectful' are simply demands for crude censorship.

If whole bodies of thought and ways of life are to be protected from 'defamation'[39] we would have to refrain too much from the frank discourse that allows democracy to function. It is necessary to clearly distinguish between the actual harm of the denial of basic equality and what philosophers Ophelia Benson and Jeremy Stangroom refer to as '[t]he pseudo-harm of causing mental pain, of causing people to think thoughts that they don't like thinking, of causing perturbation and unease'.[40]

This recent critique of free speech, or the recent form of it (an older form protected repressive Christianity for centuries[41]) has enough support to make it difficult to dismiss as marginal and it deserves a much more thorough critique than my remarks here provide. It should be clear, though, that it does not deserve, in debates about it, to be treated as the sole representative of 'equality'.

Concluding Remarks

Is liberty at war with equality then? Not if we are talking about the fundamental equality that lies at the core of liberal political philosophy. But some of our equalising projects may indeed require the sacrifice of important liberties. I have only provided what I think is a framework for dealing with the tension between such equalising missions and the protection of basic liberties. Basic equality gives support for both. There is a degree of urgency, it is submitted, in getting our thinking right about this matter of the relationship between equality and Bill of Rights type freedoms. New challenges to freedoms we have held dear, freedom of speech in particular, have in recent times, presented themselves without even the pretence of an argument that any harm beyond mere offence to some community or religious grouping is necessary before calls to limit freedom of speech are justified. To respond to the latter uncritically may produce a culture ripe for draconian laws.

The result would not be equal concern and respect. The denial of concern and respect for those who express criticism of what they see as harmful practices carried out in the name of religious or cultural dogma does not become a good thing simply because it is packaged as a contribution towards achieving equal outcomes for different ways of life. Equal concern and respect is not simply a matter of mutual admiration, it requires an awareness of other people as beings who, like ourselves, are capable of finding moral and other truths for themselves and are entitled to the rights needed to pursue this project in harmony with others and without undue hindrance.

---

39   See Laura MacInnis 'UN Body adopts resolution on religious defamation' *Reuters* 26 March 2009. Available at: www.reuters.com [accessed: 13 September 2009].

40   Ophelia Benson and Jeremy Stangroom *Why Truth Matters* (Continuum, London, 2006) 7.

41   See A.C. Grayling *What is Good?* (Weidenfeld and Nicolson, London, 2003).

The discussion of the relationship between equality and liberty was undertaken to begin to see how basic equality fits into our scheme of political values but it also unavoidably took us right into contemporary controversies about what it means to deny basic equality. That more general topic is the focus of the next chapter. It is possible to say something about the denial of basic equality in general. There are also some similarities between different types of failure to treat people as equals that are similar. Each type also has its own peculiarities to consider.

Chapter 6
Denying Basic Equality

Introduction

Having discussed the 'structural' questions of how basic equality relates to morality itself and to one other core value in political philosophy and who is, in different ways, bound by it, I will now say something more, in general, about what it means to ignore or deny basic equality. Naturally that is a broader subject than the set of questions discussed in the jurisprudence of discrimination law. Equality is a moral value which may be expressed in legal form, and its expressions are ubiquitous but, in discrimination law, only in a piecemeal way.[1]

'Equality law' usually has bias against members of groups, or types of persons in general, in mind: bias against women, homosexuals, disabled persons, members of another racial group and so on. Consider, for example, the South African Bill of Rights which states, as part of its equality provision:

> The state may not unfairly discriminate directly or indirectly against anyone
> on one or more grounds, including race, gender, sex, pregnancy, marital status,
> ethnic or social origin, colour, sexual orientation, age, disability, religion,
> conscience, belief, culture, language and birth.[2]

Although the law is open-ended the examples suggest some sort of *ejusdem generis* interpretation would be appropriate: the sort of thing the legislature had in mind was a bias against a general type of person. Its target is not only, as was once suggested, discrimination on the grounds of immutable characteristics, like race. Discrimination on the grounds of alterable characteristics such as marital status and religion are often included in modern discrimination law, as they are here in the South African Bill of Rights. But there is still, in modern human rights legislation, the sense of identifiable social groups or types of person who must be protected from discrimination.

The case of nepotism, which I referred to earlier, on the other hand, looks like a different sort of problem, one which we would deal with principally under another type of law. It does not matter that we do this of course, but we should note that phenomena as different as political nepotism and racism (although I suppose

---

1   See Sandra Fredman *Discrimination Law* (Oxford University Press, Oxford, 2002) Ch. 3 for a useful account of much of what is covered in contemporary discrimination law.

2   Constitution of the Republic of South Africa, Act 108 of 1996, s 9 (3).

the *practice* of racism includes a kind of group nepotism), for example, are both infringements of basic equality although the former might not denote discrimination against a social group or type of person in the way that racism does. Bills of Rights do not proscribe discrimination against strangers or in favour of friends and relations in general and 'ordinary' discrimination legislation is typically even more limited, in terms of the contexts, of impermissible discrimination.[3] Because the basic equality that these provisions is meant to uphold is abstract and quite general it will never be possible, or appropriate, for human rights provisions or law in general to prohibit every sort of denial of basic equality in every context.[4]

Even when a legal provision is very generally expressed, as the US Constitution's Fourteenth Amendment's 'equal protection (of the laws) clause' is, courts will restrict the meaning to something less than it could be. These judicial interpretations are often controversial. My point here is that they could not sensibly include all failures to treat people as equals because no law is likely to be so broad in its intended scope. Debates about what should and should not be included under the interpretation of any particular provision are unlikely to be about the whole meaning of basic equality although they can be better or worse interpretations of the general idea and helpful or unhelpful applications of it.[5] In what follows I only mean to give the barest outline of what it means to reject basic equality and offer a brief discussion of some of the intricacies involved in identifying its denial. I will then try to illustrate some of these intricacies by discussing the conceptually challenging idea of discrimination on the ground of culture.

What Constitutes a Denial of Basic Equality?

For a proposed policy or action to be a rejection of basic equality it will have to state or imply that it is not always morally necessary to treat everyone as equals. Obvious examples, as I have noted, are racism and sexism and much talk about equality has been about race and sex.[6] We are still concerned with race and sex. But we now think people should also not be discriminated against on other grounds, such as sexual orientation, or because they are disabled.[7] Though

---

3   I have been talking about Bills of Rights because they try to uphold basic equality by restraining governments from partial action but of course the ideal can be observed without it being enshrined in basic law or any special legislation. It is, again, just a matter of recent political and legal thought and practice that we have 'equality legislation'.

4   Fredman *Discrimination Law*, above n. 1, 67–82.

5   See Ch. 8.

6   Or 'gender' where a distinction is made between sex and gender; essentially a distinction between biological differences and social roles.

7   In some circles the very notion of 'race' is out of favour and has been replaced with 'ethnicity' although race and ethnicity are strictly speaking different things. Members of a race are thought to be biologically, but not necessarily culturally, similar. But both terms are difficult.

we might think of racism and sexism as paradigm cases of disrespect for basic equality, in terms of discrimination, their archetypal status is really a matter of the history of social activism around equality issues.

It is true, however, that in discriminating against certain kinds of people on grounds like race and sex, we are, more or less, *by definition* not treating them as equals. We are, by contrast, far from unanimous that equal concern and respect entails equal wealth or welfare.[8] It might at least prohibit certain degrees of economic inequality. Or, a commitment to basic equality may play some more indirect role in the moral assessment of our economic arrangements.

The link between basic equality and the law is also clear in the case of administrative law, which is also not dealt with in this book. Doctrines like *audi alterem partem* ('hear the other side') and *nemo iudex in causa sua* ('no one should be a judge in his own cause') obviously uphold basic equality, however their function or purpose may be otherwise described. We would fail to treat someone as an equal if we forced her to appear before a biased judge or denied her right to be heard. This is the minimum basic equality requires in legal procedure – the thinnest theory of equality before the law. Rules about fairness in contract likewise are aimed at alleviating the vulnerability of parties who are at a disadvantage. It is the equality of the contracting parties that is upheld by (for example) the doctrine of 'unconscionable bargains'. The law is replete with provisions to ensure equality though my remarks below will be mostly in the discrimination law context, as I have explained.

What most clearly unites all failures to respect basic equality is the presence of bias, or the absence of impartiality. Or, more carefully expressed, because I have accepted as justified a partiality in the personal sphere that is itself consistent with a more general impartiality born of our respect for each other as equals, it is the absence of that more general impartiality that denies our status as equals. We are biased when we act for improper motives, taking into account irrelevant considerations in our dealings with others. Basic equality requires us to be impartial as between human beings, not taking into account any consideration that contradicts or overrides our duty to treat them as equals. In other words, allowing for the partiality required to live our own lives by committing ourselves to our own justified projects, we should make no distinction between persons as such.

Unusual Suspects and Victims

The generality of equality's demands will not become more constrained thereby, but it nevertheless must be said: the perpetrators of basic inequality will not always be the usual suspects and its victims will not always be who they typically are. It is important not to have too narrow a view of the range of situations that different types of discrimination can occur in and who can be affected by them. It is not the

---

8   See Ronald Dworkin *Sovereign Virtue* (Harvard University Press, Cambridge, 2000) Ch. 2.

case, for example, that: '[d]isability differs from other types of discrimination in that it is a possibility which faces all members of society'.[9] There are clearly other types of discrimination to which anyone can fall victim.

Is there some group of people, for example, who cannot be the victims of discrimination based on race, or sex? When we think of racism we often think of whites as the perpetrators and some other group as the victims. There is so much recent history of this particular form of racism that the simplification is understandable. But that does not mean that anyone is permanently safe from the evils of racism. There are some confusing semantic issues here. In a recent discussion of racism in her book on discrimination law, Sandra Fredman expresses the opinion that racism as we know it today is not just about prejudice based on skin colour.[10] Assuming that is true, prejudice based on skin colour is still a denial of basic equality. And it can happen to anyone. And whatever else racism is thought to include can also be repeated in new contexts, as history clearly shows. Unless we *define* racism as something that only certain contemporary groups can suffer, it is an evil that may befall any racially defined group.

An example from post-apartheid South Africa may help to illustrate the point. In *City Council of Pretoria* v *Walker*[11] the South African Constitutional Court had to decide on the constitutionality of certain steps taken by the City Council of Pretoria with regard to the way it was charging for services, the way it was handling non-payment of service charges, and related matters. The council was a new, for the first time multiracial, body which replaced a number of older, racially segregated bodies. Under apartheid, the services provided to whites and blacks and the means for paying for them, differed. The delivery of services in the black townships was vastly inferior to that provided in historically white areas.

Integration of the services, including the installation of proper meters in the old black areas, inevitably took some time. During that time some differential treatment of the two groups was also unavoidable. Before meters were installed, by the new council, in the previously black areas, residents of those areas could obviously not be charged a consumption-based tariff for services. The council, more controversially, also did not want to start charging for services on a metered basis in those parts of the black areas where it had, at that stage, managed to install meters, until it had completed the installation of meters throughout the previously black townships. This second differential practice was inspired by the volatile political situation in the black townships, which were emerging from decades of intense political struggle. More controversially still, the council was taking legal steps to recover arrears in payments, in respect of council services, only from residents of the old, white, Pretoria.[12]

---

9   Fredman *Discrimination Law*, above n. 1, 58.
10   Ibid. 53.
11   1998 (2) SA 363 (CC), 1998(3) BCLR 257 (CC).
12   Para. 23.

The Court found that these practices constituted discrimination based on race in terms of the equality provisions of the interim constitution[13]. In South African constitutional jurisprudence, however, one also has to ask whether the discrimination (which does, the Court says, not mean 'differentiation') is 'unfair'.[14] That terminological curiosity aside, the Court was correct, in my view, to decide that it was not necessary for the discrimination (as their law defines the term) to be the result of hostile prejudice, for it to be unfair. Denying someone basic equality, in the absence of hostile prejudice, is as inexcusable, though more forgivable surely, as doing it for bigoted reasons is.[15] The Court was also right, I think, to find that it was unfair for the council to sue white residents of the new Pretoria for unpaid service charges while forgoing, without good reason, its right to sue black residents who had not paid.

I am not concerned here with the detail of the Court's jurisprudential assessment of the reasons given by the council for the differential treatment. I am indeed critical of some aspects of the court's reasoning, which pertain to the way discrimination and equality are understood in much recent thinking on the subject.[16] But I endorse Langa DP's general statement that:

> No members of a racial group should be made to feel that they are not deserving of equal 'concern, respect and consideration' and that the law is likely to be used against them more harshly than others who belong to other race groups.[17]

While the court did note that the respondent belonged to a racial (white) minority, it said nothing to suggest that racial discrimination could only be suffered by certain groups. While this was characterised as a case of 'indirect discrimination', which was probably not motivated by prejudice, I do not mean to suggest that discrimination against groups that have not historically been typical victims will

---

13   Constitution of the Republic of South Africa, 1993, s 8. The 1993 constitution is referred to as the 'Interim Constitution'. It was replaced by the Final Constitution, Constitution of the Republic of South Africa 1996, to complete the constitutional transition to democracy in South Africa.

14   *Prinsloo* v *van der Linde* 1997 (3) SA 300 (CC), 1997 (6) BCLR 759 (CC) para. 31. Compare Anton Fagan 'Dignity and Unfair Discrimination: A value misplaced and a right misunderstood' (1998) 14 *SAJHR* 220. Fagan argues that the Court should indeed understand 'discrimination' to mean 'differentiation' in this context. That seems right because, as he says, discrimination, in its pejorative sense is unfair differentiation and then unfair discrimination must be, according to the Constitutional Court's logic, 'unfair differentiation which is unfair'; which is surely one helping of unfairness too many. Both the Court and Fagan are trying to make the most out of a poorly drafted section. 'Discrimination' is a bad thing in human rights discourse – it was the only word the drafters needed.

15   See Langa DP's discussion of the legal history of this issue at para. 39ff.

16   See Ch. 8.

17   At para. 81.

always be perpetrated by parties innocent of hostile bigotry. We are quite capable of new outbreaks of full blown racism. But racial discrimination takes various forms and no one is immune to it. *En passant*, it may be noted that it would be a bit odd to think of the discrimination in this case as *unintentional*. There was no finding of racist motive or intent by the court but we must surely be taken, at some level, to have intended the obvious implications of what we do.[18]

What about discrimination based on sex: is that something that only women can suffer? Only if sex discrimination is *defined* as discrimination against women. But why define it that way? It might be considered a good strategy, in the fight against male domination generally, to rule out the possibility of discrimination against men – to avoid spurious claims perhaps. Or, ignoring discrimination against men might be thought a good way to suppress the surely false idea that, because discrimination against men can be serious, it is currently as great an evil as discrimination against women. But clearly discrimination on the grounds of sex is just that, and *can* be against men as well. How much discrimination against men there is in the world is a matter of fact. But that is a separate issue. The denial of basic equality is more widespread than some human rights narratives suggest though I do not mean to imply that some forms of discrimination are not more prevalent than others, or that one type of discrimination may not have a typical victim. It is also not the case that all denials of basic equality are equally harmful in terms of their effects. What I want to resist, simply, is the idea that the truth about such matters is not contingent.

To sum up: not all kinds of failure to uphold basic equality take the same stereotypical form. In particular, when a person or a group is simply favoured over another without good reason it is not always apparent that there is an awful form of animus towards those who are excluded as there typically is, for example, with the most familiar forms of racism or the condescension that is part of sexist attitudes. It is sometimes just the case that some people are unfairly favoured over others in ways that ignore their equal status as persons. Yesterday's victims can be, as in many other contexts, today's offenders.

Some Different Types of Denial of Basic Equality

Can we be more specific about what it is to deny someone or some group of people basic equality? I think we can, but in specific cases. Different considerations apply to different sorts, or categories, of the denial of basic equality. In all cases the assessment is not simple because one is not just looking to see whether in a particular situation X it is the case, as a matter of fact, that Y: in checking for consistency with basic equality one is always also making a *moral* assessment of a set of facts. This is, in particular, different from assessing a situation with some more specific equality in mind. That can be done by statistical means: what

---

18   I will return to this point in Ch. 9.

proportion of doctors in country A are women? What proportion of civil engineers are men? The answers to these questions may be data relevant to some question about basic equality in country A but they cannot constitute the whole answer to such questions. Questions about the denial of basic equality will always require the *evaluation* of facts, not just their identification,[19] and different aspects of different situations will be relevant to the process of that evaluation.

On the other hand it is the same *type* of assessment which we are undertaking in each instance and so the form of the enquiry will be similar in some ways. While there is no simple algorithm to apply to every situation, each instance of ignoring basic equality will share certain very general features. In each case we are asking whether people have been treated as equals in the sense that we have been impartial, as between persons, in our assessment of how they should be treated. In each case we are asking whether criteria have been taken into account in our decisions concerning how people should be treated which ignore their status as equals. But there are different kinds of criteria which people can use to override our status as equals. It is not possible to enter all the culprits onto a neat checklist. And a criterion used in one context to deny basic equality may be benign in another.

We can benefit, though, from discussions of the different types of denial of basic equality that we are familiar with and are aware of. In doing that we can become familiar with and appreciate some of the nuances of different sorts of discrimination, and make tentative generalisations about these. We can identify some of the individual differences, or analogies, in analysing basic equality issues in the context of familiar debates about equality and discrimination. The purpose of my references to those debates in what follows is mainly to illustrate these differences in the type of moral argument required to establish that basic equality has been denied. I will suggest that some categorising of instances of basic equality denial is useful although the categories are only useful for some comparative purposes and are not rigid.

A comparison of different types of denying basic equality is part of the general project of moral thinking about basic equality because universalisability is a requirement of all moral thought. If one form of treating people differently is wrong, all instances of it are wrong. But as we have noted, we can make mistakes about what it is, exactly, that should be universalised. The history of the incompleteness of our attempts to be impartial is well known. Some mistakes were obvious, at least with hindsight. Others might become so. To ask for racial equality while ignoring sex discrimination is clear evidence that there has been a failure to properly generalise about what it is that makes racism wrong. Of course women are different from men in some ways but not in any way that could justify the discrimination they have suffered. The grounds for discrimination are different but the reasons why race discrimination and sex discrimination are wrong are

---

19   Although, as noted in Ch. 3, knowledge and understanding of the relevant facts is always important.

similar. The differences relied upon as an excuse for discriminating are in both cases imaginary or irrelevant.

It has taken an even longer time to deal with the question of sexual orientation and that debate is not over yet. The law[20] is, in some ways, ahead of popular morality on this issue. Sociologically this may appear odd. Civil society organisations such as the mainstream religious groupings which often led the way in the struggle against racism, but did much less to counter sexism, have often failed to see why discrimination against homosexuals is wrong. It is important, though, to distinguish sociological explanations, in this case mostly to do with dogmatic religious attitudes, from good moral argument. What is required is a moral assessment of homosexuality (as a practice). If there is nothing *wrong* with it then it is discriminatory to restrict it or disparage it.

This is, in important respects, how we deal with religious equality. We only think it right to limit religious, or religiously inspired, activities which pose some serious threat to others. Sexual orientation and religion are different, in this way, to race and sex in that one is, with these, evaluating behaviour rather than trying, as in the case of the latter two types of discrimination, to see if there are significant differences just in being a certain type of person.[21] (I stress again that these terse comments about gay rights and religious toleration are not included as a proper discussion of those issues. I am trying to illustrate general matters.)

This difference between race and sex on the one hand and sexual orientation and religion on the other is thus useful to note. With race and sex the basic inegalitarian urge is to point to innate differences thought to be relevant to deciding how people should be treated. With sexual orientation and religion no judgment is made about the nature of the person (at least not in the same way as with the other two). It is behaviour and, in the case of religion, behaviour and beliefs, that the victims of these sorts of discrimination are penalised for. With race and sex, basic equality asserts the common humanity of men and women and different races. Once that is achieved we leave those differences behind and judge people on the content of their characters – on what they believe and do. With sexual orientation and religion, by contrast, we *start* with what people believe and do. The question with these is not whether some kinds of *people* are inherently inferior or unworthy (to which basic equality answers, always: no) but rather whether some types of behaviour are wrong and should be prohibited, or at least criticised. If we find there is nothing to justify the criticism, it is discrimination. We fail to treat people as equals when we punish them simply for behaving differently when our objections to their behaviour are not well founded.[22]

---

20   Or some of it. See Fredman *Discrimination Law*, above n. 1, 54–8.

21   I mean that is how we think we should approach the question of religious toleration in a modern liberal state. We think we should only restrict certain types of harmful practices.

22   Of course gay people complain that ignoring a real difference, their sexual orientation, is a denial of basic equality. That is true, and this in turn is a real difference

I do not mean there are only these two categories of discrimination. Or that this categorisation tells us all we can know about the differences between these types of discrimination. There are, as I noted, differences between racism and sexism which are relevant here. Men and women are different in much less superficial ways than racial groups are from one another. The differences do not justify the discrimination women have endured but they might be relevant to the question of what it means to treat men and women as equals now. If, for example, as Steven Pinker tells us, studies of the brain show significant differences between the sexes, that might help us to know what proportion of which sex, in the absence of discrimination, is likely to end up pursuing what sorts of careers, because of (average) differing interests. And that might in turn help us to know when to suspect that things are being skewed by discrimination.[23]

One must proceed with caution here because the quest for equality between the sexes has had to contend with many shifts in our assessments of real and imagined differences. Conservative male chauvinism relied on supposed differences that most no longer think are credible. If any educated person now thinks that men and women differ in general intelligence they are guilty of wilful ignorance. Only bad faith can support that belief in the light of clear evidence to the contrary. The anecdotal evidence is abundant and biological research supports our current intuition that men and women are equal in terms of average intelligence.[24] Other theories of purported differences, of more recent provenance, are now also doubted. Carol Gilligan's studies, for example, that suggested that men and women differ in their moral reasoning, have apparently not stood up to the scrutiny of later studies.[25] It has also been shown that, in general, it is not true that women are more empathic to everyone (only to their friends apparently) but on the other hand it is true that: '[m]en have a higher tolerance for pain [which I suspect will surprise some] and a greater willingness to risk life and limb for status, attention and other dubious rewards [which, I suppose, will surprise few]'.[26] In terms of occupational preferences perhaps the fiercest debates are about disciplines such as engineering where the representation of women is much lower even though women now study science in more proportionate numbers.[27]

---

between discrimination on the ground of religion (although some people *think* of their religion in that way too) and unfair treatment based on sexual orientation. But it should be noted that even if that orientation were 'chosen' and not innate it would be wrong to treat gays and lesbians badly on that account because there is nothing *wrong* with being homosexual in itself.

23 See Steven Pinker *The Blank Slate* (Penguin Books, New York, 2002) Ch. 18.

24 Ibid. 340. My references to Pinker's book on this and other topics should not be seen as references to the ideas of one person: Steven Pinker. The opinions he expresses there, on gender in particular, are supported by his own references to many studies.

25 Ibid. 340. Pinker cites examples of these studies.

26 Ibid. 345.

27 Ibid. 352.

The important thing for equality analysis is not whether the studies cited by Pinker turn out to be the last word on the subject, but that we do not adopt a strategic approach to factual enquiries. It is tempting to ignore suggested differences or to imagine those that suit our pre-conceived theories of discrimination. Fortunately, and predictably according to the biologists, nature has left the sexes roughly equal in the range properties which make us uniquely human. We should not shy away from such differences as we can establish and their policy implications, though the temptation to do so is great. Racial differences, as far as we know, are much less interesting in this respect. Indeed with race the major debates are increasingly about sceptical issues such as whether they even exist and as the world becomes increasingly integrated there is even less, biologically speaking, to argue about.

Another difference between racist and sexist denials of equality is the lack of obvious hostility in some cases of the latter. There is sometimes, with sex discrimination, no clear sense that one sex thinks the other is less worthy. Larry Alexander suggests: '[a]rguably, however, some people believe as a matter of moral ideal that women and men should perform distinct moral roles'.[28] I think this is quite clearly the case though here we are not necessarily talking about average preferences of women themselves. And Alexander is less convincing when he says that 'these widespread beliefs about the morality of gender roles are in many cases based not on biases or on stereotypes but on moral ideals'[29] because it does not follow that if something is morally motivated it is not the product of prejudice.[30] Whatever its provenance, the idea that a woman should, for example, not work outside the home must be the result of bad judgment, because no facts about women in general suggest the restriction is sensible. I say 'whatever its provenance' because a fallacious idea about human differences does not improve when its source is a deeply felt religious or cultural truth.

But it is true that the characteristic lack of hostility, indeed the typical intimacy of the discriminators and their victims, is a feature of much sexist discrimination. On the other hand race and sex are similar issues and they differ from sexual orientation and religion, at least in the way that I have noted. There are other types of discrimination though, the identification and understanding of which requires other nuances of moral analysis.

The question of disability, to return to the example I began with, raises its own set of problems. Here there is a significant difference between not only

---

28   Larry Alexander 'What Makes Wrongful Discrimination Wrong? Biases, Preferences, Stereotypes, and Proxies' (1992) 141 *U Pa L Rev* 149, 166.

29   Ibid.

30   Professor Alexander does not think these preferences are unobjectionable. Indeed he does not know what a moral argument in their favour would look like as he does not find sensible the kind of natural law arguments some use to justify such ideals. My only quarrel is with his suggestion that, just because they are based on some sort of moral reasoning, they cannot be based on a prejudiced distortion of reality.

disabled and other people but also between different forms of disability. And the differences are relevant to the question of how disabled people should, variously according to the type and extent of their disability, be treated. On the one hand we think disabled people should be treated the same as other people. They should be able to compete fairly on merit for prized positions in society, in employment and in public life. On the other hand we think some accommodation should be made for their disabilities. Each disability will in turn present different practical, and so moral, challenges. In some ways disabilities do close off opportunities and there is sometimes little that can be done about it. Unlike discrimination based on race, for example, discrimination against disabled people is only part of the problem; the other part is the disability itself. Efforts to deny the fact of our genetic endowments and the vulnerability of the human body are, to say the least, implausible. Disability is not just a social construct. Sometimes unfavourable treatment will be justified in the sense that we are not able to rearrange things so that a particular disabled person can achieve all that others can in a particular field. Another important difference between disability on the one hand and categories like race on the other, apart from the fact that the difference itself is indisputable, is that disability will, at least much more frequently, require different treatment. (In that regard sex may be somewhere in the middle.)

This is a big topic. I only want to note here both the complexity of the moral thinking required to decide what to do about disability and the subtle differences between different instances of the inquiry into whether basic equality has been denied. These caveats are all very well, you might say, but is there no way of cutting to the chase? Could we not, for example, at least list some criteria that we may *always* regard as morally inappropriate when deciding how to respond to people and whether to treat them differently?

Forbidden Grounds

That would seem to make theoretical life easier. If we could say, at least, that race and sex should never in themselves influence, in any way, how we treat people we would at least have something to hold constant in our deliberations about the denial of basic equality. But sex is never going to be a candidate for irrelevance. There are too many ways in which it is relevant; too many ways in which we can, for example, discriminate against one sex by expecting them to be just like the other. Height and strength requirements, to take one example, can be used in unjustified ways.

Race seems a better candidate. But all one needs to rule that out too, is some biological oddity, the prevalence of a particular disease will do, and differential treatment based on race (targeted provision of health education and counselling for example) will be justified. And note that race and sex are ruled out as candidates for forbidden criteria even before we come to more controversial matters like affirmative action. All we can say, it seems, is that our recent history is littered with examples of race and sex discrimination. That may make us (I think it should) wary of differential treatment on those grounds – especially on the ground of race. But prudent caution need not mean we are not open to the possibility that it might be justified.

Discrimination law jurisprudence is littered with slightly more abstract candidates for categories of unfair grounds of differentiation. Race and sex were once less controversial candidates because they were examples of 'immutable traits'. But as Larry Alexander bluntly points out it is not discrimination to refuse to hire the blind as truck drivers.[31] He is also right to say it is not just 'irrelevance', in itself, that makes a criterion for differentiation wrongful. The relevance of differential treatment depends on our purpose for differentiating.[32] Our reasons for discriminating may be quite functional – we might just *want* a female secretary – and so relevant, in that sense.

There is, however, something important about 'relevance' in this context. Not being dependent on a wheelchair is, obviously, an irrelevant requirement for a job as a maths teacher, because one can do the job perfectly well in a wheelchair. Even if a school would prefer not to have any teachers in wheelchairs, their preference for that is irrelevant to the *objective* assessment of what makes a good mathematics teacher. Their preference is for a certain *kind of person* rather than one for a certain kind of teacher. That preference is not literally 'irrelevant', but it is immoral. Some preferences are ruled out – we may call them 'irrelevant' if we wish – if we are to uphold basic equality. But all this does not make the denial of basic equality any simpler to identify in complex cases.

I will argue later that other attempts found in recent discrimination law jurisprudence, to reduce the idea of basic equality to some more manageable form that could be applied by courts without too much original moral thinking, are also unsuccessful.[33] That does not mean that we do not know what basic equality requires or what it means to discriminate against someone. Discrimination is treating some groups of people as if they were less inherently worthy than others. But what that means in particular instances might not be easy to say. As always, in moral analysis, different situations may require attention being given to quite different considerations. To make the demands of basic equality more concrete or simple to apply would be to substitute the abstract idea of basic equality with a more specific policy aim. But the various equalities we aim for in our actions and policy decisions also require justification. And part of that justification requires application of the more general principle of basic equality. In the next chapter I will try to illustrate the importance of asking the right sorts of questions by means of a relatively lengthy example. The relationship between culture and equality has been an important concern of political and legal philosophy in recent

---

31   Larry Alexander 'What Makes Wrongful Discrimination Wrong? Biases, Preferences, Stereotypes, and Proxies', above n. 28, 151.

32   Ibid.

33   See below Ch. 8.

Chapter 7
Discrimination and Culture

Introduction

It is in the context of the political discourse (about domestic matters) and reality of liberal democracies that I will discuss some aspects of discrimination on cultural grounds. It would be easier to point to egregious examples of cultural discrimination in countries that are not liberal and not democratic, or in the foreign adventures of some that are. But the discussion, while less vivid perhaps, is more morally interesting when there are at least two plausible sides to the argument. Which, of course, is not to say that all the arguments people make about discrimination and culture in liberal democracies are *equally* plausible.

Discrimination on the ground of culture is a difficult concept. It seems clear that it does exist, just as discrimination on other grounds does. But its component ideas 'discrimination' and 'culture' are difficult notions. We have exegetical problems with the idea of discrimination even when we are dealing with paradigm cases like discrimination on the grounds of race or sex. That difficulty is greater in the context of cultural discrimination because the notion of culture is also a complex one.[1]

Here I will apply an abstract, unanalysed, notion of discrimination to the question of cultural differences, as I will discuss the interpretation of discrimination law in general in the next chapter. This chapter says more (indeed this and the justification for criticising 'other' cultures takes up half of the discussion) about the meaning of 'culture', in the context of responses to cultural differences, and tries to get at the intended denotation(s) of that term in discussions of the moral issues raised in the consideration of fair treatment for different cultural groups.

The chapter then discusses the moral issue of cultural discrimination and first distinguishes between two types of that form of discrimination. Discrimination on the ground of culture, or ethnicity, sometimes takes the form of treating people unfairly simply because they are members of a particular group. In this respect it is like simple forms of racist, or sexist, discrimination and relatively easy to identify. Another form of discrimination against a cultural group is unfair criticism

---

1 It is not that there are no problems with the notions of race and sex. They are, I suppose, in the case of 'race' partly added to by questions about culture, although sometimes these are thought to replace them. We are supposed to have debunked 'race' but we still talk about 'racial' discrimination and racism in ways that assume people know what a 'race' is. And 'sex' can be difficult too: see Georgia Warnke *After Identity* (Cambridge University Press, Cambridge, 2007).

and/or regulation of the cultural practices of minority groups. It is this latter type of discrimination that I will discuss in this chapter.

I argue against the cultural relativism that would suggest all criticism of the practices of other cultures is unjustifiable. However, some of the ways in which democratic liberal societies are regulated will impinge more on the culture of some groups than that of others. The question of exemptions from general rules arises because of the extra burden this places on some. I discuss a recent version of the extra burden argument and conclude that it does not quite succeed in explaining why exemptions to general laws or rules should only be afforded to 'cultural' (including religious) groups rather than to all conscientious dissenters.

Definitions

It is necessary, to clear the way for the more specifically moral discussion, to address some of the difficulties we encounter with the notions of 'discrimination' and 'culture', in general. There is much controversy about the meaning (or at least the application) of the term 'discrimination' in our human rights jurisprudence.[2] Arguably there should be more debate in our human rights theorising than there is about the meaning of 'culture'. Popular discussion sometimes notices definitional difficulties with that concept; but it often ignores them when it really matters. Academic discourse about respecting cultural differences has not produced all that much lucidity either. It is necessary, therefore, to at least say what is meant here, in this chapter, by both 'discrimination' and 'culture'.

Discrimination first, but, for now, briefly. This idea has been troublesome in Bill of Rights and human rights law jurisprudence. Of course it is easy to identify some instances of discrimination. It does not require an advanced understanding of human rights theory to be able to describe the treatment of black people in South Africa under apartheid, or the treatment of women under the rule of the Taliban, as 'discrimination'. But 'discrimination' is an evaluative term and its application, like that of basic equality in general, sometimes requires, as I have stressed many times, more subtle moral argument. The issues that seem intractable today do so because it sometimes seems it is not enough to just treat everyone, or all groups, in the same way.

Of course for those who think discrimination simply, and only, consists in treating people differently on certain forbidden grounds (like race, sex or religion) life is, conceptually, a little easier. But claims, based on considerations of social justice, for *different* treatment on these sorts of grounds are ubiquitous and cannot be simply ignored or dispensed with by knock down arguments. Equally they cannot all be said to be justified simply because there is a strong case for some forms of different treatment (minimum representation for women in a post-Taliban Afghanistan legislature, for example). They must each be considered on their own

---

2   See Ch. 8.

merits, and that task is what currently constitutes much of our struggle to define 'discrimination'.

At an abstract level discrimination is a central case of failing to treat people as equals. As an evaluative term it is unavoidably this abstract but we can probably expect most to at least agree that 'discrimination', whatever it specifically entails in a given situation, means, to put it in different words, not treating people who are different with the same respect and concern that we afford to people like ourselves.

This is, it must be conceded, merely to swap one evaluative term for two. It is, however, not clear how the idea could be more specific while remaining a general principle. And a general principle it must remain until we can fashion rules from a clearer sense of what it entails in hard cases. Bill of Rights jurisprudence is littered with unsuccessful attempts to make 'discrimination' more manageable, though more will not be said, in general, about the controversies over the meaning of the term until the next chapter.[3] The law needs something more concrete than notions like 'respecting equal worth' but this chapter is concerned with the more fundamental *moral* assessment of what sorts of things constitute cultural discrimination. That assessment requires application of the general principle of equal worth. And that, as usual, once we have agreed on easy cases, like the treatment of black people in America before the revolution in civil rights in that country, includes consideration of claims for different treatment of different groups.

'Culture' is also hard to pin down. But the difficulties here are different. 'Discrimination', at least in the sense intended here, is an evaluative term. 'Culture' is not. One difficulty with 'culture' is that it is used in different senses, not all of them clear, in discussions about cultural rights. So there is the ever present danger of falling into ambiguity. This is a real semantic issue as opposed to our arguments about discrimination which are really moral arguments.[4]

There are moral arguments about culture of course, this chapter is about some of them, but we also sometimes just do not know what people are referring to when they use the word 'culture'. This is particularly the case when people talk about cultural *identity*. The problem, however, is not just that the word 'culture' has many meanings. It does, but apart from semantic issues there are also metaphysical quandaries here; questions about what sorts of cultural groups can plausibly be said to exist and which descriptions of cultural difference accurately portray the cosmopolitan reality of modern life.[5]

Sometimes it is clear what people mean when they talk about 'culture'. We know, for example, more or less, what it means to say that the English and the French differ culturally; because we understand the broad meaning of 'culture'

---

3   See Ch. 8 below.

4   That might sound strange, we do argue about the meaning of 'discrimination', but I will suggest, in the next chapter, that those discussions, for the most part, serve to obscure moral arguments.

5   Not that *only* modern life is cosmopolitan.

as the totality of someone's beliefs, values and practices and we know that the typical or average set of these for members of one of those national groups differs from that of the other group to some extent. But we do not always know what people mean by the expression 'my culture'. They might be referring to what is typical or distinctive about their, say French, culture or they might mean the totality of their beliefs, practices and values. The latter will have, in almost every case in the modern world, a great deal in common with everyone else's.

Since the latter, the total set, is seldom anthropologically interesting it is usually the former, as between these two, that we can assume is intended. But this is not always clear. Moreover, sometimes neither of these two is the intended referent when someone talks about 'my' or 'our' culture. People sometimes use these phrases to refer to something other than the totality of their actual beliefs, values and practices or the way their group's present set of these differs from that of another group. Sometimes people are instead talking about the culture of their ascendants rather than, literally, their *own* beliefs, values and practices (the two might overlap to some extent of course) and the relationship between the two is often implied rather than spelt out. The result of this ambiguity might lead to an exaggerated estimation of present *lived* cultural difference.

People also, no doubt often under the influence of the confusion just mentioned, at times talk as if human beings in the modern world could have entirely discrete cultures, and this is for the most part simply not possible because cosmopolitanism is as much a fact of our present condition as multiculturalism is.[6] As Amy Gutmann puts it, 'theorists of culture assume a rough approximation rather than a perfect match of the actual to the ideal type'.[7]

Of course not everyone has a 'modern culture' in quite the same way or to the same extent. The level of schooling provided by many European colonising powers, for the people whose lives they disrupted, sometimes did not amount to much. And the effects of that neglect are still present in some countries. And yet the encounter with European powers in recent colonial times would have confronted the colonised, in many cases, with an enormously different world view which would have been difficult to ignore in its entirety. And, as is generally the case with human beings, the typical response was curiosity rather than Luddite denial.[8] (The Europeans exported cultural relativism a little later.)

It should be noted that rapid technological and social change was not something that only the colonised peoples were facing. The Europeans had themselves been recently subjected to changes in their 'culture' which would eventually have, over a period of 200 years, '... all but totally dissolved the forms of social organisation in which humankind had lived for thousands of

---

6   See Amy Gutmann *Identity in Democracy* (Princeton University Press, Princeton, 2003) 38.

7   Ibid. at 40.

8   Michael Carrithers *Why Humans Have Cultures* (Oxford, New York, 1992) Ch. 2.

years of its previous history'.[9] We humans are all, consequently, saddled with current world views that overlap to a very great extent, and in many ways we have been facing a great period of change together.

People seem to be able to tolerate a significant degree of incoherence in their overall picture of the world but that does not mean, to take a more specifically religious example, church going Christians, now, actually have a first century world view. (One would have to employ extraordinary anthropological expertise to even imagine how to.) They typically have fundamentally the same world view as atheists or members of other religions, with a few exceptional metaphysical additions here and there. If that were not the case, and if other cultural or religious groups were also somehow living in various other centuries, we would not be sharing modes of production, commerce, consumption and communication generally to the extent that we are.

Clearly the coherence of arguments using the term 'culture' in vague ways, which ignore all this is at risk. Talk about cultural identity is a lot more puzzling than many people seem to think. What is needed for the discussion of exemptions from rules on the ground of culture, therefore, is a sense of cultural difference that can be made sense of in modern cosmopolitan, societies. For that purpose I think a useful sense of 'cultural difference', in the context of talking about discriminating against someone 'of a different culture', is a use which, first of all, refers to *a set of differences in beliefs, values and practices between groups in a contemporary society which may lead to significant disagreement about how things should be done and/or regulated.* The difference is located in the *set* of beliefs etc. Members of all the relevant groups will share many beliefs, values and practices; that is a fact about the modern world we live in. I said 'first of all', but I will only explain what else I think is required, in the definition of cultural difference, a little later in the chapter, when it will be clearer why it is required.

This sense of 'cultural difference' approximates the way we usually think of religious differences. (Religious differences *are* cultural differences; they are about beliefs, values and practices.) And so by 'discrimination against a cultural group' I will mean the same sort of thing as discrimination against Catholics or Muslims.[10] We know that modern religionists do not typically see themselves as completely defined by their religious affiliations. They are Catholic, Protestant, Jewish, Muslim or whatever, but they are, and usually see themselves, as other things too. They might also think of themselves as women, New Zealanders, liberals, vegetarians, gays or all or some of any given set of identifying characteristics. It is of course possible for a person to *emphasise* a particular

---

9   Anthony Giddens *Sociology* (2nd edn, Macmillan Education Ltd, London, 1986) Ch. 1.

10   There are, of course, differences between religious, ethnic and other cultural groupings. My suggestion is just that they are not important here.

social identity but one cannot eliminate, by a sheer act of will, the multiplicity of modern social identity.[11]

By using this sense of 'cultural difference' I hope I can avoid the semantic and metaphysical pitfalls concerning cultural identity I have referred to. The issue that I discuss below, exemptions from the application of general rules on cultural grounds, does not need (for now), within the framework of my discussion of it, any other sense of 'cultural difference'. It is not necessary, for example, to resort to the fiction of discrete cultural identities, somehow coexisting in the plethora of shared common meanings which is unavoidable in the modern world.

Saying cultural discrimination is the same as religious intolerance may engender the complaint that some people do not see their culture as a 'religion'. The riposte is that the phenomenological point is taken; but their culture *is* a set of beliefs, values and practices as much as any religious culture is. The same objection could be pressed by members of an *ethnic* group who might point out that *common descent* (another challenging assignment for those who like clear definitions) is not always a feature of religious groups though it is important in understanding ethnicity.

Common descent may lead to shared group features other than values, beliefs and practices. The fact that an ethnic group's members may look the same, to outsiders, may lead to their suffering discrimination but that feature of ethnicity and that type of discrimination are not the focus of this chapter. Common descent is also surely relevant for the consideration of responses to claims for compensation based on historical injustices; but for present purposes common descent, while it helps to constitute ethnicity, is not relevant. Claims for exemptions from generally applicable rules will usually be motivated by differences in present values, beliefs and practices rather than common descent simpliciter. The two may be difficult to separate in the case of some claims for exemptions from general rules by people who are descendants of colonised peoples, but even in that case an exemption could only plausibly be justified because the claimants actually had a present belief or value or desired activity that ran up against what the majority had decided on some issue. So that, common descent, aspect of ethnicity can be ignored here as are, of course, many aspects of cultural groups that are religious.

Some may also complain that religion typically plays a much smaller role than some cultural attachments in the life of religionists living in the modern, largely secular, societies in which our discussion takes place. That may often be true, but not always. In terms of religion, real life examples range from the staunch commitment of the Amish, or of Hasidic Jews, to the vague affiliation with their religious communities of some contemporary Methodists or Anglicans, whose involvement in religious activities may be relatively minimal. And the same applies to members of cultural groups, in the narrow sense which

---

11   Michael Carrithers *Why Humans Have Cultures*, above n. 8, Ch. 2; Amartya Sen *Identity and Violence* (Penguin Books, 2006, London) Ch. 3.

excludes religious affiliation. One may be ardently Irish, or Scottish, or mildly so; culturally speaking.

Having defended my stipulated first draft meaning of 'cultural difference' I turn to the question of what constitutes discrimination against people or groups that are culturally different.

What is Discrimination Against a Cultural Group?

Discrimination on the ground of culture, it seems to me, requires at least two sorts of ethical solicitude. On the one hand we have to protect people from the kind of prejudiced behaviour typified by racism. On the other hand we have to guard against the unsatisfactory moral assessment of actual behaviour and beliefs. Discrimination against someone simply on the ground of their *membership* of an ethnic or religious group is akin to racial discrimination. Discrimination against Jews, to take a complicated hybrid example, just because they *are* Jewish is wrong in the same way that it is wrong to discriminate against black people because they are black. Anti-Semites concoct all sorts of offensive nonsense about how Jewish people are, and then use that as an excuse to discriminate against them. The right way to respond, intellectually, to that is to point out that the stereotypes are false, or meaningless,[12] and the unfavourable treatment inspired by these stereotypes is unjustified. This is the kind of discrimination we find most notoriously in contexts like apartheid South Africa, Nazi Germany and patriarchal oligarchies but also, to a lesser extent, in contemporary liberal democracies. This form of discrimination is often, in modern secular states, forbidden by law where it occurs in, certain, public, contexts like employment and the provision of goods and services. The appropriate response to such discrimination is still the subject of debate but we understand the nature of the problem fairly well. This chapter is not concerned with this form of discrimination.

Cultural discrimination also sometimes takes the form of unfair criticism of *actual* beliefs and behaviour. Treating people differently, in ways that disadvantage them, because of what they believe and do, may or may not be a denial of their equal worth. It depends on what they are doing. This point is well understood in the context of religion. We would not be discriminating against a religion because we forbad its practice of child sacrifice. We understand there are justifiable limits to freedom of religion. We respect an adult's right to refuse medical treatment but do not allow her to refuse treatment needed by her child, and so on.

But when we talk about culture more generally we seem to have greater difficulty convincing everyone that sometimes it is just wrong to do things that

---

12   Of course some things *are* typically true of Jewish people. They do not, for example, usually believe that Jesus of Nazareth was the fulfilment of Hebrew prophecy. More mundanely, they are, in some places, represented in certain occupations to a greater degree than some groups. But these are not morally relevant facts.

happen to be integral to a particular culture; that there might be, morally speaking, a better way of doing things.

Is Critiquing Other Cultures Morally Permissible?

The point is made more easily in the realm of practical or technological achievements and the means used to achieve them. For example, as Thomas Sowell notes, Arabic numerals are not merely different to Roman numerals; they are better – if you are trying to count things.[13] In the world of ends, cultural equivalence, as the view that each value or practice of every culture is morally equivalent to every part of all other cultures, receives support from ethical relativism.

Strictly speaking, ethical relativism is, like the non-cognitivism discussed in Chapter 3, a metaethical theory; not a normative moral scheme. It is a theory about the truth of ethical statements which says (roughly): they are only true for certain people or peoples and perhaps only in certain contexts. But metaethical theories almost always imply normative commitments.[14] In the case of relativism, with regard to culture: a reluctance to judge 'other cultures'. As a normative theory ethical relativism is not convincing because to respect it one is barred from recommending it to anyone who does not already embrace it. If you are a relativist you cannot, on pain of contradiction, recommend relativism to the morally intolerant.

It is of course true that ethnocentrism and religious bigotry are real wrongs.[15] We often think our way of doing something must be the best or the only one. The anthropology that inspires cultural relativism is at least a helpful reminder that this might not be the case. Discerning whether cultural discrimination is present in a situation requires us to distinguish between two different things. Treating a group in ways that disadvantage its members for no good reason, simply because their values and practices are different, is wrong. But this is not the same as the application of even-handed principles of justice and morality. The two processes are different.

Fear of making the mistakes that we so often make when judging ways that are different from our own can make us wary of all criticism except self-criticism.[16] Ethnocentrism is discriminatory because it is the uncritical and unfair assumption that the way our group does things is better.[17] But one does not have to embrace

---

13   Thomas Sowell *Race and Culture* (Basic Books, New York, 1994) 5.

14   Bernard Williams *Ethics and the Limits of Philosophy* (Fontana, London, 1985) 73.

15   Which of course they could not be, if cultural ethical relativism were a good moral theory.

16   See David Wong 'Relativism' in Peter Singer (ed.) *A Companion to Ethics* (Blackwell, Oxford, 1993) 442.

17   Roger Scruton *A Dictionary of Political Thought* (Macmillan Press, London, 1996) 177.

cultural relativism in order to eschew ethnocentrism. As Kwame Anthony Appiah puts it: '[i]t is a poor move from recognising certain [ethnocentric] evaluations as mistaken to giving up evaluation altogether'.[18]

Everything that anyone does, or believes, is 'cultural' in the broad sense of the word. We could not criticise anything if we could not criticise something that was part of *someone's* culture – unless we define 'culture' as only the morally acceptable aspects of people's beliefs, values and practices. And that would be an extraordinary use of the word.

It is of course wrong to simply assume that our way of doing things is better and it is wrong, without justification, to force people to do things our way. It may also be wrong to press valid criticism, as criticism of a particular group, when we are guilty of the same thing, because hypocrisy is a bad thing too. This last point does not mean that no criticism of the practices of others is justified while wrongs are committed by *us*. That sort of cultural sensitivity is simply a pact of the guilty – you don't expose us and we won't criticise you.

Because it is true in general that something that is wrong in one situation might not be wrong in another, it is true in this context too. It is always possible to argue, on a case by case basis, that a particular act or practice is not immoral in a particular cultural setting though it might be in another. The practice of nepotism, for example, might not have been wrong in societies too unstable for their rulers to safely entrust power to strangers or political enemies – as long as the continuance of the ruler's governance was itself a good thing.

A better example, because it does not involve the complications of history, is given by Jeremy Waldron in an article on the justification of exemptions from general laws.[19] The case of *State* v *Kargar*[20] dealt with the application of a statute that proscribes various types of sexual contact between adults and children. Kargar, a recent arrival in the United States, was an Afghani refugee. The mother of a babysitter he had hired called the police after the babysitter told her she had seen Kargar kissing the penis of his eighteen month old son. Kargar had done this in accordance with an Afghani practice, which, according to several Afghan witnesses in subsequent proceedings, had no sexual significance. The act is, in that cultural setting, an act of love by a father though the same culture would severely punish the act if it were done for sexual gratification.[21] The lawmakers of the state of Maine surely assumed that such an act would always have sexual significance.

---

18 Anthony Appiah 'Race, Culture, Identity: Misunderstood Connections' in Kwame Anthony Appiah and Amy Gutmann *Color Conscious* (Princeton University Press, Princeton NJ, 1996) 85. See also Kwame Anthony Appiah *Cosmopolitanism* (W.W. Norton and Co. Inc, New York, 2007) for a very thoughtful discussion of this issue.

19 Jeremy Waldron 'The Logic of Cultural Accommodation' (2002) 59 *Washington and Lee Law Review* 3.

20 *State* v *Kargar*, 679 A.2d 81 (Me. 1996).

21 Waldron 'The Logic of Cultural Accommodation' above n. 19 at 6.

It would probably surprise many that this is not the case. The case is thus a salutary reminder that very different meanings can be attached to the same act.[22]

However, the awareness of relevant cultural differences is a sophistication required in the moral analysis of different cultural settings or group practices, not a reason to think such analysis is inappropriate *per se*.[23] And not every difference will be relevant to the moral assessment of a cultural practice. It is no doubt true, for example, that aspects of the historical context (including the 'culture', broadly speaking) in South Africa in which apartheid developed were unique. (History is always specific in some ways.) Those details will help to *explain* why racial segregation and dominance, as a social and legal system, developed in the specific way that it did in that country. But nothing about that context *justifies* apartheid in any way which should convince us.

It was 'culturally appropriate' for white people in apartheid South Africa to behave in a racist manner and to have racist attitudes (although there was a significant white non-racist counter-culture) but it was not *morally* appropriate. Making that moral judgment is not an act of cultural arrogance – anyone who cannot make it is just hopeless at moral judgment! Some contextual differences *explain* different outcomes without *justifying* them.

Bernard Williams discusses what he calls a 'relativism of distance'[24] Some comparisons of cultural practices can only be 'notional'. As Jeremy Waldron says, in a discussion of Williams, we cannot, now, choose to be samurai warriors and, because, as ethical theory puts it 'ought implies can', it does not make sense to suggest anyone *should* be a samurai warrior rather than something else which it is possible for us now to be.[25] It might also be difficult to say, morally speaking, that someone should or should not have been, a samurai warrior when it was possible to be one. On the other hand we can clearly say that someone should not have deliberately, and without duress, revealed the whereabouts of Jews in hiding in Nazi Germany.

Again these subtleties provide no defence for the simplistic cultural relativism I am rejecting here. The kind of 'cultural differences' that we might want to accommodate today are *present* beliefs, values and practices. These can be compared and analysed; found to be appealing or deserving of rejection. They can have prescriptive consequences for future action. The relativism that denies

---

22   The charge was eventually dismissed using a statutory de minimis exception. It would still be appropriate to ask, I would think, whether there were any harmful consequences for the children who are involved in this ritual. Even if the *motive* is innocent it might still be shown to be a harmful *practice*. I have no idea whether it is, or could be, but a culture can, we should note, have perfectly moral motives for approving a certain practice while being unaware of possible harmful effects. Medical science reminds all of us of this on a regular basis.

23   See Jeremy Waldron 'How To Argue For A Universal Claim' (1999) 30 *Colum Hum Rts L Rev* 305, 307–9.

24   Bernard Williams *Ethics and the Limits of Philosophy*, above n. 14, 161–6, cited in Waldron 'How To Argue For A Universal Claim', above n. 23, 308.

25   Waldron 'How To Argue For A Universal Claim', above n. 23, 308.

the value of such appraisal is wrong because it lets *any* difference, or at least too many, count; not just morally relevant differences. It is the sort of relativism that allows adultery, for example, to be wrong not because fidelity is a good thing in itself or because it is wrong to hurt people by breaking our promises to them, but simply because a particular community believes it is wrong.

That way of thinking is flawed whether applied to different cultural groups within a country or internationally. It is true, and fortunate, as Jeremy Waldron notes, that this obviously wrong sort of relativism is not as common in practical moralising as we might think. When people say this or that is wrong they usually mean to say just that; not 'this is wrong for us in our community'.[26] But a careless relativism is an important aspect of, at least popular, current thinking about cultural difference and discrimination. And it does not become better moral theorising simply because the difference is 'cultural'. The role of relativism in contemporary thought about culture is a large one and much more can be said about it.[27] The relationship between culture and human agency is, as I have been implying, crucial in this regard.[28] In general, I agree with the sentiments expressed by Michael Carrithers who compares his 'sociality theory of culture' with what he calls the 'culture theory':

> On balance, I argue, individuals in relationships, and the interactive character of social life, are slightly more important, more real, than those things we designate as culture. According to the culture theory, people do things because of their culture; on the sociality theory, people do things with, to, and in respect of each other, using means that we can describe, if we wish to, as cultural.[29]

Real-world multiculturalism, at least, could do with a strong dose of Carrithers's 'sociality theory'. What he calls the 'culture theory' seems to think of cultures doing things with helpless individuals. At its worst this is an example of bad faith. Of course everything we do is in a cultural context, which influences us as we influence it in turn. But that is the point: the influencing goes both ways; in the case of the morally active.

Cultural Rights

If criticism of cultural differences is not necessarily discrimination, though it sometimes is, we might conclude that what is needed is that everyone should

---

26   Waldron 'How To Argue for a Universal Claim', above n. 23, 310.

27   See Brian Barry *Culture and Equality* (Harvard University Press, Cambridge, 2001) Ch. 7.

28   See Will Kymlicka *Contemporary Political Philosophy* (2nd edn, Oxford University Press, Oxford, 2002) 221.

29   Michael Carrithers *Why Humans Have Cultures*, above n. 8, 34.

simply be treated the same. All should be judged by and made to live by the same rules, which are determined in a democracy by majority decisions made under fair conditions. But the rejection of cultural relativism does not, however, necessarily entail the rejection of all demands for different treatment on cultural grounds. It is not only by making diversity *per se* a moral value that we can have reason to think that we should sometimes treat people differently on cultural (including religious) grounds.

Because a commitment to treat people as equals does not always require equal treatment, though it often does, reasonable people will disagree over whether it is ever morally appropriate to treat people differently according to cultural difference. Argument is required to reach a conclusion either way on that point. Cultural difference does not *obviously* entitle us to equal, or different, treatment. I do not mean we have no intuitions about this; we do, but they pull in different directions.

Current debates about multiculturalism are the setting for serious thought about what it means to deny the basic equality of others by unfairly ignoring, suppressing, attacking or failing to respect or support the culture of others. There is a considerable literature on the purported strengths and weaknesses of multiculturalism's various policy proposals.[30] Because there is little disagreement about the more obvious forms of discrimination, as with race and gender the contemporary debate about culture can be said to be organised around the question whether or not we should have 'one law for all'.

Will Kymlicka thinks the onus has shifted partly to those who do think we should all be treated the same to show that this is not discriminatory.[31] I am not so sure about this. There may be no point in thinking in terms of a presumption of equal treatment with general application.[32] But when certain differences are used to justify different treatment, race and sex in particular, we should be wary because of our racist and sexist past, and ongoing discrimination on these grounds. Religious and cultural accommodation may make us less suspicious but we should still think carefully before accepting proposals for different treatment on these grounds because they too have been grounds on which people are typically discriminated against.

Claims for different treatment on cultural grounds are typically expressed as claims about rights.[33] Very different sorts of claims for minority cultural

---

30   See Kymlicka *Contemporary Political Philosophy*, above n. 28, Ch. 8 for a useful review of recent debates. A less sympathetic assessment of multiculturalism, as a policy, may be found in Brian Barry *Culture and Equality*, above n. 27. See also Jacob T. Levy 'Liberal Jacobinism' (2004) 114 *Ethics* 318 for a critique of *Culture and Equality*.

31   Will Kymlicka *Contemporary Political Philosophy*, above n. 28, 366.

32   Peter Westen *Speaking of Equality* (Princeton University Press, Princeton, 1990) Ch. 10.

33   It is interesting to note, once again, that discussion about discrimination and culture (an equality issue) is also a debate about the right to be different (a liberty issue).

rights may be made. Some, to mention a few well-known types, are to do with governance; some are about claims for funding of cultural projects, while others are about justifying exemptions to the application of general laws.[34] I will only comment on the last type. They are harder to justify than one might think, or so I will argue.

I should perhaps note here that I am not talking about laws which are just plainly, intentionally, discriminatory in themselves. If atheists are made to say prayers at state functions or Muslim women are not allowed to wear headscarves in the workplace (where it is safe to do so) or at university then the law, or the absence of legal protection in the case of the Muslim women, is the problem. The appropriate remedy for unfair, and pointless, laws is usually repeal or inclusion of the needs of relative outsiders in new generally applicable laws, not a system of exceptions.

Of course there is much to think about in the assessment of the fairness of laws in terms of even-handedness in the treatment of cultural and religious groups. Some issues seem straightforward. Why do we persist, in New Zealand, for example, with trading restrictions on Easter holidays? Other issues are harder. Is a ban on certain religious methods of killing animals justified if the discomfort caused to animals by using them for consumption, for the rest of us, is also not easily morally justified?[35] For now I want to focus on considerations applicable to laws untainted by such considerations, but I will return to this source of possible imbalance, briefly, later in this chapter.

The way United States courts dealt with the right to 'free expression' of religion[36] until recently, is perhaps the best known model we might use for

---

34   See Jacob T. Levy 'Classifying Cultural Rights' in Ian Shapiro and Will Kymlicka *Ethnicity and Group Rights* (New York University Press, New York, 1997). Levy categorises cultural rights as follows:

1.   exemptions from generally applicable laws which penalise or burden cultural practices (discussed here);
2.   assistance (e.g. affirmative action);
3.   self-government;
4.   external rules which protect cultures from the actions of outsiders;
5.   internal rules for enforcing group members' conduct;
6.   recognition and/or enforcement of cultural laws (e.g. family law);
7.   guaranteed or facilitated representation of minorities in government bodies;
8.   symbolic claims (e.g. disputes over public holidays).

As Levy notes, a typology might instead focus on the identity of the recipient of the rights. Cf. Will Kymlicka *Multicultural Citizenship* (Oxford, Oxford University Press, 1995).

35   Linda Barclay 'Liberalism and Diversity' in *The Oxford Handbook of Contemporary Philosophy* (Oxford, London, 2005) 155, 159.

36   This right is protected by the First Amendment to the United States Constitution which also forbids the establishment of a state endorsed religion.

considering claims for cultural exemptions in general to laws of general application.[37] The protection given religious freedom in the First Amendment to the United States Constitution, as interpreted by courts before the United States Supreme Court *Employment Division* v *Smith*,[38] while controversial and not always perfectly coherent, is inspired by the seemingly plausible idea that restrictions of the same freedom can be a greater burden for some people than for others.[39] If the burden is greater and imposing it is not strictly necessary, then it seems to follow that not all exemptions from general rules constitute unfair special treatment. It seems reasonable therefore to consider them on a case by case basis. Not every desired exemption can be granted because the rule may serve a purpose that is too important[40] but it may, in this context as in others, not always be morally necessary to treat people equally: that may be the wrong thing to do.

If the argument for exemptions on religious grounds makes sense in some cases, it seems reasonable to extend that to cultural differences in general. That may appear to be the best way to deal with claims for cultural equality by the descendants of colonised peoples who are minorities, for example, at least in terms of demands for exemptions from general laws, or similar claims of – ethnic minority – immigrants. But basic equality demands that we consider too, in terms of exemptions from general laws, the situation of others who may also resent the intrusion of law into their chosen way of life and whether we have a reason for distinguishing their claims from those who make cultural claims for exemptions. What exactly is the additional burden that is imposed on this latter category of claimants and what is its moral significance?

Brian Barry argues that an extra burden *in itself* is not sufficient to justify granting an exemption. If the law is not fair in that it affects one group in a particularly harsh way Barry says we should see if the law can be modified in a way that its purpose will still be fulfilled while not producing such an onerous

---

37   Until the Supreme Court decision in *Employment Division* v *Smith* 494 US 872 (1990). That case changed, in the view of many at least, the test which applies to laws burdening religious freedom. Before *Smith* it was generally thought the government had to show a 'compelling state interest' in imposing the burden. For a history of the law before *Smith*, and subsequent attempts to revive it, or what the revivalists thought the law had been, see Erwin Chemerinsky *Constitutional Law* (3rd edn, Aspen Publishers, New York, 2006) Ch. 12; cf. Christopher L. Eisgruber and Lawrence G. Sager *Religious Freedom and the Constitution* (Harvard University Press, Cambridge, Massachusetts and London, 2007); see also Martha Nussbaum *Liberty of Conscience* (Basic Books, New York, 2008).

38   494 US 872 (1990)

39   See Chemerinsky *Constitutional Law*, above n. 37, 1204–1206.

40   A 'compelling state interest' as the US courts sometimes put it. We cannot, for example, exempt people from the law forbidding murder, for cultural or religious reasons, even if we are willing to think about modifying, for example, our doctrines of provocation or mitigating circumstances to take cultural difference into account. See Jeremy Waldron 'The Logic of Cultural Accommodation', above n. 19, 3.

burden for this or that minority group.[41] As noted already, good law does not impose unnecessary burdens. But apart from some pragmatic considerations about what to do about existing exceptions in UK law Barry is not keen on what he calls the 'rule-and-exemption' approach. The simple fact that a rule burdens one group more than another does not justify the granting of an exception, in Barry's view.[42] The law against rape only burdens rapists but that does not make it unfair.[43] Something more is needed other than the unequal impact. Barry does not think a general rule plus exemption can never be justified but he does think that usually the case for the rule will be strong enough to exclude the possibility of justifying an exemption or the case for an exemption will be strong enough to justify removing the rule. The rule and exemption approach, says Barry, is not the panacea that multiculturalists sometimes take it to be.[44] Well, what can be said for it?

Jeremy Waldron thinks one reason why a cultural or religious group might have an extraordinary, and morally relevant, burden placed on it by a general law of universal application is that the members of such groups may be doubly regulated, by state law *and* by the rules of their religious/cultural community.[45] Unlike the ordinary objector they might not be asking to be free from constraint altogether – they are pulled in different directions by two opposing sets of regulations. It is not the intensity, Waldron argues, of the preference not to be restricted by a rule which counts as the added burden.[46] He is right to note that, because the preference may be more intense, on occasion, in the case of the ordinary objector who just does not like the rule. The feeling torn is, Waldron says, not just a matter of 'subjective conviction'[47]; it is socially grounded. As he puts it:

> Because of the positive existence of a scheme of regulation rivalling the state law, the person we are considering is already under a socially enforced burden, established as part of an actual way of life, a burden grounded in the actually-existing and well-established regulation and coordination of social affairs afforded by a religious or a cultural tradition. Others claiming an exemption simply as a matter of liberty or personal conscience might not be under any burden comparable to that.[48]

Well, why is peer pressure, from one's cultural group, to conform to a law which conflicts with a state law more of a burden than individual conscience? Individual conscience too, can be a burden. The individual objector need not be a libertarian

---

41 Brian Barry *Culture and Equality*, above n. 27, 40.
42 Brian Barry *Culture and Equality*, above n. 27, 34.
43 Ibid.
44 Brian Barry *Culture and Equality*, above n. 27, 62.
45 Waldron 'The Logic of Cultural Accommodation', above n. 19, 16.
46 Waldron 'The Logic of Cultural Accommodation', above n. 19, 24.
47 Ibid.
48 Waldron 'The Logic of Cultural Accommodation', above n. 19, 24. I am not sure this description of the burden would apply equally to all religious and cultural groups.

fundamentalist who thinks just *any* restriction of freedom is a great loss. He may understand the difference in kind between not being allowed to drive the wrong way on a one way road and not being allowed to criticise the government.[49] He too may be torn, between following state law and the dictates of his conscience. Furthermore the latter will come from somewhere. As the cultural theorists are eager to remind us, no norms are culture free.

Conscientious objectors, of various stripes, have communities too. They also feel the burden of dual regulation. The dominant culture in western democracies has been troublesome for these subcultures too. Human rights legislation sometimes recognises this in provisions about 'freedom of conscience'.[50] I have not overlooked Waldron's use of the word 'might' in the passage just quoted; I just mean to emphasise it was needed.

Waldron also thinks some cultural groups might be disadvantaged by ignorance of the law if they are newcomers. It is true that familiarity with the dominant culture and its laws will not usually be a problem for subcultures which constitute a *counterculture*. But this, the problem of ignorance of the law, can be better remedied by education for new migrants, which Waldron suggests, although I also agree that sometimes ignorance of the law should be a valid defence or a mitigating factor.[51] But for anyone: 'cultural' impediments to knowing about or understanding the law are present in the nearest poor neighbourhood.

Waldron does acknowledge that his suggested reason for allowing religious or cultural, but not other, exemptions from general laws does not apply to cases where the law changes and people in the *mainstream* culture have to suddenly submit to a regulation which may go against the grain of their upbringing and the culture (including the legal culture) they had hitherto been a part of.[52] I agree that this sort of new regulation, which challenges existing mores, does make it difficult to distinguish between 'cultural' objections and others. But I think that any conscientious objector too might have the sort of dual burden that Waldron is discussing. What may be acceptable to the majority may be unacceptable to all sorts of minorities, not just ones with an 'identity'.

Waldron says he is not sure if anyone has ever given a satisfactory explanation of how it can be fair, if there is room for an exemption from a given law, to give the benefit of it only to groups who claim it on religious (or cultural) grounds.[53] I think we are still some way from finding a good answer. The extra burden idea, which Waldron is trying to give new life to in the article referred to here, is an initially plausible one. If members of majority cultures want to claim that contemporary

---

49   See Ronald Dworkin *Taking Rights Seriously* (Duckworth, London, 1977) Ch. 12. Dworkin argues convincingly here that not all liberty is equally important.

50   See, for example, s 15 of the Constitution of the Republic of South Africa, Act 108 of 1996. What exactly courts are supposed to do with such provisions is another matter.

51   Waldron 'The Logic of Cultural Accommodation', above n. 19, 25–7.

52   Waldron 'The Logic of Cultural Accommodation', above n. 19, 27–8.

53   Waldron 'The Logic of Cultural Accommodation', above n. 19, 21–2.

modern society should, as far as possible, be neutral on questions about the good life, then they should take the trouble to ensure that minorities enjoy that autonomy too. But the difficulty of identifying exactly which *sorts* of minorities should be exempted on occasion remains. And that difficulty does threaten to undermine the plausibility of the fairness of the rule-and-exemption approach.[54] Our commitment to basic equality may inspire the idea of limited justifiable exemptions but it also requires equal consideration of the concerns of others.

I said I would return to the problem of laws which, while otherwise harmless, in a sense, establish the dominant culture as such. I will only comment here on the response to this issue which suggests it be dealt with by the rule-and-exemption approach. Religious holidays, Sunday closing laws and conscientious objector (to military service) options for some groups but not others, are common examples. To have broad categories of exemptions to include relative outsiders seems only fair in the presence of such favouritism. And that has been carried out to some extent in liberal societies, although anomalies still exist. In the body of law that I referred to as a sort of paradigm case for this discussion, First Amendment freedom of religion law,[55] a seminal case, that of *Sherbert* v *Werner* is instructive here.[56]

Mrs Sherbert, a Seventh Day Adventist, worked in the South Carolina textile industry. Saturday, not Sunday, is the Sabbath according to that church's doctrine. She had worked, at Spartan Mill, for many years before becoming a Seventh Day Adventist but only later, after continuing to work a five-day week after joining that faith, did the problem of working on Saturdays arise. When it did she was unsuccessful in her unemployment insurance claim because she had lost her job, and failed to take up alternative employment for (religious) reasons which were unacceptable in terms of state law. Her First Amendment objection to this was eventually upheld by the United States Supreme Court, the majority holding that she had been made, unfairly, to choose between her religious duties and her rights under the unemployment insurance scheme. The Court observed that mainstream Christian denominations had been spared that choice. An attempt to uphold basic equality was thus an important part of the rationale for the decision. As Martha Nussbaum puts it, writing about the case in her recent book on religious freedom in America: 'it [equality] can be said to be what drives the whole argument'.[57] This is because the extra burden is unfair, as between Seventh Day Adventists and traditional Christians.

Nussbaum is arguing here about First Amendment law. She cannot stretch that law to cover cultural issues, let alone questions of 'individual' conscience[58]

---

54   See Brian Barry *Culture and Equality*, above n. 27, 40.

55   To be more exact: those that fall under the First Amendment's protection of the 'free exercise' of religion.

56   *Sherbert* v *Werner* 374 US 398 (1963).

57   Martha Nussbaum *Liberty of Conscience*, above n. 37, 137. It being unlikely for Christians, at least then, to have to work on a Sunday.

58   The inverted commas serve as a reminder that the word 'individual' can be misleading in this context. Individuals have consciences, perhaps only individuals can, but

Yet she understands well the question of fairness we are struggling with in this context. She discusses it in terms of religious reasons *compared* to non-religious reasons because she is writing a book about religion, but the problem is the same. Her argument (if you replace 'religion' with 'culture' using the latter in the way I have suggested), to include non-religious reasons as far as possible when thinking about exemptions under the First Amendment, goes a long way to protect basic equality, but she would not countenance scrapping the whole Free Exercise clause enterprise just because all non-religious (for my purposes 'individual') dissenters cannot be accommodated. Nussbaum's argument is constrained by her topic but she does say '[t]he ideas of the Free Exercise tradition are ... ideas of equal respect for all citizens' consciences, 'delicate' accommodation of conscientious scruples, and fairness to minorities who live in a majority world'.[59] But if that is the case then adding, as she suggests the Court, over the years, was right to do, a couple of conscientious objector (to military service) cases involving people who were not really religious[60] to exemptions allowed for religious sensibilities is not really enough.

Nussbaum is aware of this and is, I said, constrained by the law itself. She does however base her argument largely on basic equality, as I argued earlier one well might, and says that ideally what one is looking for is respect for each individual's conscience.[61] This is why, she says, we should include 'quasi-religious' searches for ultimate meaning.[62] Nussbaum is not trying to include individual objectors simply because religious objectors might be protected; she rightly sees that what is being protected in both cases is the same thing: respect for persons' moral personality.

That is worthy of respect of course; I have argued that our nature as moral beings is a large part of how we are right to consider ourselves each other's equals.[63] But if that is what we are trying to protect with systems of rules plus exceptions, then we ought to remember that we already have a way of doing that; simply by having a liberal democratic system of government. We ought to remember that because we will often disagree about the conclusions of serious moral thinking about social policy: that is why we protect people's rights to argue and vote.

If we are to go further than that, it seems then, if we agree to exceptions based on cultural grounds, we are bound as a matter of fairness, as a matter of basic equality, to consider any conscientious objection to a law or rule that the majority favour but do not regard as needing complete enforcement. It still does not seem at all clear that we can, fairly, limit this enterprise to exemptions based on 'cultural' grounds, let alone religious grounds.

---

not in any isolated or completely private sense.

59   Martha Nussbaum *Liberty of Conscience*, above n. 37, 174.
60   *United States* v *Seeger* 380 US 163 1965.
61   Martha Nussbaum *Liberty of Conscience*, above n. 37, 168.
62   Martha Nussbaum *Liberty of Conscience*, above n. 37, 169.
63   See Ch. 3.

I also said I would return to the draft definition of 'cultural differences' I stipulated for the purposes of this discussion: *a set of differences in beliefs, values and practices between groups in a contemporary society which may lead to significant disagreement about how things should be done and/or regulated.* The problem is over-inclusiveness. Cultural difference in this broad sense seems to include more types of disagreements than the ones this topic is supposed to be about. (It would include, for example, the differences between the beliefs and values of the Greens and the Liberal Party in Australia.) And yet the definition does not misuse the word 'culture' in any obvious way. If it is said what is missing is the burden of dual obligation which may come from a religious or non-religious 'cultural' context, then I have argued that the inclusion of these provides protection for almost anyone. If what is lacking in my definition is a sense of the seriousness of the issue at stake, that can be rectified by replacing the word 'significant' with something sterner. That would be equally futile. We then end up searching for 'matters of conscience' as a subset of seriously held moral opinions about public regulation.

I don't think we are finished with this topic, by any means, but I do not think we have got very far with it either. That does not mean our striving has been in vain. Democratic decision making is not a perfected art and we always have to think of ways to alleviate the plight of those pulled in directions the majority have not chosen. It is just not quite clear yet that a right to exemptions from general rules on cultural (including religious) grounds makes sense.

There are many more conundrums to do with culture and discrimination, as the reader will no doubt be aware. Logically these are problems in political philosophy first and then in law. But the law today, in matters of discrimination generally, is a contested site. It seldom speaks with one voice, although nations often declare themselves to be implementing international agreements when they enact them. And what consensus there is, in anti-discrimination law in general, frequently amounts to a house built upon sand. It is to the law of equality protection and promotion to which the final three chapters will be devoted. The next chapter, on discrimination provisions generally, will mostly be about the central difficulties in the interpretation and application of that law. Some of these difficulties raise hard moral questions which are relevant to the subject matter of the final two chapters dealing with indirect discrimination, and affirmative action. It is there that these moral questions will be discussed.

Chapter 8

Equality's Law

Introduction

The most obvious purpose of equality laws is to uphold or promote basic equality. By this I mean that if the idea of basic equality expresses what is morally important about equality then it is that idea which serves most naturally as our moral reason to introduce anti-discrimination laws. To uphold basic equality, lawmakers may try to make governments conform to basic equality. This they may do by means of Bill of Rights provisions that constrain the legislative and executive branch of government from denying basic equality to those they are responsible for. They may also apply ordinary human rights legislation to the government itself. To promote basic equality, laws may restrain the practices of private citizens by making them conform to it in certain areas of communal life or aim at achieving a particular equality with provisions that may apply to both government and private parties.

In this chapter I am not directly addressing the justificatory question about what sort of laws we should have. I am mostly concerned with problems concerning the interpretation of current laws, but the nature of that interpretation cannot be divorced from discussion about why the law is there. I am also not trying to provide a general review of this area of law. I only want to comment on the merits of some contemporary approaches in equality law exegesis.

I want to note, first, the difficulty in interpreting these laws, caused by their usually very general terms and then go on to discuss some recent approaches to interpreting and evaluating them and assess these according to how well they relate the point of these laws to the moral idea of treating people as equals. I conclude that the approaches that I discuss do not do that well and that is to the detriment of our moral understanding of these laws. Anti-discrimination law has an overtly moral purpose – it does not exist to make our societies more efficient or more technologically sophisticated – and so its interpretation, evaluation and development are not well served by approaches that are not clear about its moral point.

Provisions in Bills of Rights[1] prohibiting the denial of basic equality or attempting to ameliorate the effects of discrimination are even more abstract and less like a rule than the other rights typically found in a Bill of Rights. The idea of freedom of speech for example, while it has been the subject of a large and

---

[1] Those found in ordinary human rights legislation are usually more specific but can also be difficult to interpret because the meaning of 'discrimination' can be elusive.

sometimes confusing jurisprudential analysis, has at least recognisable contours. We argue about how much freedom of speech we should have and when it should be restricted, rather than about *what it is*. We know what freedom of speech is: the right to express ourselves freely. It is true there is a difference between speech and expression in general but when the meaning of one is extended to include the other we know what we have ended up with. So even when the 'meaning' of freedom of speech is widened to include expression, after arguments about things like flag burning[2] and naked dancing,[3] we still have a recognisable thing to study and discuss.

Another way of saying this is that at one level it makes sense to say that it is a matter of *fact* whether there is a certain level of freedom of speech in country A today. More specifically we can know as a matter of fact whether particular forms of expression, giving a Nazi salute or inciting imminent violence, are prohibited in country A. The same is not true, at least not in the same way, for basic equality. We can say the people of country A seem to be more committed to basic equality than the people of country B but we cannot demonstrate that simply by pointing to certain facts about those countries; we first have to argue about what it means to say one treats its people like equals to a greater extent than the other. This is because, in the metaethical terminology I have adopted,[4] basic equality is a value not a fact. The existence, or presence, of freedom of speech on the other hand is a fact. You either have certain types of it or you do not.

This may strike some as odd because we can also think of freedom of speech as a value. It *is* a value. But what we mean when we say that is that there *should* be freedom to express ourselves within certain prescribed limits. Of course it is difficult to work out what the limits should be. That is what we argue so much about with regard to free speech. Sometimes the policy arguments about the appropriate limits of free speech are left to the legislative branch but sometimes it is up to courts to decide on the limit. The meaning of all broad constitutional provisions can be difficult to determine; but with 'freedom of speech' the meaning is not really unclear, it is just broad. And we know the broad meaning is not the intended meaning because no one wants to allow direct incitement to violence. We just do not always know what to leave out, but eventually someone or some institution decides and then we know, as a matter of fact again, what is in or out.[5]

The value of free speech is explored, in parliaments and courts, in discussions about autonomy or truth, or the prerequisites for democracy, rather than in talk about the meaning of the concept 'freedom of speech' and those discussions can

---

2   See Erwin Chemerinsky *Constitutional Law* (3rd edn, Aspen Publishers, New York, 2006) 1067.

3   See Chemerinsky *Constitutional Law*, above n. 2, 1027.

4   See Ch. 3.

5   Unless the lawmaker uses vague terms, like 'obscenity', without being clear about what is meant.

be as difficult as ones about basic equality. But the judicial task must be harder, it would seem, with basic equality, because there we *only* have the background value: there is no plain fact of the matter about whether basic equality is being observed or not. With rights to speech or association, or movement, there are. Of course the difference, in terms of the difficulties in interpretation, between anti-discrimination provisions and free speech clauses should not be overestimated. Even when permissible limitations to free speech are included in a law they can be very difficult to interpret or apply. But there is at least a definite *something* − free expression − that you might want less or more of in particular contexts.

Still, if law can take a concern for autonomy[6] or whatever we take to be the background value(s) justifying freedom of speech and turn that into a rule specifying a right to a particular freedom, albeit in terms lacking instructions about the scope of the freedom, why can it not do something similar with basic equality? So far equality law lacks even that level of concreteness. The law story usually starts with the United States Bill of Rights which speaks more generally about 'equality before the law'. That is not quite as broad as 'basic equality', but it is still a reference to a value rather than a specific instruction to (United States) State and Federal government institutions not to do A in situation X. We immediately have to ask what 'equality' or 'equal protection' requires here. Does the law always have to treat us the same way? Obviously it does not. So what distinctions are permissible? Any except those based on race? And so on from, in the United States, *Brown*[7] to *Bakke*[8] and beyond.

Recent law usually talks about discrimination, not basic equality. Recent constitutional provisions are typically more elaborate than the US one but no less difficult to interpret, ultimately, apart from the fact that they commonly allow what are apparently some forms of affirmative action. Their claim to an essence one can depend on might be thought to be the idea of discrimination. But 'discrimination' cannot even be as determinate as 'free speech'. The addition of certain grounds of discrimination does help, even though these are not always meant to be exhaustive. But, as the case law makes clear it is not, I have argued it should not be,[9] simply a matter of proscribing 'forbidden grounds' of differentiation. Differentiation on the specified grounds is sometimes upheld even in the absence of affirmative action provisions. So what is discrimination?

Some insight into the meaning of 'discrimination' could be gleaned by looking at a dictionary. It will allow a meaning that is just 'differentiation'.[10] But one would expect a human rights lawyer to pick the one about prejudicial distinctions. But

---

6   I have suggested a commitment to basic equality itself is part of the justification for upholding liberties like freedom of expression. See Ch. 5.

7   *Brown* v *Topeka Board of Education* 347 US 483 (1954).

8   *Regents of the University of California* v *Bakke* 438 US 265 (1978).

9   See Ch. 6.

10   *The New Shorter Oxford English Dictionary* (Clarendon Press, Oxford, 1993) 689.

which are these? Distinctions which take irrelevant considerations into account? But which are these again? I have cited Larry Alexander noting relevant distinctions are any which are important to us.[11] The idea of basic equality is not subjective in that way, it condemns distinctions which do not take the concerns of all affected parties into account but it does not assume that all concerns have equal weight. Assessing the importance of different concerns involves making value judgments which, naturally, is often very difficult.

What some legal commentators have done, with some prompting by the courts, is to try and make the task more manageable by specifying what sort of 'equality' is important or valuable or by working out what 'discrimination' *really means* and, in at least one case, by suggesting discrimination might be best understood without reference to equality at all. My complaint about their efforts is that recent jurisprudence, which attempts in various ways to circumvent the abstractness of basic equality by substituting other, more limited, notions of equality or by suggesting alternative rationales for anti-discrimination provisions, distorts the moral analysis of the policy objectives or leaves it incomplete. It does this because it does not clearly relate these policy objectives to the moral point of talking about equality – our commitment to basic quality. No law can implement the whole of what basic equality requires but whatever we take the specific purpose of equality law to be it should be consistent with basic equality and we should be able to explain how it relates to that value.

I will first propose that we rethink the value of comparing 'formal equality' with 'substantive equality' in the way these terms are used in much recent writing about equality. I think this way of talking has not offered a means to solve any of the issues that those committed to equality argue about. I will argue that the underlying concerns of 'substantive equality theorists' are better able to be discussed once we accept that 'equality' is a larger, more abstract concept than any particular aim to equalise the distribution of a particular social good. The disavowal by substantive equality theorists of 'formal equality' (which is usually interpreted to mean 'equal treatment'), does have a point. But the point is not well made, because the terms in which it is expressed do not clearly convey what is intended by the best interpretation of that point. Those said to be committed to 'formal equality' are also making an important moral point, in my view, but it too, is cast in unhelpful terms. There is, in the terms that I do not think are helpful, a real moral debate to be had (or continued) between the advocates of 'formal' and 'substantive' equality but it will only be fruitfully conducted in clearer language. Both sides of this debate are suggesting that something be made equal and both confuse their policy choices with the ideal of equality itself.

I will also counsel against the suggestion that equality, or discrimination, should be explained in terms of other large concepts. Cases and commentaries in constitutional law in some jurisdictions have in recent years at times expressed

---

11   Larry Alexander 'What Makes Wrongful Discrimination Wrong? Biases, Preferences, Stereotypes, and Proxies' (1992) 141 *U Pa L Rev* 149, 151.

the idea that discrimination is in large part a matter of treating people in ways that negatively impacts on their *dignity*. Apart from the obvious problem − that this approach adds to the analytic burden because we now have to explain what 'dignity' is and when it is impaired − explaining a value in terms of another value might reveal a lack of confidence in our ability to explain the first value at all. While I do not share that scepticism I will suggest that the dignity of humanity in general, the worth of persons qua human beings is indeed part of the explanation of our *commitment* to basic equality. I have argued this already, in different terms, in my discussion of our reasons for valuing basic equality. I will argue that dignity in that sense is not itself a value, not a candidate for inclusion in our canon of human rights and that respect for it is an even more abstract idea than basic equality. Dignity in another, more subjective sense, that of our particular estimation of our self worth, the dignity that can be offended or impaired, may or may not in particular instances be worthy of human rights protection or moral concern generally. Whether it is will depend on the moral reasonableness of its foundation in a particular instance. And because of this last point the impairment of dignity in this sense is not the essence of an offence against basic equality.

The perceived need to use other values, or indeed other ideas which may or may not represent values, to explain the meaning of equality or the purpose of legislation promoting or upholding equality may also lead to the eschewal, if not of equality, of explanations of discrimination law in terms of equality. I will argue that Hugh Collins's suggestion that 'social inclusion', rather than equality, is the aim of such laws gets some of its plausibility from the fact that he is using the word 'equality' in a specific restricted sense which he does not relate to the general moral principle of basic equality. Because of the seemingly endless debate about what sort of equality is envisaged by the laws it might be tempting to replace the idea altogether. The problem here is we do not know much about the philosophical underpinnings of 'social inclusion' either. How does *it* relate to the major Enlightenment values of equality, liberty and community? Until this question has been satisfactorily answered it seems premature to judge that we are wrong to think of anti-discrimination law as 'equality law'. It is not in the straightforward sense that, for example, the law on civil procedure is about the nuts and bolts of civil procedure. But, anti-discrimination law can only make sense morally if it is understood as an attempt, however clumsy the attempt might seem, to uphold basic equality.

Substantive Equality?

An Odd Dichotomy

Discrimination law is usually seen as an attempt to uphold equality. The abstractness of the notion of basic equality has led to the development of various conceptions of the idea. It is common, especially in discrimination jurisprudence, to find the idea that there is a merely *formal* idea of equality which should be rejected in favour of a *substantive* equality.[12]

Louis Pojman and Robert Westmoreland are influenced by this view when they write: '[w]e can divide egalitarian theories into two types: *formal* and *substantive*'.[13] As an 'illustration' of the former they give Aristotle's formula: equals should be treated equally and unequals should be treated unequally.[14] This formal notion does not tell us, they say, what is wrong with a Connecticut law of 1650 which read: 'If any man after legal conviction shall have or worship any other God but the Lord God, he shall be put to death'. The only value formal equality upholds, according to them, is consistency.[15] Pojman and Westmoreland think there is another kind of equality, 'substantive equality', which does have a specific content, or rather that there is a range of substantive equalities each with a specific content.

But it is not clear why these authors think the 'likes should be treated alike' formula is, on its own, a 'type of egalitarianism' which must be compared to the 'other type': substantive equality. 'Egalitarianism' is a cluster of moral theories, concerned with justice. And, as the authors point out,[16] Aristotle knew (and everyone since surely knows) some substance or other must be provided to complete the idea that, as Aristotle had it, justice means treating equals equally.[17] It has to be decided which differences are morally relevant because that is the morally interesting question – when one starts with the likes should be treated alike formula. The equal right to follow the one true religion in their Connecticut example has a substance, just not a very attractive one if you believe in the right to be free from religious discrimination.

If we think the toleration of religious differences is a value in sound political philosophy the Connecticut law was not morally justified. If on the other hand we agree with the absolutist views of the early New England Congregationalists, it was justified. It is not helpful, therefore, to think that we are working with two different theories, one 'formal' and one 'substantive'. Any call to equalise the distribution of something will have its 'substance', stated or not. The trouble with Pojman and Westmoreland's discussion is that they have not started with the moral essence of equality – the requirement to treat people as equals. The problem, in terms of

---

12 The concept has quasi synonyms. In some cases the (equally indeterminate) expression 'equality of outcomes' is used interchangeably with 'substantive equality', and 'procedural equality' with 'formal equality'.

13 Louis P. Pojman and Robert Westmoreland (eds) *Equality* (Oxford University Press, New York, 1997) 2.

14 Ibid.

15 Louis P. Pojman and Robert Westmoreland (eds) *Equality*, above n. 13, 3.

16 Ibid.

17 Aristotle *The Politics* (Oxford World Classics, Oxford, 1995) Book III Ch. 12 1282b14.

basic equality, with the Connecticut law, is that it does not fulfil this requirement. It treated people with non-conformist views with less concern and respect. Their religion was forbidden just because *it was theirs*.[18]

The logic of the formal/substantive distinction is thus elusive. But its use persists. A full-blown example, in the specific context of the debate on the proper role of discrimination law, of the use of the terms 'formal' and 'substantive' equality, which illustrates the futility of current uses of these notions to solve equality's dilemmas, can be found in an article by Catherine Barnard and Bob Hepple titled 'Substantive Equality'.[19] The article is specifically about UK and European anti-discrimination law but will serve as a typical example. The authors provide an, at times, interesting and thought-provoking analysis of how that law sometimes produces undesirable results. The discussion is seriously marred, however, by the constant use of the terms 'formal or procedural equality' and 'substantive equality', the latter taking equally elliptic sub-forms such as 'equality of results'. The use of those terms by these writers, in itself, does not provide anything in the way of justification for the types of outcomes they suggest are desirable.

The essay opens with the question '[t]o what extent is EC and UK equality law moving away from the liberal notions of non-discrimination towards an approach based on substantive equality or equity?'[20] Information about the intended senses of the key terms is provided in a section titled 'Concepts of Equality' where the authors tell us that '[t]he liberal notion of formal equality is one of consistency – likes should be treated alike'.[21] This conception, they say, only supports the prohibition of direct discrimination. In general, the authors say, the principle of 'consistent treatment' does not guarantee any particular outcome.[22]

It is not clear why the authors think that their truncated Aristotelian principle, 'likes should be treated alike', even implies a ban on direct discrimination. The example given by Pojman and Westmoreland, just cited, demonstrates the contrary. 'All those who do not conform to prevailing dominant religious beliefs should be punished' is perfectly consistent with 'likes should be treated alike'. One may, to take other examples, discriminate against blacks or women consistently with that 'principle' if one does not think those groups *are* like whites or males in the relevant respects. And a rule which makes direct discrimination on account of race or sex unlawful, by contrast, *does* have precisely *that* substance. And it will

---

18 Of course the law makers, like the modern drafters of apartheid's laws, may have thought their reasons were more substantial but we think that they, like their racist counterparts, were wrong about this.

19 Catherine Barnard and Bob Hepple 'Substantive Equality' (2000) 59 *Cambridge L J* 562.

20 Ibid. 562.

21 Ibid. 562.

22 Ibid. 562–3.

produce a 'particular outcome' though perhaps it will not achieve all that one thinks ought to be achieved as a matter of social equity.[23]

Turning to 'substantive equality', Barnard and Hepple do distinguish between variants of that notion but in the end none turns out to have much specific content. They cite Sandra Fredman who they say has identified different 'overlapping approaches'.[24] But the sub-categories discussed by Professor Fredman are equally unhelpful. The first is 'equality of results'.[25] This is another indeterminate concept. Which results should we aim for? This subcategory is again divided into three more. In their discussion of these, some idea of what our authors want as policy outcomes does emerge. Barnard and Hepple are in favour of proscribing indirect discrimination as well as direct discrimination but believe only affirmative action will produce 'equality of results'.[26]

Affirmative action has many results of course but so does equal treatment of races and the sexes. The evaluative element is still missing. Perhaps what is meant is that affirmative action has mostly good results. But of course that would not be because it is founded on a 'substantive' equality rather than a 'formal one'. Not unless 'substantive' just means 'real' or whatever solution to the cluster of social issues we usually discuss under the rubric of 'equality' an author happens to prefer.

The next substantive equality discussed by Barnard and Hepple is 'equality of opportunity'.[27] This would only be a truly 'broader'[28] substantive equality, our authors say, if it embraced, again, positive action in favour of disadvantaged groups or measures that dealt with labour inequalities in a (yet to be explained) substantive way.[29] Equality of opportunity can mean different things of course[30] but each interpretation of that ideal will have its own substance. The other two 'substantive' approaches are taken from legislative schemes and, again, it does not appear at all from this article what is peculiarly 'substantive' about them or 'formal' about the alternatives.

---

23   Such a rule proscribing discrimination could be described as 'liberal' I suppose, although many conservatives and left-wing radicals would endorse it. Why Hepple and Barnard think that nothing more in the way of discrimination law could have a liberal justification is not explained. They must be aware, for example, of the support for affirmative action by prominent liberals such as Ronald Dworkin.

24   Sandra Fredman 'A Critical Review of the Concept of Equality in UK Anti-Discrimination Legislation' Working Paper No. 3, Cambridge Centre for Public Law and Judge Institute of Management Studies, November 1999 paras 3.7–3.19, cited in Barnard and Hepple 'Substantive Equality', above n. 19, 564.

25   Barnard and Hepple 'Substantive Equality', above n. 19, 564.

26   Ibid. 565.

27   Ibid.

28   Ibid. 566.

29   Ibid. 566.

30   See Peter Westen *Speaking of Equality* (Princeton University Press, Princeton, 1990) Ch. 8.

In the rest of the article which discusses, first, developments in UK and European indirect discrimination law which threaten equality of results,[31] the authors argue that the point of indirect discrimination law is sometimes not understood in those jurisdictions, focussing too much, as they think it does, on how individuals are affected by certain practices rather than on the disparate impact those practices have on disadvantaged groups. Properly expressed, Barnard and Hepple suggest, the law would provide valuable protection for those groups which are indirectly discriminated against. This is an interesting and important argument, but if I am right about their use of the terms 'formal' and 'substantive' it is incomplete.

Barnard and Hepple are also unhappy that affirmative action is not more fully embraced by British law. They note that EC law in this regard 'has moved closer to the aim of substantive equality'.[32] But we are not told exactly what that aim is. The, in my view, confusing use of 'formal equality' as if it indeed had a substance (the prohibition of direct discrimination, only) and could be better or worse than some other type of equality, when of course it does not have a content precisely *because it is formal*, is not complemented with any clear definition of 'substantive equality'. Nor could it be, because 'substantive' is being used in a vague commendatory way while at the same time seeming to denote something specific which could itself be subject to evaluation.

Professor Fredman, to whom Barnard and Hepple often refer, employs the same terms in her subsequent book on discrimination law.[33] This book's theoretical discussion is marred by the employment of the same vague terminology adopted by Hepple and Barnard. Fredman sometimes seems to understand the vacuous nature of substantive equality terminology. When she discusses equality of results she writes about the different outcomes that could be aimed at: a good result for this individual, for her group, or for the institutions in which we work and live. Achieving any of these outcomes may mean giving up on another.[34] But despite this recognition of the indeterminacy of 'results' Fredman still thinks that formal equality will be improved by being 'allied to a more substantive approach'.[35]

It is, to some extent, clear what Barnard and Hepple, and Fredman and others who use these terms in the same puzzling way, want. They want something more than equal treatment for groups that have been discriminated against in situations where equal treatment seems to perpetuate unfair disadvantage. Some might agree that something more is needed. The prohibition of 'indirect discrimination', and affirmative action come to mind. But the boundaries of the mischief of indirect discrimination and the question of appropriate remedies for it are not settled (we would not still be discussing them if they were) and cannot be settled by reference to an empty slogan. Imposing liability for unintentional 'indirect discrimination'

---

31   Barnard and Hepple 'Substantive Equality', above n. 19, 568.
32   Ibid. 583.
33   Sandra Fredman *Discrimination Law* (Oxford University Press, Oxford, 2002).
34   Ibid. 11–14.
35   Ibid. 11.

(as opposed to devious, and clearly intentional indirect discrimination) may in any event not be morally straightforward.[36]

Substantive egalitarians also typically favour affirmative action ('positive action' in the UK) but even if they think that all thoughtful egalitarians do, which is of course not the case, they cannot assume that all will know what they mean by programmes of affirmative action that more nearly approach the aim of 'substantive equality'. Throughout their discussion it is clear these authors are not really comparing form and substance. They are comparing different policies, all of which have moral implications and, therefore, a 'substance'. They are disqualifying some policies by labelling them 'formal' and privileging others with the label 'substantive'.

The Point of 'Substantive Equality' Discourse

The way of talking about kinds of equality that I am criticising here is widespread. It will be familiar to readers of jurisprudential debates about discrimination law in, *inter alia*, North America and the UK. It also features occasionally in more general political philosophy. I do not mean to suggest, therefore, that Barnard and Hepple, or Fredman, are isolated purveyors of a rare confusion. They are, to the contrary, part of an establishment. For some time it has been *de rigueur* to commence any discussion of equality law by noting (but not critically analysing) the difference between 'formal' and 'substantive' equality.[37]

My comments thus far, therefore, might seem glib if I did not make a serious attempt to understand what the advocates of 'substantive' equality are getting at. I think the moral point being made by some is that one standard conception of equality, formal equality, is a sham which needs to be displaced by a more authentic one. Formal equality is shallow; substantive equality is deep, and gets to the heart of the matter. Professor Fredman has a well-known quote at the beginning of her book: '... to labour in the face of the majestic equality of the law, which forbids

---

36   See Jeremy Waldron 'Indirect Discrimination' in Stephen Guest and Alan Milne (eds) *Equality and Discrimination* (Franz Steiner Verlag Wiesbaden GMBH, Stuttgart, 1985) 93. Cf. Christopher McCrudden 'Changing Notions of Discrimination' in Stephen Guest and Alan Milne *Equality and Discrimination* (Franz Steiner Verlag Wiesbaden GMBH, Stuttgart, 1985) 83; on indirect discrimination in general see Larry Alexander 'What Makes Wrongful Discrimination Wrong? Biases, Preferences, Stereotypes, and Proxies', above n. 11, 206–16; Linda Lye 'Title VII'S Tangled Tale: The Erosion and Confusion of Disparate Impact and the Business Necessity Defense' (1998) 19 *Berkeley J Emp & Lab L* 315. Ms Lye's article is a useful history of the US jurisprudence – the idea's provenance.

37   See Rory O'Connell 'Cinderella Comes to the Ball: Art 14 and the Right to Non-discrimination in the ECHR', *Legal Studies*, 29(2), June 2009, 211–29. O'Connell's article approves of recent decisions in the ECHR for reasons almost identical to those which led to Hepple, Barnard and Fredman disapproving of earlier Article 14 decisions. No justification is offered by O'Connell as to why, for example, affirmative action is a good remedy for group disadvantage. It just is, because it's 'substantive'.

the rich as well as the poor to sleep under bridges, to beg in the streets, and to steal bread'.[38] The point of the aphorism could be expressed in different ways and it was written in a specific historical context, but the essence is: applying the same law to all does not necessarily afford everyone equal benefits.

The point of talk about substantive equality could be understood, then, as giving equality some substance that is *worth having*. It could be argued that 'substance' in substantive equality means 'worthwhile substance'. The idea not being that formal equality is indeed literally empty but rather that it is empty, at least some of the time, in the sense of being an empty gesture. By analogy if we refer to a book as having 'substance' we do not mean literally that there are books with no content, just that this particular book is a better read. So the point is not that 'formal equality' is literally formal; it is rather that equal treatment does not require all that equality mandates.

But if substantive equality theorists are just saying they are trying to apply the dictates of equality more rigorously their language could be a lot plainer. If that frankness were adopted the question would immediately arise 'more thoroughgoing in what way?' and then the moral argument could proceed, or continue, without prejudice. The argument could then be about the moral point of our talk about equality and what it entails. The 'equal treatment' school also thinks its conception of equality is more rigorous. There is still much to debate.

The substantive equality school might switch metaphors at this point and say that what must be avoided is a *mechanical* approach to equality: the equal treatment of different groups which have different circumstances and different needs is sometimes perfunctory. This may be true but again it amounts to saying: 'their approach is unthinking, ours is sensitive'. And the problem is the same complaint may be made about a proposal to treat two groups differently. It too may be mechanical, assuming certain significant differences between the two groups which do not really exist or assuming that any difference in overall group outcomes must be the result of discrimination and that rectifying the imbalance does not pose new moral quandaries. The critics of affirmative action, for example, also sometimes suggest their opponents are not concerned with 'real' equality but simply with numbers (proportionality).[39] So it seems synonyms of 'substantive' do not make the theoretical point of the underlying idea any clearer or the idea of 'equality' being advanced any more convincing.

Of course it is not just a matter of getting the terminology right, precisely because there are still unresolved moral issues that sensible people can argue about. But the language we use to discuss these issues, or more strictly the way we use it, must not suppose or give the impression of supposing the moral correctness of one point of view. And positively it must help us find good answers. The debate

---

38   Anatole France *Le Lys rouge* (Calman-Levy, 1927) 106, cited in Fredman *Discrimination Law*, above n. 33, 1.

39   See, for example, Jim Sleeper 'Affirmative Action's Outer Limits' in Nicolaus Mills (ed.) *Debating Affirmative Action* (Dell Publishing, New York, 1994) 309.

between substantive and formal equality theorists should ideally continue in a spirit of openness to the opposing view.

It is, on the one hand, not entirely obvious that grounds that could be used to discriminate *against* people should *never* be used as reasons to treat people differently. All one has to show to disprove that is one instance in which race or gender or something like that *is* relevant to the fair distribution of a social good.[40] But the equal treatment school could concede that while still insisting that a high degree of caution be applied to all suggestions that we differentiate on that sort of ground. It is quite plausible to argue that that caution be exercised, given our notorious propensity, as human beings, to act in a prejudiced way. Even when we do not suspect our motives, we should at least be wary of preferential policies based on things like race and sex and demand that they be demonstrably justified.[41] The opponents of the equal treatment school might also pay more attention to the effects of preferential treatment on *all* affected parties. And so on. These are issues in important debates about the implications of our commitment to treat one another as equals. These debates are far from over and will not be advanced by the use of vague slogans.

Finally I want to stress that it is the *way* certain terms have been used that I have found unhelpful. I am not suggesting that 'formal' or 'substantive' are generally unhelpful words. Such a suggestion would be odd. I only claim the way they are used in our recent discrimination jurisprudence is not productive. The notions could be usefully employed. In terms of formal equality, the treat likes alike formula is in a sense empty, until we decide who we are talking about; but we can treat that information as implied by a proper understanding of our shared humanity. The formula would then be elliptical rather than empty.

Robin West, writing about the way the law upholds what she thinks of as 'formal equality', says:

> By 'treating likes alike', through law, we recognise and reaffirm a universal and complex human nature, and the equal moral worth of all who fall within the legal regime. When we recognise someone 'as like us', and therefore entitled to like treatment by law, we acknowledge that shared humanity, and acknowledge the inclusion of all in a circle constituted by mutual recognition and sympathy.[42]

We could, tongue in cheek, call Professor West's interpretation of formal equality 'substantive formal equality'. It is interesting to note that not only would direct discrimination be barred by West's reworking of 'formal equality' but possibly also some forms of indirect discrimination. Indeed treating likes alike, as understood

---

40   Breast cancer screening programmes for women would be one example.

41   I do not mean to suggest that the caution should be uniform. I am sure it is more problematic to justify differential treatment on the ground of race than of sex.

42   See Robin West *Re-Imagining Justice* (Ashgate Publishing Limited, Aldershot, 2003) 149–50 and Ch. 4 generally.

by West, may also offer a justification of affirmative action and much else that some human rights lawyers would like to see accepted. It all depends on the development of the ensuing moral argument. Her treatment of formal equality – she calls it a 'humanistic interpretation of formal equality'[43] fills the notion of formal equality out to get to its moral point; and that of basic equality itself. The same could be done with 'substantive equality'. That term too could be used to refer to something more substantial than simply the idea of a social policy which brings about some specific outcome of which we happen to approve. Until it is, it offers little in the explication of the abstract language of discrimination law.

Equality and Dignity

A Structural Relationship

The seemingly inevitable indeterminacy of 'substantive equality' means that its theorists will have to come up with candidates for the substance it refers to. The recent tendency in jurisprudential thought to think that discrimination consists at least in large part in the denial of dignity[44] to those who are treated differently on certain grounds is thought by some to be a promising contender.[45] I do not think that idea is needed at all, strictly speaking, to explain the point of discrimination law but 'dignity' can play a role in the explanation of our *commitment* to equality. I will try to explain that role. In doing that I will distinguish between two senses of 'dignity'. One of these, I will argue, may be employed in the explanation of our commitment to equality; though it is itself too abstract an idea to offer any specific help in the application of discrimination law. The other sense of the word is not implicated in our explanation of why equality is worth upholding or in what it means to fail to do so.

Any attempt to explain the relationship between equality and dignity must explain what role the notion of dignity may play in the formation of political and social values and then explain how that relates to the concerns we are trying to evince in our talk about equality and discrimination. If 'dignity' is, in its primary (dictionary) sense, the 'quality of being worthy'[46] we first have to ask what that

---

43 Ibid. 149.

44 See Fredman *Discrimination Law*, above n. 33, 17; David Feldman 'Human Dignity as a Legal Value, Part 1' (1999) *Winter Pub L* 682; David Feldman 'Human Dignity as a Legal Value Part 2' (2000) *Spring Pub L* 61; L.W.H. Ackermann 'Equality and the South African Constitution: The Role of Dignity' Bram Fischer lecture delivered at Rhodes House, Oxford, on 26 May 2000; Denise G. Réaume 'Discrimination and Dignity' (2003) 63 *La L Rev* 645.

45 See Réaume 'Discrimination and Dignity', above n. 44.

46 *The New Shorter Oxford English Dictionary* (Clarendon Press, Oxford, 1993) 671.

means in terms of *human* dignity. What is it about human beings that makes us think we are worthy of respect at all? I think this question is the same as the one we might ask when justifying our commitment to equality itself. Why, in spite of all sorts of individual differences that distinguish them from each other, do we consider human beings to be equals who should be treated with equal consideration? I have answered this question in Chapter 3 and the answer given there is our reason to accord persons a *human* dignity. The human characteristic of moral personality which helps to structure our common set of needs inspires our attribution of worthiness to humanity in general.

We could always decide that only some human beings are worthy. But if we decide they *all* share a common dignity we would have a reason to believe that all should be treated as equals. I am suggesting that dignity's role is foundational. It *inspires* the value we call 'equality'. There are, then, three parts to the story about equality and dignity. First there are assessments about what makes human beings special. Second, because of these qualities we say humans have a particular dignity. Then we draw ethical implications from this, including our commitment to equality.

It makes sense therefore to talk, as Sandra Fredman does, about '[t]he primacy of individual dignity and worth as a foundation for equality rights'.[47] Fredman writes, though, as if dignity itself is the fact about human beings that we should respect. In a sense that is right. But dignity is something that is attributed to us because of something else – the thing or things that make us special as humans. Without the 'something else' the ascription of dignity would be pointless.

I nitpick because Professor Fredman thinks that talk about 'dignity' in equality rights discourse replaces talk about 'rationality' and that this is an improvement because we might think that some people, women for example, are not fully rational.[48] But human characteristics are what justify the *assignation* of dignity to persons. If women are not rational, they do not share the dignity accorded to men. Dignity cannot replace rationality (or any other core human attribute) as a foundation for equality because rationality is (a candidate for) the foundation of human dignity.

Fredman writes as if those who think that women are not the equals of men, because they lack rationality, just have a different idea of 'equality' to ours.[49] Their idea would be that rational creatures are alike and women are not rational and so not like men and we therefore do not need to treat them as equals. If equality can now be explained in terms of dignity rather than rationality the sexist argument is undermined.

But if we accord a common dignity to humans *because* they share a common rationality (amongst other attributes or because of some other common attribute which inspires a general respect for persons) commitment to equality as a value

---

47   Fredman *Discrimination Law*, above n. 33, 17.
48   Ibid. 18.
49   Ibid.

is a further step, justified because there is no good reason to think our individual differences are such as should cause us to be fundamentally less concerned about anyone (or any group). Those who do not think our important attributes such as our rationality or our moral personality and our need for suitable conditions for these to flourish, are those we have in common with others – black or white, male or female, Muslim or Christian – have no need for the notion of equality that plays a central role in modern political and legal philosophy. There is no point in thinking they just have a different one to ours.

Dignity and Equality in the Courts

How does my suggested link between dignity and equality differ from that suggested by recent discrimination jurisprudence? First a caveat and disclaimer: courts will express things differently in different cases and will only sometimes be interested in developing doctrine. They will usually not think of their efforts as theoretical treatises and it would be unrealistic to think they should. Legal commentary of the sort typically found in law journals might attempt to be more systematic but it will usually also be more concerned with predicting, and influencing, what the courts will do next than with abstract jurisprudential reflection. Here I merely notice a trend which I think is, in part, trying to get at what I have just said about equality and dignity. Recent jurisprudence also suggests another link between the two which I will suggest is confused or a mistake. Neither approach will produce the Holy Grail of a discrimination law which is easy to apply.

The source, or the most recent source, of talk about equality being based on the idea of dignity is recent Bill of Rights jurisprudence. L.W.H. Ackermann[50] writes in his paper on South African constitutional law about the 'role of dignity' with regard to equality law.[51] He and the other judges of his court developed ideas from Canadian constitutional jurisprudence where the purpose of the Canadian Charter's discrimination provision has been stated, in the seminal case *Law* v *Canada*,[52] as being:

> to prevent the violation of essential human dignity and freedom through the imposition of disadvantage, stereotyping, or political or social prejudice, and to promote a society in which all persons enjoy equal recognition at law as human

---

50   SC, retired Justice of the Constitutional Court of South Africa.

51   Ackermann 'Equality and the South African Constitution: The Role of Dignity', above n. 44, 11.

52   *Law* v *Canada (Minister of Employment and Immigration)* [1999] 1 SCR 497. See *President of the Republic of South Africa and Another* v *Hugo* 1997 (6) BCLR 759 (CC); 1997 (4) SA 1 (CC) for a South African example of the application of 'dignity' to discrimination law analysis. See also *Quilter* v *Attorney-General* [1998] 1 NZLR523 (CA) for an application of the idea in New Zealand.

beings or as members of Canadian society, equally capable and deserving of concern, respect and consideration.[53]

Leaving aside the reference to 'freedom', the idea that dignity is 'violated' when equality is denied is almost consistent with what I have argued here about the relationship between equality and dignity. (I will explain the 'almost' in a moment – also note that the citation already refers to basic equality in other words and it is thus already clear that nothing more specific is going to be produced.) If our commitment to basic equality makes sense because of our descriptive equality and dignity is accorded to humanity because of attributes we share, then the dignity of those denied treatment as an equal is also, *ipso facto*, denied. We should treat people with equal concern and respect if we think that, despite their individual differences, they are of equal worth.

When Ackermann says, expounding on the jurisprudence of his court, that the essence of (unfair) discrimination is the impairment of human dignity[54] we are *ad idem* if he means that to deny someone equality's protection is to exclude her from the dignity accorded others, to suggest she is not worthy. Only the sense of 'dignity' used here, so far, will be helpful in this regard. The dignity, in one of its secondary senses, that one 'stands on' – in the sense of a person's estimation of his own worth – is not always morally interesting. I said the quote from *Law* v *Canada* almost expressed what I am trying to say. The use of the word 'violation' is problematic. Talk about 'violation of dignity' or the 'impairment of dignity'[55] being the essence of discrimination could be misleading if it leads us to think that a perceived attack on someone's sense of her own importance was a necessary or sufficient condition for a claim that her intrinsic equal worth had been ignored.

I have suggested that the dignity of human beings, qua human beings, provides us, because we think the qualities which justify according that dignity to our species are shared, with a reason to uphold basic equality. That we have that dignity is an 'objective' assessment which we think is consistent with the facts about who we are as persons. Strictly speaking, dignity, in this sense, cannot be 'impaired' or 'violated'. It can only be ignored or denied. It is not a substance or a quality that can be diminished but a fact, albeit a social or 'institutional' fact.[56]

---

53   *Law* v *Canada (Minister of Employment and Immigration)* [1999] 1 SCR 497 at 529.

54   Ackermann 'Equality and the South African Constitution: The Role of Dignity', above n. 44, 14–15.

55   Ibid.

56   See John Searle *The Construction of Social Reality* (Penguin Books, London, 1995) 1–2. The propositions of chemistry that would be used to describe the composition of a ten dollar note express 'brute' facts. Its worth in our economic system is an 'institutional fact'. Sometimes institutional facts are termed 'socially constructed' facts, but that usage should not be confused with the idea that *all* facts are socially constructed.

A person's sense of self worth (of her 'dignity' in that subjective sense) on the other hand, might be based on that general fact about the dignity of humankind but it could be based on something else. If, for example, I say of a hired killer that his life's work serves no valuable purpose and is in that sense meaningless, my words may very well 'impact on his dignity' but not in any sense we should care about.[57] Of course most people understand, at least intuitively, the objective basis of human dignity. So the denial of our universal dignity we share as a species will often be widely and sorely *felt* by its victims as an indignity in the second 'injured feelings' sense of the word 'dignity'. Ackermann, for example, clearly empathises with the indignity, in this secondary sense of 'dignity', felt by black people in South Africa under apartheid.[58] But the felt indignity of apartheid is what its victims *should* feel; it is what they are *entitled* to feel because they have been denied inclusion in the group of people whose concerns should be accorded respect consistent with the dignity (in the first sense) ascribed to them as members of the human race (but note, as I will explain in a moment, this is an appropriate *response* to discrimination – it is not what *constitutes* discrimination).

The dignity people demand, however, is not always that which we should grant them, as the example of the hired killer illustrates, and so the dignity whose role in the explanation of our commitment to basic equality I have acknowledged cannot be the subjective sense of self worth, the loss of which is caused by being treated in what a particular person on a specific occasion feels is an 'undignified' way. In some cases the fact of being treated in a way that offends one's dignity in that sense will be a denial of the dignity we should attribute to all persons, in other cases it will not.

When Iacobucci J. says, in *Law*,[59] the Canadian case cited above, that: 'human dignity means that an individual or group feels self respect and self worth', he is right, but only in the secondary meaning of the word. Feelings of self worth and self respect may of course be diminished when human equality is ignored; this is typically the case when some people are systematically badly treated, as people were under apartheid. And this is surely the kind of case the judge has in mind. But this is not the essence of the relationship between dignity and equality.[60] It is the 'objective' dignity we ascribe to humankind that is ignored by discrimination although we naturally expect, and are often right to predict, certain negative feelings will be experienced by one who has been discriminated against.

Iacobucci J. goes on to say: '[h]uman dignity is harmed by unfair treatment premised upon personal traits or circumstances which do not relate to individual

---

57   See the discussion of essentially the same point in Feldman 'Human Dignity as a Legal Value, Part 1', above n. 44, 687.

58   Ackermann 'Equality and the South African Constitution: The Role of Dignity', above n. 44, 5–7. See also Grant Huscroft 'Discrimination, Dignity, and the Limits of Equality' (2000) 9 *Otago Law Review* 697.

59   *Law*, above n. 52, 530.

60   See Réaume 'Discrimination and Dignity', above n. 44, 684.

needs, capacities, or merits'.[61] It might well be, though which sense of 'dignity' the judge means is not clear. Such treatment, being an infringement of the right to equal respect as a human being, does ignore (not 'harm' strictly speaking, in this sense of 'dignity') the dignity of some which is accorded to all by liberal humanism. That is what I have argued is the important conceptual link between equality and dignity. But dignity in the second, subjective sense (as his honour had just defined 'human dignity') *might not* be injured by unfair treatment and might be injured by other things as well – not all of which are morally important.

It might be objected that I am stipulating that some forms of indignity do not matter morally. It might be thought I am suggesting it is alright to offend some people at least in certain ways, if we do not think their dignity is worth preserving. That is not quite right. My riposte is to stress again that the two meanings of 'dignity' used here denote different things. Everyone's dignity *as a human being* is to be respected if we are to uphold equality (amongst other values). What I am suggesting though is that the human dignity we respect as humanists has content. We have to have a viewpoint about what human beings uniquely are and their special worth if we are to think they should be accorded certain rights on the basis of that worthiness. We might disagree about what that is but our views will have to be reasonable if we want them to be plausible. The indignities, on the other hand, people feel when we do not take their abilities or achievements (or luck) as seriously as they do, have whatever content their subjects honestly say they do.

The 'dignity-centred'[62] approach in recent constitutional jurisprudence is aware that a simple assertion of impairment to dignity is not enough. But it does not clearly distinguish the two senses of 'dignity' I have used here. To return to the judgment of Iacobucci J. in *Law* again, his honour notes that the claim that the treatment has impaired one's dignity must be reasonable. But what makes it reasonable? Justice Iacobucci says, in essence, that the test is whether the reasonable person, under the same circumstances, would feel his or her dignity had been impaired. Various things are to be taken into account, such as 'society's past and present treatment of the claimant and of other persons or groups with similar characteristics' and 'the larger context of the legislation'.[63] Dignity, Iacobucci J. says: 'concerns the manner in which a person legitimately feels when confronted with a particular law. Does the law treat him or her unfairly, taking into account all of the circumstances regarding the individuals affected and excluded by the law?'[64]

Fairness is the crux here (the rest is practical advice about how to assess the law or challenged act, in context, for its fairness). The proof that dignity has been impaired in the appropriate sense seems to be the existence of unfair treatment, the denial of equal concern – basic equality – which we discover through considering all the appropriate aspects of the context in any given case. So it seems the

---

61   *Law*, above n. 52, 530.
62   Huscroft 'Discrimination, Dignity, and the Limits of Equality', above n. 58, 705.
63   *Law*, above n. 52, 532–3.
64   Ibid. 530.

assessment of whether a person has been denied treatment due to her as an equal is necessary to make a finding about whether a person's dignity has been violated which is, literally, a process of legitimating people's feelings.

We must ask here why we are looking for this reasonable 'sense of impaired dignity'. We were supposed to be deciding whether someone *has been discriminated against* but talk about people's dignity in the sense of feelings almost makes this of secondary importance. It is, by analogy, a bit like thinking the purpose of a murder trial is to establish whether the deceased's relatives have an appropriate sense of loss. Determining whether someone has been discriminated against is not a question of how one *feels* at all. It is, in the Bill of Rights context, about whether the law has dealt with a person or a group in a way that denies her or her group the equal consideration that a commitment to equality requires. When the law does discriminate, its effects are typically bad ones but although one of these bad consequences may be injured feelings, a 'demeaning of dignity', it might not be.

Making the presence of a felt injury to someone's dignity a requirement of a breach of equality does not just include too much then, it also excludes some cases of discrimination. Not all breaches of basic equality need result in a loss of one's sense of one's own dignity. The victim of the breach may realise that she is being treated with less than equal concern and respect but not *feel* any loss of dignity. Moreover we can discriminate against people in subtle ways and there is always the problem of false consciousness. We might convince the victims of discrimination that the treatment they receive is what they deserve. All this being so one can agree with Grant Huscroft that: '[w]hatever else may be said about the Court's dignity-centred approach … it facilitates a substantial reduction of the protection the right [not to be discriminated against] might otherwise afford'.[65] That result may or may not please the law's makers but it is not a consequence of the meaning of 'discrimination' or 'equality'.

Even the reader who was satisfied with all my reasons why the protection of dignity in the second sense identified here could not be what discrimination law, or equality in general, is all about, might be anxious that that argument has unhappy consequences in another area of human rights thinking and law. If that were true it would count against my argument; especially if my conclusion contradicted something we took as settled and well founded. The worry is this: I seem to have provided reason, in arguing that our sense of our own dignity may or may not be worthy of protection, for thinking there could be no general *right* to dignity in that sense. I have already said that dignity in the first sense I use here is not a value which could be protected by a right. And now I have said not all instances of dignity in the second sense are worth protecting. So there can be no general 'right to dignity' in either of the senses of 'dignity' I have used. But do people not deserve to have a wide-ranging right to dignity?

---

65 Huscroft 'Discrimination, Dignity, and the Limits of Equality', above n. 58, 707.

Is There a Right to Dignity?

In Constitutional jurisprudence judges have to give effect, in some jurisdictions, to a right to dignity alongside the rights to free speech, freedom of movement, of association and so on. It is not clear, if my argument is sound, what this right could amount to. I think that uncertainty is justified but it seems best to start with what the right is thought to amount to. It might be noted first that the right to dignity does not appear to enjoy the same status as the other rights just mentioned. Not all modern jurisdictions have provisions specifically protecting 'dignity'.

As David Leibowitz and Derek Spitz note, in their discussion of the dignity provision in the South African Bill of Rights,[66] The United States, Canada and India have no such provision in their constitutional protection of human rights[67] though the German Basic Law does include such a provision. These writers do not provide much in the way of explanation of the content of the right to dignity. They declare instead:

> It is in the demarcation of the boundaries of the concept of dignity, and not solely in the manner in which the right to its protection is specifically phrased, that the true extent of that protection is to be identified.[68]

This is of course to leave the matter of definition entirely in the hands of the courts. Nothing the courts did in South Africa in the first few years of its new constitutionalism carved out a place for a right to dignity like that enjoyed by freedom of speech or freedom of religion. There was a lot of talk about its importance and its role as a foundational value and, as noted, its role as the essence of unfair discrimination[69] but not much about its own essence.

Later developments in South African constitutional dignity jurisprudence have not essentially changed the role of the idea since Leibowitz and Spitz wrote. Professor Stu Woolman's more recent treatment, for example, of the South African provision, illustrates again the abstractness of the notion of dignity, and its principal role as a background idea that helps to explain our commitment to certain, more specific, rights.[70] It is clear from Woolman's commentary that 'dignity' in the

---

66   Section 10 Constitution of the Republic of South Africa, Act 108 of 1996, which reads: 'Everyone has inherent dignity and the right to have their dignity respected and protected'.

67   David Leibowitz and Derek Spitz 'Human Dignity' in Matthew Chaskalson et al. (eds) *Constitutional Law of South Africa* (Juta and Co Ltd, Cape Town, 1996) Ch. 17, 17–1. Nor do we have such a provision in the New Zealand Bill of Rights Act 1990.

68   Ibid. 17–5.

69   Ibid. 17–5 – 17–6A.

70   See, for example, Stu Woolman, 'Dignity', in Woolman, Roux, Klaaren, Stein and Chaskalson, *Constitutional Law of South Africa* (2nd edn, Jutas, Cape Town, 2002) Ch. 36.

sense of human worth (as has been described here) is not usually directly applied, and that there is no general right to protection (not even one subject to the usual limitations imposed on all rights) from every sort of indignity, although the courts have granted protection under s 10 of the South African Constitution from forms of subjective indignity that South African law previously had allowed, and even inflicted.[71]

I suspect this lack of a clear dignity right is due to those wishing to protect human rights wanting to because they respect human dignity *in general*. Constitutions, international human rights documents, and courts all refer to 'human dignity' as much as, or more than, they refer to any person's sense of his own dignity in a subjective sense. Saying there is a 'right to dignity' is just an unhappy way of saying our common dignity is a *source* of, or inspiration for, rights and should be respected in general.

In the secondary sense of the word it is morally right to preserve another's dignity if his sense of self worth is appropriate, or, even if it is not, when there is no reason to disillusion him. The law may sometimes help; the tort of defamation comes to mind.[72] But a right not to be treated in *any* way that offends one's dignity, however dubious the dignity is that one stands on, is not justifiable.

This conclusion is consistent with the ordinary law's protection against certain attacks on our subjective sense of self worth. As Leibowitz and Spitz note, in the South African context, for example, the (Roman Dutch) common law 'recognizes actions for insulting words, contemptuous behaviour, wrongful deprivations of liberty including wrongful arrest, and invasions of privacy'.[73] Different jurisdictions have different lists but I do not know of any that offer a *general* protection against the loss, caused by others, of subjective feelings of self worth – apart from those which forbid all criticism of certain persons. No one who recognised the dignity of humanity in general would support the retention of such laws.

David Feldman would agree that '[t]he notion that dignity can itself be a fundamental right is superficially appealing but ultimately unconvincing'.[74] He has the matter about right, in my view, when he says '... one clearly has an interest in having one's human dignity respected, and this may support more specific rights'.[75] This is because dignity or, more precisely, respect for dignity,

---

71   See, for example, *National Coalition for Gay & Lesbian Equality* v *Minister of Justice* [1999] 1 SA 6 (CCSA). This case, and others in which s 10 has been applied, might seem to apply a general right to 'dignity', but inasmuch as they are concerned with a person's sense of their own 'dignity' the cases protect it only in a limited range of circumstances. To the extent that those cases purport to protect the 'dignity' of humankind in general, they are attempting to apply the philosophical basis for all human rights, rather than a particular right.

72   See Feldman 'Human Dignity as a Legal Value, Part 1', above n. 44, 684–5.

73   D. Leibowitz and D. Spitz 'Human Dignity', above n. 67, 17–10.

74   Feldman 'Human Dignity as a Legal Value, Part 1', above n. 44, 682.

75   Ibid. 689.

is too large a concept to be encapsulated in just one right. The problem is abstractness at a very grand level. Human dignity justifies a commitment to equality and various rights but respect for it in general is an even more abstract notion than equality.

It is only in the secondary sense in which people may or may not be treated in a way which conforms with their sense of self worth, that we could talk about rights and duties relating to dignity directly. We only extend those rights and duties sensibly where people have a sense of self worth worthy of protection and we might say here that if the dignity X stands on *is* consistent with the dignity we deem her to have as a human being then it is clearly morally right to uphold it and perhaps to do so by legal means, subject to other considerations. We can note here that our commitment to basic equality can inspire the protection of dignity in what I have called its secondary sense. If we allow some people to be tortured or slandered just because we do not care for them or their *type*, we deny them the esteem due to equals.

Our efforts to use the law to 'protect' dignity are thus twofold. We might use the law to ensure that people are treated 'with dignity'. Prohibitions on corporal punishment, invasive medical treatment without consent, abuse of prisoners and harassment may all, perhaps indirectly, preserve our dignity in the secondary sense I discuss here.[76] But the variety of rights we find in a typical Bill of Rights and laws preserving basic equality generally, acknowledge and are inspired by the inherent dignity, or worth, of humanity. And so are the specific dignity laws just mentioned; these are only justified because of (and only if they are justified by) our general human dignity.

This may sound too neat. But we should not always be suspicious of simplicity. I think some current discussions of this topic are too wedded to the idea of indeterminacy in matters conceptual. It is important, as David Feldman reminds us, to remember that there are different senses of the word 'dignity'.[77] But it is equally important not to think that there are so many that we cannot really be sure what we mean when we talk about it. In theorising about anything we have to choose the senses of concepts we want to employ and then use them, consistently. Constitutional theory is a purposive activity. It will find useful some aspects of any concept and not need others. We should not give in, in thinking about equality and dignity, to the linguistic relativism that is common in much talk about equality itself and leads to an endless variety of 'meanings'. I am confident, in any event, that explanation of the link between dignity and equality (and probably human rights in general) only needs the two I have used here.

---

76   David Feldman 'Human Dignity as a Legal Value, Part 1', above n. 44; David Feldman 'Human Dignity as a Legal Value Part 2', above n. 44. Feldman discusses these and other examples in these articles.

77   Ibid. Feldman refers to many senses of the word and develops his own taxonomy which is very expansive.

Summing Up

Attempts to give content to the right not to be discriminated against, by explaining that upholding equality means respecting our dignity, will not make the law clearer.[78] We can say that distinctions made by the law, in the case of government discrimination, which treat us with less than equal concern and respect ignore human dignity; but we still have to work out when the law does or does not treat us with equal consideration. It will sometimes be clear that it does not, but there will be hard cases. Difficulties will arise because equality is a moral concept; moral argument is required to apply it. But that argument is about the best understanding of equal concern for persons. Rephrasing that as a duty, or an element of a duty, to respect each person's inherent worth does not make basic equality's meaning any more concrete or give it a content it was lacking.

Note also, finally, that the justification of our belief in basic equality can be expressed in terms that make no reference at all to the idea of 'dignity'. 'Human dignity' is simply a placeholder for all that we think makes people, as persons, special. Indeed we could explain our commitment to all of our political morality without reference to it. To say that we have that set of values because we respect human dignity is not really to say anything more than that our political morality is inspired by our respect for humanity *per se*. There is nothing wrong with using the placeholder 'dignity' as a summary of what we think is special about human beings. But we should not expect that it denotes something previously overlooked which will explain what it means to discriminate against someone.

Social Inclusion

Both the 'substantive' and 'dignity' discourses have a dual purpose. On the one hand they are attempts to understand equality. They both assume that any attempt to understand discrimination law requires an understanding of what equality entails.

---

78   See Réaume 'Discrimination and Dignity', above n. 44, 672–95. Professor Réaume uses the notion of dignity to give content to the idea of equality but I think she is using the values that human dignity inspires to explain what dignity is. If, as she says, the violation of dignity involves prejudice, stereotyping and the distribution of important benefits in ways which suggest some are more important than others, then it sounds, once again, as if the impairment of dignity is being defined in terms of the denial of equality – and not vice versa. Like the Canadian Supreme Court, whose decisions she is analysing, she ends up with a still very broad idea of equality, which is where you will end up when you are dealing with an idea which just is very abstract. And it will not become more concrete by turning it into talk about an even more abstract notion – human dignity. Compare Emily Grabham 'Law v Canada: New Directions for Equality Under the Canadian Charter' (2002) 22 *Oxford J. Legal Stud.* 641, 653. Grabham notes the abstract nature of 'human dignity' which can mean different things to different judges. Interestingly enough, she is quite sanguine about our ability to discern the meaning of 'substantive equality'.

They are thus jurisprudential contributions to constitutional and human rights theory. They are also attempts to explain and give guidance in the interpretation of discrimination law, which is sometimes called 'equality law'. Both these ways of talking about equality are also contributions to the exegesis of such laws. Hugh Collins's recent discussion of Social Inclusion and its relationship with equality and discrimination law is also both theoretical and exegetical but it is not an attempt to deepen our understanding of the idea of equality *per se*.[79] He is concerned with understanding and suggesting what he thinks is a more coherent purpose or justification for discrimination law than that provided in terms of conceptions of equality. He does not say that discrimination law is not, at least in part, motivated by a commitment to some sort of equality but he thinks that because conceptions of equality pull in different directions something else is needed to make sense of an area of law which would otherwise be incoherent.

It will strike some as odd that discrimination law can be seen as serving, primarily or largely, something other than equality. Infringements of basic equality may not all amount to discrimination in the sense of that word which is used in modern human rights law. When we talk about discrimination in that context we mean something like the unfair treatment of a group of people, usually based on what we take to be a generally irrelevant characteristic like race or sex and motivated by a hostility towards and lack of respect for that group. But basic equality may also be infringed just by leaving out of consideration in a moral argument any person likely to be affected by it. It might seem semantically unconvincing to label every instance of that 'discrimination'. But there does seem to be an obvious link between equality and discrimination. Racist and sexist policies, for example, seem to be clear examples of the infringement of basic equality and, equally clearly, core examples of discrimination.

Collins argues, however, that attempts to explain anti-discrimination law in terms of conceptions of equality have failed.[80] He thinks this is because different conceptions of equality are used and they conflict. He notes the tension between the equal treatment school and the substantive equality theorists, which I have been discussing.[81] He is of course right to think that how equality justifies discrimination laws cannot be explained until we know what we mean by 'equality'. And it is not just a matter of choosing one of the currently competing theories because both equal treatment and differential treatment seem to be required at different times by the same body of law. Collins notes various attempts to deal with this tension in anti-discrimination law but thinks they all fail.[82] And they surely must if the conflict is real and there is no underlying theory which can explain apparent contradictions.

There are, however, different ways of responding to these doctrinal puzzles and saying that anti-discrimination law should rather be justified by something

---

79   Hugh Collins 'Discrimination, Equality and Social Inclusion' (2003) 66 *M L R* 16.
80   Ibid. 17–21.
81   Ibid. 16–18.
82   Ibid. 17–21.

other than equality is just one of them. It could simply be argued, for example, that one of the conceptions of equality used is the right one and that the other one, and law which it gives expression to it, should be jettisoned. Perhaps not all anti-discrimination law is worth keeping because not all thinking about equality is sound. Or one could argue, as I have, that the competing conceptions of equality used to explain discrimination law are muddled or at least incomplete and are themselves in need of reform or better explanation. It would not follow from this that a better explanation of what equality is about would reveal the meaning and purpose of any particular anti-discrimination law framework: a better understanding of equality may provoke a substantial revision of this law instead. But we can only know anything about this once we have thought more carefully about what 'equality', as a moral concept, requires.

Collins does consider the Dworkinian 'strategy' of replacing 'equal treatment' with 'treatment as an equal' but says this will not work because the law as it is is committed to the 'equal treatment principle'. But if the law is committed to treating people equally, without exception, regardless of race and sex and so on, and if we think that is not always consistent with treating people as equals, then perhaps we should change the law. The law does, in affirmative action provisions and in other ways, allow differentiation on grounds that are otherwise thought invidious but of course that law is controversial and difficult to interpret. If the law as it stands is at odds with itself in some respects surely a plausible solution is to revise our philosophy, work out what we value because of our commitment to basic equality and other important values and then see if we can devise law to give better effect to it. No mean feat of course. But surely that is at least a reasonable alternative to looking elsewhere, beyond equality discourse, to find the meaning and purpose of existing anti-discrimination law.

Collins simply assumes that 'equality' in this context of the justification of anti-discrimination law is either the 'equal treatment principle' or some 'substantive' equality. He does not try to resolve this debate between equality theorists. He thinks what we really need to decide is when it is *fair* to treat people in the same way and when it is not. And he thinks a conception of equality might not be necessary to explain what 'fairness' is.[83] He does not explain that. He goes on to say that apart from equality justifications, one sometimes finds that it is argued that discrimination law is justified for economic reasons or, more importantly, according to Collins, by the idea of Social Inclusion (SI).[84]

Social Inclusion is a term of 'Third Way' politics which 'tries to distance itself from egalitarian ideals associated with traditional socialist movements, whilst promising more practical and effective measures towards a fairer society than those offered by traditional socialist societies'.[85] The socially excluded are not just the poor but also those who are excluded from meaningful citizenship because of

---

83 Ibid. 21.

84 Ibid.

85 Ibid. 22.

their membership of some disadvantaged group. (These sound like the wards of Equality.) SI is, Collins goes on, not concerned with universal equality of outcomes but prioritises the needs of completely excluded groups. SI is also perfectionist because it decides that there are some things the socially excluded need and sets about getting these rather than just aiming at an equality of resources. Ultimately the aim is social cohesion – what used to be called 'solidarity'.[86]

Social cohesion seems an admirable goal, if the perfectionism does not spill over into authoritarianism. And Collins does go on to argue how the goal of SI might be seen to be expressed in anti-discrimination law, or some of it. But that is not reason enough, in my view, to replace equality as the background value which inspires our attempts to outlaw certain forms of discrimination. As I have argued, Collins has only shown that some current strands of talk about equality are at loggerheads and not that no better understanding of equality can explain what we think of as equality law. Moreover he compares SI with ideas of equality as expressed in current legal rules and decisions rather than as moral principles. And while the origin or sources of SI and its political rationale are discussed, its moral force is not, although attempts are made to illustrate it.

SI is meant to have moral bite. It is meant to be seen as a good thing but Collins does not really offer more than an adumbration of a political or moral philosophy of it or justify his claim that SI is a 'theory of distributive justice'.[87] He does not compare it to equality except in the sense of 'equality' in the confused use of the idea in much recent human rights jurisprudence. Perhaps after thinking about it we would conclude that a policy of SI is consistent with basic equality, or something we should do in our current circumstances *because* we believe in basic equality. SI, while still itself, as Collins admits, somewhat indeterminate, may more directly explain anti-discrimination law in part but not because the law has little to do with equality. That would be because basic equality is a deep or background value and not an alternative *policy* as a particular equalising goal might be.

Once again it is useful to stress the difference between equality as an aim and equality as the fundamental commitment to treat each other as equals. It is not easy to read off the terms of modern anti-discrimination law from the latter but to admit that does not rule out a justificatory relationship. Collins is comparing SI with equality as possible justifications of discrimination laws. But by 'equality' he means equality in the first sense as a particular aim to equalise the distribution of something.

Modern discrimination law is not, as he says, an attempt to equalise incomes or welfare. It is not a socialist project in any traditional sense. If 'egalitarian' denotes only the equal distribution of wealth or welfare then discrimination law does have a different aim. We would of course hope that law which forbids discrimination against groups who were often disadvantaged because of discrimination would improve the welfare of those groups because we know that discrimination can

---

86   Ibid. 21–6.
87   Ibid. 41.

cause poverty. But discrimination law might do other things as well. It might contribute to a broader sense of well-being by including excluded groups in a more meaningful sense of citizenship; what SI aims at.[88]

Collins also argues that SI is about *priority* rather than equality. This a reference to the debate initiated by Derek Parfit about whether, when deciding how to distribute social goods it is better to aim for a distribution between people that will make them equally well off or to give priority to those who are worst off.[89] Parfit describes this as a choice between *priority* and equality but makes it clear that he is not talking about basic equality. As he says:

> Most of us are Egalitarians, since most of us believe in some kind of equality. We believe in political equality, or equality before the law, or we believe that everyone has equal rights, or that everyone's interests should be given equal weight. Though these kinds of equality are of great importance, they are not my subject. I am concerned with people's being *equally well off.*[90]

The sense in which Parfit says we are egalitarians is a reference to basic equality. That equality provides one way of assessing any equality we want to achieve between individuals or groups of people. And if SI advocates think that some kinds of equality should be eschewed in favour of policies that 'include' the most excluded groups in society, their theory must also pass basic equality's test, as must Parfit's prioritarian idea. That test is not an 'equal treatment' test nor is it the requirement that there should be equality of any particular result. It is the requirement that all persons affected by what we do are treated as equals with equal consideration.

Conclusion

I think there is still much more basic thinking about equality to be done before we can understand all of what we are, or even *should*, be trying to do with discrimination law. The underlying value of equality which discrimination law is usually thought to be upholding does not present us with a simple rule to follow. It is obviously not easy to conclude from a commitment to equality exactly what laws we should have in place to uphold that ideal. And most people would agree that we are not clear about the exact meaning (or application) of many of the anti-discrimination laws that we have passed; even if, because certain types of invidious discrimination are of great concern to all of us who favour having these laws, we are pleased that we have passed them. Some of the difficulties experienced with interpreting

---

88   Ibid. 22.

89   See Derek Parfit 'Equality or Priority' in Matthew Clayton and Andrew Williams (eds) *The Ideal of Equality* (Macmillan Press, Basingstoke, 2000) 81.

90   Parfit 'Equality or Priority', above n. 89, 84.

discrimination law might apply to other aspects of human rights law and Bills of Rights in general,[91] but equality's law seems in need of special attention.

The situation is not entirely bleak. What equality requires is not always hard to fathom. Black people in South Africa or the United States, or women in Afghanistan, do not need to take advanced courses in human rights to understand that they are being discriminated against. The essence of the right to be treated as an equal (and its denial) is easy to grasp in an intuitive way. We are, accordingly, clear about the purpose and meaning of some of the law and about what it might achieve in certain contexts.

That clarity and moral certainty does evaporate as soon as we get to hard questions about when it is right to treat people who are members of disadvantaged groups differently, in ways that are meant to *benefit* them. Those hard questions cannot be solved by applications of the popular slogans of recent equality jurisprudence. What, however, are courts supposed to do in the meantime? If the notion of 'substantive equality' does not, by itself, produce anything more concrete and if the application of the concept 'dignity' is also unhelpful in this regard, what are we supposed to do about hard cases in discrimination law?

I am not suggesting that the Dworkinian injunction to 'treat everyone with equal concern and respect', which I have often used as the equivalent of 'basic equality' solves that problem; that slogan expresses the idea of 'equality' in terms as abstract as the idea itself – it just *is* a formulation of that idea. At the moment there is no clear solution to the problem and that is because the law for the most part expresses a moral abstraction rather than a clear set of rules, and the moral dilemmas underlying our discussions of this area of law are unresolved. Concrete proposals about what to do next will be more useful only after greater resolution of these dilemmas.

Even in jurisdictions like New Zealand, or South Africa, where the law clearly allows some forms of affirmative action and tries to respond to the problem of 'indirect discrimination', puzzles abound as to the meaning, point and justification of the remedies provided.[92] There are of course other areas of law whose meanings are difficult to fathom. But that is not a good excuse for creating new ones. I think, therefore, that we should at least be wary of introducing any new 'equality law' until we are clearer about its justification in general. A good example of what not do is provided by post-apartheid South Africa. That country rightly turned its back on a history of some of the worst forms of discrimination imaginable, but it now

---

91   If, instead of the particular freedoms enumerated in Bills of Rights, we gave legal protection to 'freedom' generally, we would be faced with the same difficulty. Not because respect for human autonomy is a mysterious notion which can only be explained in terms of something else, but because it is a large idea whose implications will sometimes be hard to work out.

92   See Grant Huscroft 'Freedom from Discrimination' in Rishworth et al. *The New Zealand Bill of Rights* (Oxford University Press, Melbourne, 2003) 366.

has more equality law than seems sensible.[93] The problem of working out what it means to develop and uphold a defensible conception of equality is not solved by simply passing more law.

There is, for now, I fear, not much advice for Judge and Co. Or too much — none of it particularly helpful if courts are looking for an explanation of 'discrimination' that would relieve them of the burden of being policy formulators and legislators. But, positively, there is much that academics and others can do to sort out what it is we should be doing to give effect to our commitment to treat each other as equals.

Law aimed at protecting individuals from discrimination is in need of much jurisprudential attention. Partly this is because it cannot be viewed, or is, at any rate, no longer viewed, in isolation from attempts to ameliorate the effects of past discrimination. Although the issues are clearly related, and indirect discrimination and affirmative action have already been referred to often, the topics dealt with in the final two chapters have an added dimension that a law simply proscribing 'direct' discrimination need not have. With direct discrimination there is no innocent bystander issue. Apart from the argument that taxpayers' money is wasted administering them, laws prohibiting direct discrimination can only be said to be a financial threat, if fines or damages are to be paid or reputations tarnished, to wrongdoers. The justification for laws against indirect discrimination, at least when these are targeted at the mischief of 'disparate impact' *unintentionally* caused, is a more difficult task. As is the justification for affirmative action.

Laws prohibiting indirect discrimination or allowing affirmative action may cast unfair burdens on sectors or groups; that should rightfully be spread across the whole community. This argument is notorious in the affirmative action context but it is also a consideration, which has been noted and should receive further attention in discussions of indirect discrimination.

---

93   The reader may peruse the (South African) Promotion of Equality and Prevention of Unfair Discrimination Act (4 of 2000) for a nice introduction to the enormous exegetical task facing South African human rights lawyers. I have no doubt that the intentions of the South African legislature in passing this and other pieces of equality law were honourable, but their policy formulation was not always well articulated in the legal products of that process.

Chapter 9
Basic Equality and Different Treatment

Introduction

Many of the controversial policy issues which pose ethical conundrums in contemporary social and legal thought about human rights involve policies or policy proposals which treat people differently on grounds which are seen by some as *prima facie* discriminatory. Although basic equality does not require equal treatment in every case, treating people as equals does mean we may not treat any person or group of persons more favourably or less favourably without good reason. It is not surprising therefore that many are suspicious of, and likely to scrutinise for fairness, any preferential treatment on grounds that were previously, or are currently, used for discriminatory purposes (or are similar to those which might be so used). That suspicion is warranted in cases that we have not already analysed and settled. We understand why there are different tennis contests for women and men but we still argue about affirmative action for women in tertiary education, or whether there should be remedies for indirect, unintentional, discrimination, against women and other underrepresented groups.

Just as suspicion about preferential treatment on those grounds is understandable, it is not extraordinary that there is concern when outcomes, in a particular context, are less favourable for groups which have been discriminated against. Again some of these different outcomes are not interesting. We do not expect many women to fare well in tennis matches against the world's top men players. If we did we would not now have separate competitions for the sexes. But many are concerned, for example, about the fact that there are, relatively, very few women in certain prized occupations – engineering being one topical example.

These two causes for uneasiness, the existence of preferential policies for historical victims of discrimination (or currently vulnerable groups) and inequalities in desired outcomes, can pull in opposite directions. Evidence of unequal outcomes may be used as data to support the case for increased preferential treatment which will in turn increase the restlessness of those who are sceptical about all such policies or practices. This tension is most apparent in the contexts of race (or culture) and sex which are the areas in which we are most likely to be talking about remedies for indirect discrimination, or affirmative action.

I am of course lumping things together which will sometimes require different sorts of prudential and moral analysis. But there is a common thread. There is a view which says that overcoming the denial of basic equality means treating people equally, regardless of race, sex, religion, culture, sexual orientation and other similar 'forbidden grounds'. That idea is strongly challenged by a second thought, more prominent recently, which claims that equal treatment, even on those grounds, is not always fair and may constitute discrimination. Basic equality's principal entailment, that treating people as equals does not always mean treating them equally, means that there is no knockdown argument which can dispose of the second idea by relying on the meaning of 'equality'. The idea that the 'forbidden grounds' are not always forbidden, that is to say they *should* not always be, is not absurd – it is just controversial – like its denial. I have argued that there are indeed no convincing candidates for absolutely forbidden grounds of differentiation[1] and I will provide more counter examples here. The question of precisely when differentiation on such grounds should be allowed is an open, largely unresolved one.

The moral issues will have to be decided on a case by case basis. One general point seems worth making though. It is wrong to admit any claim for preferential treatment[2] simply because someone or some group can point to a disadvantage or (descriptive) inequality of result it would alleviate: basic equality must be satisfied and other relevant considerations also taken into account.

In terms of individuals: Jones cannot be awarded his diploma in crisis counselling if he does not pass the exam and complete his coursework requirements even though, if he does fail, the neutral rules about what must be achieved to earn a passing mark will have a negative impact on him. The fact that a policy produces unequal outcomes *per se* is not necessarily morally important. If Jones is unable to get a job as a crisis counsellor because he failed to get his diploma in terms of the rules applied to successful fellow students, then, all else being equal, there is no wrong to remedy. Even those who think we should compensate people for the 'brute luck' of inequalities imposed by nature at birth or by later accident, or for the inequality of nurture we may experience, agree that we are to some extent in charge of our destinies.[3] If we are, then some unequal outcomes, at the level of individual persons at least, are morally irreproachable.

Different outcomes for groups are more worrying. The groups we think of here are those constituted by race or sex, ethnicity, religion and the like. It is not a cause for moral concern that there is *a* group of people that does not have the ability or the commitment required for medical school. It is a cause for concern when the

---

1   See Ch. 6.

2   I use the phrase 'preferential treatment' in its most broad sense. I do not mean by it that some are being preferred *unfairly*. That is what I am trying to assess. Also: providing remedies for unintentional discrimination may seem to have nothing to do with preferential treatment at all. I simply mean that here too the idea that one standard is good enough for everyone, regardless of group membership, is being challenged.

3   See Ronald Dworkin *Sovereign Virtue* (Harvard University Press, Cambridge, 2000) Ch. 2.

group that does study medicine is almost entirely male and from one racial or ethnic group.

But even inequality of outcomes for these kinds of groups might not always be morally relevant. While different outcomes for groups will sometimes be the result of discrimination against the worst off, we cannot assume that will always be the case. If we could, then we would feel justified in correcting all such imbalances that we became aware of. That suggestion is quickly reduced to absurdity by asking whether we should provide preferential access to training facilities for all long distance runners who do *not* come from Kenya or Ethiopia.[4] Ronald Dworkin repeats a story about a Harvard University President who once argued that the number of Jews entering Harvard should be limited to prevent them from being disproportionately represented amongst Harvard's graduates. (The President thought they were too intellectual.)[5]

Other humorous or sinister examples (the one about the historical Harvard President is both, I suppose) are not difficult to think of. Not every inequality of outcome offends equality in its moral sense. There is just nothing to be done, by way of preferential treatment for everyone else, as a matter of fairness, about group sporting advantage that is not the result of unfair tactics. The relative average success of a contemporary ethnic group in some area may itself have something to do with past discrimination *against* that group. That is hardly a reason to favour all other groups in some way in order to counter-balance that success. I do not mean to imply though, that preferential treatment can always be justified as long as it is trying to remedy past discrimination against the preferred group, or that it could not possibly be justified absent such discrimination. My point here is only that unequal group outcomes are not always cause for morally motivated intervention.

The example of Jones and his diploma I used a few paragraphs ago does beg an important question. Sometimes we are not questioning, on its own terms, one of the various hurdles we use to limit access to things like educational and job opportunities. Sometimes we are questioning, instead, the point of the hurdle itself as an aspect of the social institution which imposes it. Our complaint may not be that Jones did not deserve to fail his course. It might be that we simply think the requirement of a diploma is itself unfair. Perhaps because it excludes from the crisis counselling profession those who are not good at academic studies but who may have, what we might take to be more important, a strong intuitive sense of what support is needed by people in crisis situations. Someone else might think a diploma is necessary. It is a matter for debate. The point is some complaints about the denial of basic equality can be more radical in this way, challenging a social structure rather than just an isolated application of a rule. This kind of complaint

---

4   Whatever one might think is the cause of the success of so many athletes from that region. See Marek Kohn *The Race Gallery* (Jonathan Cape, London, 1995) 76–82 for an interesting discussion of recent explanations of this phenomenon.

5   Ronald Dworkin *Taking Rights Seriously* (Duckworth, London, 1977) 230–31.

cannot be rejected out of hand simply because it suggests the rules of the game should be changed. Perhaps they should. It all depends. But the fact that the rules produce different outcomes is not in itself reason to change them. To sum up, one cannot argue:

1. Basic equality does not always require equal treatment.
2. Group X is proportionately less successful, well off etc.
3. Therefore members of group X should receive preferential treatment to remove the disadvantage regardless of its provenance, its effect on group X, or the consequences for others of adopting the preferential policy.

The general point made here has direct application to the debates on indirect discrimination and affirmative action. What does basic equality have to say about these issues? I have noted, many times, the very abstract nature of basic equality. One clear implication of that is while much can be ruled out in terms of social policies which do not show a concern for all affected persons, it is not possible to find a solution for the quandaries we have around the problem of dealing with discrimination by any simple application of the idea of equality. That does not mean these are not equality issues. They are, in a more direct sense than the basic liberties are because we can argue meaningfully about those without relying on equality; although I have shown the arguments can go awry when we forget that egalitarian reasons for limiting basic liberties can often be outweighed by egalitarian considerations for upholding them. Arguments over issues like indirect discrimination and affirmative action, however, seem to be only about equality and so every argument for and against every measure proposed to deal with discrimination should be measured against the idea of equality itself. As I have shown in the chapter on culture and discrimination, the idea of cultural rights can be inspired by the thought that being subject to general laws can sometimes place unfair burdens on minorities of various sorts. But the solution to the problem, granting cultural rights, seems to come at the cost, if the concerns I expressed there are valid, of unfairness to others – itself a failure to apply basic equality.

My discussions of measures preventing indirect discrimination and the chapter on affirmative action will both, again, illustrate the need to consider not only the obvious connection between basic equality and the rationale for such measures but also, here too, the question whether these measures themselves impose unfair burdens on some social actors or groups. The assumption that they do not seems to me to be a recurring failure in recent equality jurisprudence.

A disclaimer about what follows: I am discussing policy issues for the purposes of general evaluation. I am not attempting to state the existing law, in a particular jurisdiction or generally, on indirect discrimination or affirmative action. I will only refer to instances of that law for broad evaluative purposes. I also do not offer much detailed policy advice. I know the devil is often in the detail but general principles also need to be established. Before we can meaningfully say how technical matters such as the burden of proof in indirect discrimination cases should be resolved we should be clear, or clearer than I think we are, about matters of culpability and liability, in general, for different sorts of outcomes. My intention is only to suggest some of the moral implications of a consideration of these issues in the light of our commitment to basic equality and other values that cohere with that one.

I also do not assume that 'indirect discrimination' or 'affirmative action' mean quite the same thing in all jurisdictions or settings where these terms, or synonyms for them, are used. Indeed part of the reason for thinking about indirect discrimination is that there is some confusion about what it amounts to and it is well known that many people support some forms of affirmative action but not others. But there are common themes around these ideas, which are, in my view, worth discussing before we get to more localised analyses. The fact, then, that my discussion focuses a lot on North American cases and quandaries does not mean that I think we should always do as the Americans do. I could not intend that for they are, of course, divided amongst themselves on these issues. The context of many of my examples is merely an acknowledgement of the lively debate about these issues in those countries and of the fact that despite our fervent claims to be different we do tend on the whole to end up with similar human rights laws and their attending conundrums. It does of course behove us to transplant carefully and we do not always do that, but many of the general points we need to argue about are the same.

Indirect Discrimination

The idea of indirect discrimination, found in some constitutional and ordinary anti-discrimination law provisions, tries to deal with the problem of policies and rules which have an unintentional, disproportionate and unnecessary adverse impact on certain groups. 'Certain groups' usually means already disadvantaged groups although the provisions of such laws may sometimes apply to members of groups that are not disadvantaged in general. The kinds of groups we are talking about are those which it is generally assumed will on the whole be as well off or successful as any other, absent discrimination.

The idea that discrimination can be unintentional is an important and difficult notion. It raises awkward questions about fault and responsibility which should be considered when thinking about types of disparate impact that we think should be remedied. Ignoring these questions of culpability can itself constitute a breach of basic equality. Some indirect discrimination is not only unintentional but may be a quite unforeseeable result of a 'facially neutral' measure or requirement. I will argue that private actors should not exclusively bear the costs of such remedies when they are not to blame, or not solely to blame, for the existence of the troublesome imbalances.

A commitment to basic equality will constrain us from intentional discrimination. In certain limited contexts it is justifiable to require private actors to forgo their liberty to commit the wrong of discrimination. But it is not fair to require those covered by anti-discrimination law to bear the entire burden of group disadvantage that is not intentionally or carelessly caused by them. An argument for imposing strict liability for causing any sort of disparate impact which negatively affected disadvantaged groups would have to convince us of two things. First, that the goal of alleviating the disadvantage could only be achieved by imposing the responsibility for ameliorating the condition of disadvantage entirely or disproportionately on certain actors covered by discrimination law. And second, that the result would be good enough to outweigh considerations of fairness due to those bound by the law. I do not think there is a good argument for either of these conclusions.

After talking about it for over 35 years it still takes a while to explain exactly what 'indirect discrimination' is. Basic equality is denied in acts of direct discrimination. A state, for example, denies the right to vote to a racial group or to women generally or a private sector company hires on a racially exclusive basis or refuses to appoint women to senior positions in the organisation. The 'directness' is said to lie in the fact that a particular ground of differential treatment was intentionally used and the purpose of the differentiation was discriminatory. The 'indirectness' of indirect discrimination is thought to reside in the fact that there is no requirement of motive or intent in legal rules prohibiting it. The important thing is the effect of the rule or practice. We can discriminate against people inadvertently, as it were. As Jeremy Waldron points out, covert discrimination is something else again.[6] If A introduces a new, but unnecessary in terms of his business needs, educational requirement for new employees, with the intention of excluding a racial group whose members are less likely to meet it, there is an indirectness involved, but it is not morally significant.

Some think the point of talk about indirect discrimination just is to ensure that the law covers situations where the discrimination is indirect in that factual sense, perhaps because that is where covert discrimination is most likely to reside. Indirect discrimination, on that view, could be intentional or unintentional.[7] It is true that discrimination which is indirect, in the sense that the use of one ground to differentiate may lead to a disproportionate adverse impact on another ground, may be intentional or unintentional. But if it is intentional it is no different, morally speaking, than (factually) direct intentional discrimination is. To say that someone has discriminated against someone else is to make a moral judgment. It is not a factual assessment of the technique by means of which discrimination was achieved. This is true even if the legislation seems to not intend a pejorative

---

6   Jeremy Waldron 'Indirect Discrimination' in Stephen Guest and Alan Milne (eds) *Equality and Discrimination* (Franz Steiner Verlag Wiesbaden GMBH, Stuttgart, 1985) 93, 95.

7   See, for example, Janet Kentridge 'Equality' in Matthew Chaskalson et al. (eds) *Constitutional Law of South Africa* (Juta and Co Ltd, Cape Town, 1996) Ch. 14, 14–24B–1426B.

connotation to be placed on the term 'discrimination'; intending instead that the word means mere differentiation. Such legislation will at least be implying that many instances of differentiation on certain grounds are morally wrong.

It might be thought that if someone differentiates on one ground and that has the effect of unfair disadvantage on some group not referred to by that ground that the discriminator could argue that, because the initial differentiation was not on a forbidden ground, there was no discrimination. But that argument assumes discrimination cannot be executed in a complex way. It can. This can be made clear by realising (or stipulating if necessary) that 'discrimination', in the context of human rights discourse, is a moral term. It is a judgment we can make of individual acts or of patterns of behaviour. Intentional indirect discrimination is no different from direct (in that mechanical sense) discrimination. The interesting thing to think about here, therefore, seems to me to be whether 'discrimination' in its pejorative sense can be unintentional, not if it can be achieved by circuitous methods.

Talk about indirect discrimination, in the sense of unintentional discrimination, is an extension of the usual dictionary meaning of 'discrimination' because no prejudiced attitude is required.[8] Christopher McCrudden says that this expansion of the meaning of the term 'discrimination' amounts to a 'persuasive definition'[9] which philosopher C.L. Stevenson defines as 'one which gives a new conceptual meaning to a familiar word without substantially changing its emotive meaning'.[10] The idea encourages us to think of indirect discrimination in the way we now think of direct discrimination – as a bad thing. Persuasion does not always work. Jeremy Waldron thinks most people will not transfer the emotive (morally negative) meaning they attach to the idea of intentional discrimination to the concept of indirect discrimination.[11]

Perhaps most people now (Waldron made the point 25 years ago) would still not think a policy is as bad as they think direct discrimination is, simply because it has an unintentional disparate impact on some group, even if that group is relatively disadvantaged and even if the offending policy is not 'necessary' in some suitable sense. Waldron is clearly not perturbed by the failure of the persuasive redefinition of 'discrimination' to make people think indirect discrimination is as bad as the direct kind because he does not think indirect discrimination is as bad as ordinary discrimination based on prejudice.[12] He rejects the argument which says it must be

---

8   *The New Shorter Oxford English Dictionary* (Clarendon Press, Oxford, 1993), 689 defines discrimination in the relevant sense as 'an unjust or prejudicial distinction'.

9   Cristopher McCrudden 'Changing Notions of Discrimination' in Stephen Guest and Alan Milne *Equality and Discrimination* (Franz Steiner Verlag Wiesbaden GMBH, Stuttgart, 1985) 83, 91.

10   C.L. Stevenson 'Persuasive Definitions' (1938) *XLVII Mind* 331, 333, cited in McCrudden 'Changing Notions of Discrimination', above n. 9, 91.

11   Waldron 'Indirect Discrimination', above n. 6, 93.

12   Ibid. 94–5.

as bad, if the effects are as bad. Not because he thinks the effects are not important, but because the infliction of the harm caused by discrimination motivated by conscious prejudice is worse.

Waldron notes that when the concept of indirect discrimination was introduced into United Kingdom anti-discrimination law, the idea of intention associated with it was not its distinctly legal sense.[13] I think perhaps it would help, in sorting out our moral attitudes to direct and indirect discrimination, to think about culpability for discrimination in something like traditional legal terms. Discriminating on a particular prohibited ground involves, Waldron says, more than *mens rea* because it seems to include *motive*.[14] Indirect discrimination on the other hand does not even include intention. Our different moral attitudes to murder and manslaughter may explain, by analogy, to a limited extent at least, why we condemn direct discrimination more than the unintentional sort.

Resort to legal categories here might lead to a more extensive taxonomy. Perhaps discrimination can be intended, caused by recklessness, or be the result of carelessness, each with an attendant level of moral impropriety. Outside the usual legal categories it might also just be the result of a not unreasonable inadvertence. I am suggesting that we could see matters of discrimination in this way, not that this reflects most people's current intuitions.

The idea that I am suggesting we might adopt would not be that indirect discrimination is as bad as the direct sort. Instead of being a persuasive definition where the definition but not the emotive content is altered, the extension of meaning might be accompanied by a new range of emotive content, so the idea of indirect discrimination could simply indicate that discrimination may, like homicide, be more (or less) culpable and that not all forms of it, or of discrimination generally, are equally as bad. Of course some people do think the two forms of discrimination, as the law defines them, are equally bad. But they might just be misled by unexplained semantics. The two forms might be as bad in terms of some of their effects but actions are immoral in a different way when they are also intended to have harmful results.

If we want to justify keeping the idea of indirect discrimination we need to distinguish it, then, as Waldron does, from covert discrimination but we also need to make it clear that it is not as bad as direct discrimination. 'Bad', that is, in terms of the condemnation we heap on those we deem culpable. Of course using the same word might make this difficult. It helps, by analogy, to be able to say 'this is *murder* but that is *manslaughter*' and, although there are more or less serious cases of each, we generally think one is worse than the other.

---

13   Ibid. 94.

14   Ibid. It is only in this sense that the South African case, *City Council of Pretoria* v *Walker*, discussed in Ch. 6, was not about direct discrimination. But I think discrimination in its ordinary pejorative sense includes unthinking acts of discrimination that can't really be described as unintentional, though perhaps not *motivated* by prejudice in any hateful sense of 'prejudice'. This is an issue which might benefit from further attention.

This way of thinking about indirect discrimination will not be convincing if discrimination is simply not something that can be done unintentionally. Grant Huscroft thinks it obviously can be. Writing in the New Zealand Bill of Rights context he says, of the assumption that the right not be discriminated against can be unintentionally infringed:

> There is nothing remarkable in this proposition; all rights may be infringed intentionally or inadvertently, and there is no reason to suppose that the protection of the Bill of Rights depends upon a showing that the rights infringement was deliberate – though of course that may well be relevant to the remedy that a court may afford once an infringement is established.[15]

Huscroft does not offer any examples or an argument for his conclusion. Is it true of the right to freedom of expression for example? If we censor the works of D.H. Lawrence we infringe the right intentionally. We do it on purpose. But might we not pass a law to protect consumers from misleading conduct without reflecting on all the possible free speech implications? Freedom of religion might seem an easier case still because the lawmaker might not even be aware of the existence of the offended religion. A law is passed instituting some sort of health or environmental regulation making it impossible, or very difficult, for a particular religion to conduct its worship and, as it happens, no one involved in the lawmaking process has any idea it will affect some group's religious practices. That might or might not in the circumstances be careless but perhaps not, as a matter of fact, intentional. So it seems it is true of rights like that. If this sounds a bit odd that might be because our religion and speech are typically protected from government rather than private interference. We are not much concerned whether the interference is intentional or not. We just want it stopped. With equality rights we are, however, in the business of restraining private actors as well, in the name of a communal good, and the question of unfair, because unshared, burdens arises.

How does someone unintentionally fail to respect another as an equal? The idea of indirect discrimination is a legal one and it is defined in laws and by courts, although I am suggesting it might make sense as a moral idea. The remarks of McCrudden and Waldron[16] that I have cited were made in the specific context of the English Race Relations Act and the Sex Discrimination Act.[17] Those laws followed an idea from an interpretation of the provisions of the United States Civil Rights Act.[18] The idea of indirect discrimination is now found in the law of various states and in international instruments. It is not always easy to abstract from legislative and case law differences but it seems clear that the different

---

15   Grant Huscroft 'Freedom from Discrimination' in Rishworth et al. *The New Zealand Bill of Rights* (Oxford University Press, Melbourne, 2003) 366, 386.

16   1976.

17   1975.

18   Title VII 1964. The seminal case is *Griggs* v *Duke Power Co.* 401 US 424 (1971).

terminology used in these various provisions is intended, at least, to refer to roughly the same phenomenon. Different terms are used. The US term 'disparate impact' may seem to suggest something different from 'indirect discrimination' because literally there can be a disparate impact without there being any discrimination but the term 'disparate impact' is elliptical. It means 'unjustified disparate impact'. But wherein lies the lack of justification?

Is it *wrong* to use rules and practices which have an unnecessary, albeit unintentional, adverse impact on particular groups? 'Unnecessary' is rather vague. We are trying to work out if it is unfair as between persons. That assessment differs depending on whether we are evaluating the effects of legal rules and state practices, or, on the other hand, the behaviour of private individuals or organisations. Governments may not discriminate intentionally and it is not unreasonable to require them to take some care not to act in such a way that the interests of, especially, the kinds of groups which have been the victims of intentional discrimination are unnecessarily harmed. Even if the avoidable disparate impact is not the result of carelessness, but simply an unforeseeable unintended consequence, a concern for basic equality might require some sort of corrective action on the government's part. The costs, of taking care not to cause such outcomes or of correcting for those caused by inadvertence are, in the case of the state, borne equally among the citizens. The question of culpability is not relevant in the way it is in the private sector. This is because we are not as concerned with whether, or to what extent the government has done something wrong, although we do think it should not be careless. We just want to avoid a certain outcome. In the case of unintentional discrimination on the part of the government then, we would only worry about liability, in terms of cost, which would be an undue burden on everyone – including those who suffered the disparate impact.

We should be more concerned about culpability, or the lack thereof, in the case of the private sector because taking steps to avoid disproportionate impacts does involve costs. The costs are borne by those engaged in a particular activity, such as employers, and not amongst the citizenry equally and it does not seem just to impose those costs in a partial way when there is no fault. In this private context it seems sensible to worry, with Waldron, that this unfairness might lead, on the part of employers, to 'bewildered amusement' or indifference to racial and sex based injustice.[19] Those concerns are certainly relevant when one is trying to advance the goal of a particular equality or equalities. If legal provisions about indirect discrimination are going to make people indifferent or hostile to the goals of racial or sexual equality that is certainly one reason not to have them. The unfairness of disproportionately burdening some to achieve these goals is also worrying in principle. Lest anyone argue such laws are much more accepted now

---

19   Some sort of hesitancy led to the omission of an indirect discrimination provision in the English 1995 Disability Discrimination Act but the concept is now a part of many anti-discrimination laws in various jurisdictions.

than 30 odd years ago, we should remember that enthusiasm cannot be inferred from silence.

My concern with Waldron's analysis, though, is that he treats everything which 'indirect discrimination' might refer to as morally equivalent:

> In the case of *indirect* discrimination, the wrongness of the employers' actions is nothing more than that they are not doing their bit to promote racial or sexual equality; it seems odd, then, to respond to *that* by requiring them to do *more* than their fair share?[20]

In cases where the reasonable employer, or whoever is covered by such legislation, would not have foreseen that its practices would have the offending disparate impact Waldron's concern seems right. In such cases it does not seem right to impose all the costs associated with avoiding the unequal outcome on private parties, because they will not have done anything wrong. Perhaps greater advertence would have helped but it would not be reasonable for the law to require it. But what about cases where the reasonable employer *would* have foreseen that a condition for employment or promotion would have a disparate impact on a particular disadvantaged social group?

The idea of indirect discrimination comes from a United States case that suggests that kind of carelessness.[21] In *Griggs* v *Duke Power Co.* the company had openly discriminated against blacks until the coming into force of the Civil Rights Act of 1964[22]. Blacks were restricted, before that date, to the operating department, the 'Labor Department', that paid the lowest wages.[23] That was no longer lawful after the passing of the Act and the issue in the case was the legality of conditions placed by the company on appointments and transfers after that. When the company terminated its policy of direct discrimination it required a high school diploma for transfer from the Labor Department to the other departments. This had been a requirement for initial assignment to these departments since1955.[24] There were, however, white people working in these departments who did not have high school diplomas but who had nevertheless performed satisfactorily. Some of these white workers had achieved promotions.

On the date that Title VII of the Civil Rights Act became effective the company also imposed another condition for placement in any department, apart from the Labor Department, to which blacks had hitherto been confined. Now satisfactory scores on two aptitude tests and a high school diploma were required for placement in these departments. A high school diploma was still enough to transfer into these

---

20   Waldron 'Indirect Discrimination', above n. 6, 98.

21   *Griggs*, above n. 18. The case is famous but, perhaps because of this, summaries of the key facts sometimes differ and so I will set the facts out in some detail.

22   *Griggs*, above n. 18, 427.

23   Ibid.

24   Ibid.

departments from the Labor Department. Soon after this the company allowed existing employees who had not matriculated from high school to transfer from the Labor Department and the Coal Handling Department (another 'outside' department) to an 'inside' department if they passed two tests, both of which were not intended to measure the ability to do a particular job. The disadvantage to blacks of these entrance and transfer requirements was clear as was the fact that they were not necessary. They were shown to be unnecessary by the fact that whites had done well without satisfying them, and they disadvantaged blacks because blacks had received less of the kind of education needed to succeed on those sorts of tests.

Strictly speaking, as Brian Barry notes,[25] the fact that black employees had received an inferior education, as blacks in the United States had in general at that time, might have suggested that blacks who had not matriculated from high school were much less educated than whites who had not finished high school. So it did not necessarily follow, from the fact that whites did not need a high school diploma to do some of the more desirable jobs, that blacks who were similarly unqualified would have the required skills. But, as Barry argues, that does not mean blacks should not have been given the opportunity to show what they could do.

The District Court and the Court of Appeals found that discrimination under Title VII had to be intentional and this had not been established.[26] The US Supreme Court disagreed:

> The objective of Congress in the enactment of Title VII is plain from the language of the statute. It was to achieve equality of employment opportunities and remove barriers that have operated in the past to favor an identifiable group of white employees over other employees. Under the Act, practices, procedures, or tests neutral on their face, and even neutral in terms of intent, cannot be maintained if they operate to 'freeze' the status quo of prior discriminatory practices.[27]

There is no mention, in this statement of the meaning of indirect discrimination, of the fact that the use of the 'practices, procedures, or tests' might be justified. But, in setting out the questions it had to decide, the Court did make it clear that the reasonableness (in terms of 'business necessity') of the practices is relevant. The Court did not directly discuss the moral culpability of the company other than to accept the lower courts' findings that there was no discriminatory purpose. But while the Court did not specifically say the discrimination was covert, it did say: '[t]he Act proscribes not only *overt* discrimination but also practices fair in form,

---

25   Brian Barry *Culture and Equality* (Harvard University Press, Cambridge, 2001) 101.

26   *Griggs*, above n. 18, 428.

27   Ibid. 429–30.

but discriminatory in operation' (emphasis added).[28] Why the contrast between indirect discrimination and *overt* discrimination? If the Court was implying the company had acted *covertly* then it did not really believe the disparate impact was unintentional.

As Larry Alexander says: '[t]he case could be viewed as establishing an evidentiary and procedural framework for smoking out covert uses of forbidden criteria'.[29] But covert discrimination is intentional discrimination and that is not what we are talking about. If that, dealing with covert discrimination is the purpose of indirect discrimination provisions then they are over-inclusive covering, as they do, genuinely unintentional discrimination as well.[30] But, if *Griggs* could be seen, rather, as implying: 'under these circumstances the company *should have known* that its requirements for placements and transfers would unnecessarily burden a community trying to recover from decades of post-slavery discrimination' then there would at least be a potential match of liability and costs.

Perhaps the company's intentions, or motives, were mixed. The court accepted, as evidence of its lack of discriminatory intent, the fact that it had instituted a policy which assisted employees by paying two thirds of the cost of high school tuition. But perhaps the company should have been more careful not to unnecessarily limit the immediate appointment and transfer of black applicants and employees. Perhaps that was indirect discrimination in the sense that it was culpable but not deliberate.

If we think the company in *Griggs* was negligent we might not have qualms about making it change its ways, with all the cost that implies. And we might not worry that other employers will have to take care not to have practices that have the undesirable impact. That will cost too. But so might, for example, taking care not to cause avoidable damage to the natural environment in which a business operates. On the other hand, if we cannot say that a particular practice which has caused a disparate impact, and which is not really necessary, was instituted at least carelessly, then it does seem that imposing liability involves imposing an unfair, because disproportionate, burden on the defendant. One that makes him more responsible for the problem of group disadvantage than it is fair to do.

If that is right then part of indirect discrimination law is itself unfair. Some might ask: 'should we care about that specific unfairness in the context of attempts to remedy such serious social ills? In the private sphere it is employers, and others bound by human rights legislation, who have intentionally discriminated against women and minorities in the past so why should we worry about

---

28   Ibid. 431.

29   Larry Alexander 'What Makes Wrongful Discrimination Wrong? Biases, Preferences, Stereotypes, and Proxies' (1992) 141 *U Pa L Rev* 149, 207.

30   See Waldron 'Indirect Discrimination', above n. 6, 95–6; McCrudden 'Changing Notions of Discrimination', above n. 9, 84.

imposing costs on these people now?' That is the sort of casual approach one sometimes finds in defences of affirmative action programmes, but it is too glib. Apart from not explaining why only *some* people should pay for these past wrongs it ignores the fact that some employers are women and some are members of minority groups and the rest are not all equally (or at all) to blame for the current disadvantage of less well off groups. The intuitive sense that some have, that it is not wrong to burden employers, and other stakeholders in their businesses, with the costs of preventing disparate impact becomes less convincing as we move further away from a time when intentional, prejudiced, discrimination was more widespread, though there are arguments worth considering about compensation for that earlier discrimination.[31]

It could be argued that the focus on fault altogether misses the point of disparate impact discrimination. The purpose of the law, as Chief Justice Burger said in *Griggs*, is to equalise opportunities and remove barriers. It is a procedural tool but it is aimed at a goal of greater representation.[32] McCrudden says: drop the word 'discrimination'; call it 'inequality of opportunity' if you prefer.[33] That would remove the stigma but not the cost. Somebody has to pay and the same people who pay are those whose freedom, to employ who they will, is limited. Larry Alexander notes:

> Interestingly, not even the most sweeping civil rights laws ... have ever been applied to discrimination *against* employers by prospective employees, or to discrimination *against* sellers by prospective buyers.[34]

Partly that omission is motivated by a respect for freedom, but it is also just easier to target employers and suppliers. That is not as objectionable in the context of intentional discrimination. Regulation, like all politics, is the art of the possible. But convenience is not enough when there is no fault, even if it is, as I have suggested it might be, in the case of diminished fault. And, in any event, no one has suggested that resort to no fault liability for indirect discrimination is the only possible way to deal with group disadvantage.

Interestingly enough, the development of disparate impact jurisprudence in the United States Supreme Court has found it difficult to let go of the idea of intent, let alone fault. I have already noted how the Court, in *Griggs*, contrasted indirect discrimination with 'overt' discrimination, suggesting the former might be covert; and thus intentional. In *Albemarle Paper Co.* v *Moody*[35] the Court found that, under Title VII the plaintiff might show that even a practice which was *prima*

---

31   See below Ch. 10.

32   McCrudden 'Changing Notions of Discrimination', above n. 9, 84.

33   Ibid. 91.

34   Alexander 'What Makes Wrongful Discrimination Wrong? Biases, Preferences, Stereotypes, and Proxies', above n. 29, 204.

35   *Albemarle Paper Co.* v *Moody* 422 US 405 (1975).

facie justified under the 'business necessity' defence was not necessary because there were alternatives available that did not cause disparate impact. If the plaintiff could show this, the Court said, it would be evidence the employer's practices were a 'pretext' for discrimination.[36]

As Linda Lye notes, this seems to indicate that indirect or disparate impact discrimination is perfectly intentional, just hidden.[37] While the essence of the case made indirect discrimination easier to prove, conceptually the idea might appear to have been restricted. The Court has also evinced a concern that the requirements of Title VII indirect discrimination might impose a burden of costs on employers that is too great. In the words of Justice Blackmun in *Albemarle*:

> I fear that a too-rigid application of the EEOC Guidelines [for proving 'business necessity'] will leave the employer little choice, save an impossibly expensive and complex validation study, but to engage in a subjective quota system of employment selection. This, of course, is far from the intent of Title VII [Civil Rights Act 1964].[38]

This trend continued. In *New York City Transit Authority* v *Beazer*,[39] on the question of intention the Court said:

> The District Court's express finding that the rule was not motivated by racial animus forecloses any claim in rebuttal that it [the company's exclusionary practice regarding drug use] was merely a pretext for intentional discrimination.[40]

Again the Court seemed to be importing a requirement of intent into disparate impact jurisprudence. The *Beazer* Court also lessened the burden involved in establishing a business necessity defence. This process of redefining indirect discrimination continued until the business necessity defence was considerably less onerous than in *Griggs*. References to 'facially neutral' employer practices, in the disparate impact context, being a 'pretext' for intentional discrimination continued.[41] Those comments are consistent with the diminution of liability as time passed.

---

36 Ibid. 425.

37 Linda Lye 'Title VII'S Tangled Tale: The Erosion and Confusion of Disparate Impact and the Business Necessity Defense' (1998) 19 *Berkeley J Emp & Lab L* 315, 325. Ms Lye's article is a useful history of Title VII disparate impact jurisprudence. I rely on her account a lot for that history but she does not discuss the possible unfairness to those subject to no-fault discrimination law which I am discussing here.

38 *Albemarle*, above n. 35, 449.

39 440 US 568 (1978).

40 Ibid. 587.

41 *Wards Cove Packing Co.* v *Antonio* 490 US 642 (1989) was the culmination of these trends. See Lye 'Title VII'S Tangled Tale: The Erosion and Confusion of Disparate Impact and the Business Necessity Defense', above n. 37, 332–3.

This process of watering down disparate impact discrimination was strongly disapproved of by some.[42] Clearly employers had to do less in terms of diversifying their workforces as time went by. I would suggest, though, the Court's retreat from all the potential implications of *Griggs* need not be seen as a retreat from race and gender equity. It could rather be seen simply as a concern about imposing costs on employers who had not intentionally discriminated. What was left after the last case in this pruning of Title VII discrimination jurisprudence was, apart from clearly intentional discrimination, enough perhaps to cover covert discrimination and some reckless or careless discrimination.[43] Very roughly speaking, to be sure, but the Court clearly was concerned about an undue burden being placed on employers and kept slipping into talk about intent – exactly what you would expect from those concerned not to stretch 'discrimination' too far beyond the idea of intentional unjust behaviour and reluctant to impose burdens of cost on employers (and others covered by the law; but not everyone) not shown to operate from any discriminatory intent.

Disparate impact law under Title VII of the Civil Rights Act in the US thus reflects both concerns about unequal outcomes for groups and concerns about how to deal with these in ways that are fair to others. The first of these concerns is also evident in some UK jurisprudence. Catherine Barnard and Bob Hepple,[44] who are in favour of an expansive application of the indirect discrimination idea, criticise trends in the fast changing world of sex discrimination prohibition. Their complaints, like those of Lye and other American scholars who criticise the watering down of indirect discrimination in the US, are about courts confusing direct and indirect discrimination and the lowering of the standards of justification for practices which have disparate impacts.[45] They do not really consider questions about fairness to other affected parties.

Summing Up

My suggestion is that where carelessness or recklessness is proved, the remedies for indirect discrimination in the private sector should be milder than those for intentional discrimination and should be aimed at imposing better practices.

---

42   See Lye 'Title VII'S Tangled Tale: The Erosion and Confusion of Disparate Impact and the Business Necessity Defense', above n. 37.

43   Congress did intervene. The Civil Rights Act 1991 was an attempt to restore the pre *Wards Cove* law but it did so in uncertain terms and many of the same disagreements bedevil subsequent cases. See Lye 'Title VII'S Tangled Tale: The Erosion and Confusion of Disparate Impact and the Business Necessity Defense', above n. 37.

44   Catherine Barnard and Bob Hepple 'Substantive Equality' (2000) 59 *Cambridge L J* 562, 567.

45   See also Sandra Fredman *Discrimination Law* (Oxford University Press, Oxford, 2002) 106–15.

Perhaps the term 'discrimination' should be replaced with a milder one too. Where there is no fault but there is an undesirable disparate impact (each jurisdiction must decide which are important and why) it does seem unfair to ask private parties to bear the entire burden of ensuring equal opportunity. Basically that leaves two alternatives. Either, in the absence of fault there should be no liability for disparate impact or all should share the burden of the costs of remedying it – the state should pay the costs of monitoring and correcting disparate impact. A government agency could be empowered to monitor large businesses and fund changes required to avoid policies that inadvertently – unforeseeably – have the undesired outcomes.

If employers are not in any way required to change policies or practices which unforeseeably disadvantage certain groups that does not necessarily mean that nothing should be done about such disadvantage. We can look for other solutions which do not unfairly tax one section of the community, and which do not involve prohibiting disparate impact. We might want to do that to eliminate the need to interfere with the private activities of employers in that respect when they have not been careless in the requirements they have insisted on.

Even in the private sphere employment is, of course, only one area, although probably the most prominent one, in which the question of indirect discrimination could arise. And I have not said anything about the public sector other than to point out that the burden of avoiding indirect discrimination is in that case automatically spread amongst the citizenry equally. The remaining issue there is to decide which sorts of disparate impacts to worry about. That is a very big issue though and each type of situation would require its own discussion. I think it is clear that the promulgation of law is ahead of our jurisprudence in this area. My comments here are only meant to illustrate this and how it is important, in particular, to ensure that our efforts to achieve equality respect the basic equality of all affected persons.

Some of the issues that arise with indirect discrimination are common to group directed policies. Objections to such policies are usually better known as arguments against what is most commonly known as 'affirmative action'. Responding to no-fault discrimination raises some of the same moral questions that affirmative action does. I will address some of those questions under that heading. That new heading is required. I think there are differences between plain anti-discrimination laws, indirect discrimination laws and affirmative action though there are similarities between these three that might be overlooked. We might be happy to have plain anti-discrimination laws but not indirect discrimination laws or affirmative action. We might distinguish the latter two because they are redistributive policies not necessarily linked to any fault of those who might have to pay for them.

Cass Sunstein argues that if we thought this, or anything, evidence of a 'sharp discontinuity' between affirmative action and ordinary discrimination law we would be overlooking the fact that not all plain anti-discrimination law is about prohibiting actions based on bias or prejudice.[46] Discrimination law typically prohibits sex discrimination based on prejudice against women but it is also unlawful, under such laws, to use sex as a proxy, say for 'workers who are likely to need time off to look after sick children'. The use of sex as a proxy in that way is not irrational *per se*, because it might be efficient for the business concerned. It does not necessarily evince a hatred of women or a desire to devalue them. The likelihood of women with children caring for them when they are sick, as opposed to their fathers caring for them, might, Sunstein plausibly suggests, itself, at least partly, be the product of discrimination. But that does not mean the employer who uses sex as a proxy in this way is biased against women in the sense that he thinks all women are intrinsically less useful in the workplace.[47]

Discrimination is wrong, however, because it is wrong not to treat people as equals. If I exclude women from my workforce or fail to promote them or train them because I think it is in my own, rationally calculated, interest to have workers unlikely to need leave to care for another, I do, intentionally, deny the women I exclude equal concern and respect. Women who never take any sick leave at all will be excluded although men who take a lot will not be. People, women, who are more often expected to look after sick children will be excluded in favour of those who are not as likely to – men. We use proxies all the time of course but not all of them are discriminatory in this way.

Sunstein's point that we do not only prohibit – when we do forbid discrimination – discrimination motivated by an irrational prejudice, is well made however. The denial of basic equality does not always involve the presence of an attitude of prejudice. But 'statistical discrimination' as Sunstein calls it,[48] is intentional, and that makes it different from one sort of indirect discrimination that I have been discussing. And it is also less costly – to avoid it: just don't do it. The ban on statistical discrimination is also different from affirmative action. The latter tries to help disadvantaged groups that have been discriminated against. It does not always respond directly to the wrongdoing of the discriminator, who may not even be around anymore.

Statistical discrimination is intentional and it intentionally and unfairly excludes individuals. It is not just a practice that 'has the harmful long-term consequence of perpetuating group-based inequalities'.[49] It is true that, in a way, all discrimination law, defined broadly, deals with (past or present) group disadvantage but it is, in principle, one thing to prevent discrimination from happening now and another to try to deal with the effects of past discrimination. Even if affirmative action is best seen as a response to present disadvantage, it is a more comprehensive response

---

46   C. Sunstein 'The Anticaste Principle' (1994) 92 *Mich L Rev* 2410, 2417–8. Sunstein does not claim there is *no* difference between anti-discrimination law and affirmative action.

47   Ibid.

48   Ibid. 2416.

49   Ibid. 2418.

Chapter 10
Affirmative Action

Introduction

Basic equality's role in justifying affirmative action can seem an intuitively straightforward one but there is an equally strong widely felt moral intuition to the effect that affirmative action is precisely the kind of thing we should avoid if we are committed to basic equality. We need therefore, as I have intimated throughout this book, to go beyond these intuitions and embark on a difficult process of considering the interests of all parties affected by our choice of affirmative action as an attempt to right the wrong of discrimination. Though so much has been written about affirmative action I think an assessment of the main arguments still yields the conclusion that it is hard to say whether the practice of affirmative action is consistent with fidelity to basic equality. Even in the country which has studied affirmative action more carefully than any other, the United States, the research that has been done does not seem to clearly establish that affirmative action is worth the trouble, the moral trouble in particular.

On the other hand it is not at all clear that affirmative action does no good. This factual issue is an important part of the assessment of affirmative action. It is relevant to our consideration of whether the use of affirmative action affords the respect which is due to equals to the parties affected by it. The practice of affirmative action is also cumbersome and expensive compared to the alternative of just forbidding new discrimination. It must work to be worth the trouble.

Its efficacy is related to its fairness because the expense of affirmative action is borne partly by those who only benefit from it, if they do, very indirectly and the principal burden is placed disproportionately on a very small group of people – those who are not chosen for places or positions because of it – who are not all members of the most socio-economically privileged classes in countries in which affirmative action is practised. But the fairness of affirmative action can also be raised as a prior, distinct question: is affirmative action fair to those who are not chosen even if it is a useful means of advancing disadvantaged groups? Not every means of doing that will be consistent with basic equality.

It is the *motivation* for affirmative action which seems to be most clearly, positively, related to a commitment to basic equality. Affirmative action is seen by its defenders as a means of achieving greater equality of beneficial social outcomes for disadvantaged groups. It is most often thought of as a response to disadvantage caused by past discrimination. The discrimination in question was obviously a breach of basic equality and so it is plausible to think that sincere attempts to undo the harm caused by that discrimination must be in the service of that ideal. But, as with any measure to achieve social justice, affirmative action must itself be *shown* to be consistent with basic equality and other worthwhile social values. This means its effects on *all* affected parties must be taken into account. It will again not be enough to demonstrate how affirmative action is able, if it is, to produce an equal distribution of certain outcomes amongst various groups of people. And, to discredit affirmative action, it will not be enough to simply point out that it treats different groups of people differently on 'prohibited grounds'.

Affirmative action is an 'equality' issue, but the context in which it is debated is complex and does not merely require a simple application of one value. The issue is certainly not resolved simply by hitting on the correct conception of equality and then applying it – at least not in any straightforward uncontroversial way. If it were then we could choose one which stipulated that equality never allows distinctions on grounds like race or, on the other hand, one which says it does if this benefits a disadvantaged group by producing desirable outcomes that make the circumstances of the groups involved more equal. Supporters of the first conception could argue that they are being 'consistent' and supporters of the other conception could argue that they are giving equality 'substance' by taking into account the context in which the preferential treatment is given.

In these terms the debate about affirmative action never gets very far. The first conception argues that affirmative action is wrong by definition, it is just more discrimination on the grounds of race or sex. Any example of a white person or a man not getting or keeping any opportunity or position they would have if they had been black or female is then evidence that discrimination has taken place. The other conception argues affirmative action is right by definition because 'equality' means achieving equal outcomes for different groups. Neither of these conceptions of equality is entailed, in any straightforward way, by a commitment to basic equality. Both of them incompletely state the point of that ideal. Basic equality does require that people are treated consistently in the sense that they should be treated as equals but the context does help to determine what that means in particular situations. On its own, consistency ignores the different effects that our treatment of others produces because it ignores the different circumstances in which we find individuals and groups. A preoccupation with context, on the other hand, can make us forget to consider, at all, the effects of our policies on the interests of people other than those whose circumstances we want to improve.

If it is conceded, however, as an application of the idea that treatment as an equal does not always require equal treatment, that not every differentiation on a prohibited ground is discrimination on that ground, then the conceptual apparatus of basic equality does seem ready to embrace affirmative action. I think there is a small class of group-based policies which may be justified by means of this straightforward application of basic equality. But justifying affirmative action itself is a far more complex process.

It is not clear that all group-based policies and practices should be called 'affirmative action' even though the term is generally used in a very broad way to describe different programmes in very different situations. The paradigm cases of affirmative action are preferential access to jobs and education or training for jobs and careers. It is possible to think of a programme, aimed at a particular group, and excluding others, which would not raise the hackles or engage the critical faculties of opponents of preferential hiring or access to educational opportunities.

Because equal treatment is not always required by basic egalitarianism, and because this is widely intuitively understood, we hardly notice unequal treatment in innumerable contexts. We do not notice it as between the sick and the healthy or when a teacher gives his advanced students better grades and his failing ones extra tutoring. In terms of 'forbidden grounds', sex is not much of a problem in this regard because of the obvious biological differences between men and women. For example, the relatively high incidence of female breast cancer as compared to male breast cancer makes breast cancer awareness aimed at women and screening programs for that type of cancer for women seem unexceptionable. Separate sports programmes, I have noted, for men and women are also not remarkable. *Not* to have them would clearly be unfair.

It is not impossible for some things to pan out on racial or ethnic lines as well, in certain contexts. Physical differences between the groups we call races may be of little significance as compared to sex differences but the environmental adaptations that produce these differences may result, for example, in medical needs which are more or less group specific.[1] This may sometimes justify uncontroversial group specific policies. If there are, or if there were to be programmes aimed at a particular racial grouping who were, say, particularly susceptible to a certain disease, the fact that the programme was not aimed at everyone is not likely to be contentious. Possible candidates might be programmes to deal with Tay-Sachs or sickle cell anaemia.[2] In terms of *cultural* ethnic differences, different cultural patterns may give rise to different needs and culturally specific solutions need not be controversial though they will be more so if they rely, for their justification, on general disparities in the health or well-being of group populations. And they will be contentious if they consist of general separate treatment. The reason for the potential controversy is that the link between the need and the exclusive treatment will not always be apparent. But group-specific policies might be justified in the absence of a perfect match between need and group membership if it can be shown that ethnicity is an appropriate proxy.

Exclusive, or practically exclusive group need may be practically indistinguishable then, from individual need and policies aimed at one sex or racial/ethnic group may not be even superficially ethically distinguishable from the treatment received by individuals. If we think we should respond, as a community, to anyone's need of a particular sort then basic equality insists we should include everyone who has that need whether it be an individual, a family, or some wider

---

1 See Steven Pinker *The Blank Slate* (Viking, New York, 2002) 143–4.

2 See Amy Guttmann 'Responding to Racial Injustice' in Kwame Anthony Appiah and Amy Gutmann *Color Consciousness* (Princeton University Press, Princeton, 1996) 117. Guttmann notes these two diseases are not quite racially exclusive.

grouping. At some point here we will run into difficulties in justifying different treatment which are hard to assess although they do not amount to 'affirmative action' as the term is commonly understood. But there will be some uncontroversial cases like the breast screening example or health education programmes aimed at a particular community.

Affirmative action, however, is not usually suggested as a response to a naturally occurring need or an obvious cultural predicament. We mostly think about it as a response to discrimination.[3] Controversy usually arises because most or some of the discrimination is in the past although many of its effects are in the present, and it is difficult to work out how to ameliorate these harmful effects in ways that respect human rights. That difficulty is considerable. Discussions of policies and practices known variously as 'affirmative action', 'positive action' or 'positive discrimination'[4] constitute one of the most heated and intractable moral debates of our time. Affirmative action certainly ranks with issues such as abortion in terms of our inability to resolve the matter to most people's satisfaction. It can also be as unpleasant to talk about as abortion is. Focussing as it must on groups and their relative success and prospects for the future, it necessarily involves talking about people in terms of broad, and not even always sensible, categories. That in itself can be awkward but the context of affirmative action debates makes our discussions sound at least superficially patronising and distasteful as well.

Unless, that is, we think affirmative action is simply another tool to be used to prevent *present* discrimination, and even then to a certain extent we have to talk about the *fact* of and not simply the reasons for group disadvantage. This is not a cause of discomfort when discussing the relative sophistication of the ancient Greeks compared with less advanced nations of that time but it obviously is when discussing the relative position of contemporary groups. But affirmative action is not just an emotive topic. It presents us, like abortion again, with a substantial intellectual challenge. It is therefore important that we think carefully about the principles and facts related to this issue. Facts which are relevant to the moral assessment of affirmative action include facts about group differences and their causes and facts about the effects of affirmative action and its prospects for improving the circumstances of disadvantaged groups. These facts are not settled yet and an assessment of our current best understanding of them is necessary in any attempt to evaluate affirmative action in terms of its compatibility with basic equality.

---

3   This is far from always being the case. Affirmative action for Pacific Islanders in New Zealand appears to be simply justified, by its advocates, on the grounds of need. I mean that is the, mostly unstated, apparent reason for it.

4   There are many other terms for this type of group-based preference. More of them are listed in Thomas Sowell *Affirmative Action Around the World* (Yale University Press, New Haven, 2004) 2. I will use the well-known 'affirmative action', as Sowell does, to refer to these practices generally but I will only discuss, for the most part, the more paradigmatic instances of it.

'Affirmative action' can mean different things in different discussions so I will first say a little bit about the concept and its application around the world. I will then discuss two principal rationales for affirmative action and try to assess the reasons they offer for practising affirmative action in the light of our commitment to basic equality. I will argue that the *forward looking* rationale for affirmative action is a better candidate for moral approval than the justification which relies solely on past discrimination. The past discrimination argument's thesis about the present cause of disadvantage of certain groups is in part plausible, but it has more difficulty establishing what should be done about that. This is because it is not clear, from its premises about the condition of groups, exactly who should be compensated by whom and precisely what compensation is due.

The forward looking justification for affirmative action offers a better explanation for giving the direct benefits of affirmative action to certain members of the disadvantaged group. In some cases better representation in desirable positions seems likely to benefit the whole group indirectly by providing a link between communities, which are segregated in various ways which limit equality of opportunity, and more well off groups. The role of the members of groups who have to give up opportunities they would otherwise have had is more difficult to explain in terms of both the justifications for affirmative action I discuss here.

It is, on the one hand, reasonable to think that the increased social stability and harmony that a divided society can achieve by the integration of different groups which brings about a better equality of opportunity and desirable social outcomes is a benefit for everyone in that society. That includes the 'victims' of affirmative action. It is not accurate therefore to characterise affirmative action as prejudiced discrimination, because such discrimination takes little or no account of the interests of the persons discriminated against. It is necessary, on the other hand, to ask why a certain group of people is singled out to pay the cost of achieving the upliftment of the disadvantaged. To justify that would seem to require at least a demonstration that such policies work and that something else which spreads the burden of achieving inter-group justice would not work as well.

There is, in America at least, some research which suggests that affirmative action works, but it does not convince everyone. After more than 30 years of affirmative action in the United States one might have hoped for better evidence that a policy which people in that country feel so strongly about – whether for or against – was at least achieving its stated goals. Finding that evidence, if it is there, should be the priority of supporters of affirmative action everywhere. It is also important that such affirmative action programmes that we do think are worth having in the meantime are tailored to achieve only goals that will improve the circumstances of disadvantaged groups. They should not simply be aimed at some nebulous achievement of 'diversity'.

Attempts to resolve the issues mentioned in the last few paragraphs are best understood as ways of applying the principle of basic equality to the problem caused by the ongoing effects of past discrimination. Writing on affirmative action usually suggests this, if only implicitly. My view of this work is that while much of it is thoughtful it does not typically realise the force of opposing arguments. My conclusion is that there is still much work to be done. I hope this will be evident from my summary and critique of the debate thus far.

The Meaning of 'Affirmative Action'

Before I begin discussing the two main types of arguments for affirmative action I should include a word or two about what affirmative action is. The term has many related meanings. If affirmative action can be as broadly defined as Julio Faundez characterises it, it can have many rationales. Faundez says: '[a]ffirmative action involves treating a sub-class or group of people differently in order to improve their chances of obtaining a particular good or to ensure that they obtain a proportion of certain goods'.[5] Defined this broadly the policy could be a response to any group inequality, however caused. Certainly, if one takes an international perspective, there are group preferences that do not fit into the past discrimination mould into which affirmative action for blacks in the United States, or South Africa, might seem quite easily to fit. Not if the past discrimination is supposed to have been carried out by some group that was not now preferred.

Thomas Sowell, whose work on the history of group differences and responses to those differences I shall refer to often in this chapter, describes how the *bumiputeras*, the indigenous people of Malaysia, were in some ways privileged in colonial times but later became the beneficiaries of a sort of affirmative action.[6] He notes:

> Non-Malays faced strong restrictions against owning land in Malaya and the colonial government provided free education for Malays, while leaving others to educate their children however they could. Malays were also preferred for jobs in the colonial bureaucracy.[7]

And in colonial times the Chinese immigrants, who now experience the disadvantage of Malaysian affirmative action, did not have the political or social power to oppress or exploit the Malays.[8] Sowell also mentions, amongst other somewhat odd examples, an exception to China's one child policy, granted to ethnic minorities in the 1990s.[9] Identifying the motivation for such policies, let alone finding a plausible justification for them would take some time.

It is clear then, that 'affirmative action' can be used, with some semantic plausibility, in ways that make the term at least as unruly as 'discrimination' or 'indirect discrimination'. To keep the subject at all manageable it will be better to

---

5   J. Faundez *Affirmative Action* (International Labour Organisation, Geneva, 1994) 3.
6   Sowell *Affirmative Action Around the World*, above n. 4, 55–9.
7   Ibid. 58.
8   Ibid.
9   Ibid. 9.

stick to preferential access for disadvantaged groups to education, jobs (including training and advancement) and other business opportunities. I will do that for the most part and, again, as I did with indirect discrimination, I will be considering the basic idea rather than the details of any legal system.

The Past Discrimination Argument

The rationales for affirmative action rely on quite complicated assessments of what has happened and what is happening in the relationship between various groups in a particular society. Sorting out the relevant facts will always be difficult. What those material facts are will partly depend on which rationale for affirmative action we are relying on. Arguments for affirmative action thus have to pick a rationale and a setting. The most common rationale is the one about past discrimination. To assess the past discrimination argument for affirmative action it will help to pick a context where it seems plausible. For reasons already stated the example of affirmative for blacks in the United States is a good one.

A defence of affirmative action for blacks in the United States, based on the past discrimination theme, might look like this[10]: if there had been no discrimination against blacks during their time in America they would have been successful in proportion to their numbers. Affirmative action for blacks in America is thus justified now to the extent necessary to remedy any disproportionate lack of success for African Americans. Affirmative action is needed to compensate for past discrimination, though its use must be limited to the amount of preferential treatment for blacks that is required to give them their due.

We must stipulate that by 'no discrimination' we mean that we are imagining that Africans were immediately and completely accepted into American society when they first arrived in the settlements which now compose that country. Not only were they not enslaved, no discriminatory laws were passed restricting their social freedom or industry. They were also not in any way socially discriminated against, for example because they looked different. In those circumstances we would expect groups of that size to fare equally well on average unless we thought races were genetically different in some way that meant some would inevitably lag behind. Since that, genetic, explanation is racist and arguments about culture cannot explain why blacks would have a separate culture, absent discrimination, we are left with discrimination as the only plausible explanation of (race) group disadvantage.

---

10   The argument for affirmative action in the following paragraphs is essentially that of Ronald Fiscus in *The Constitutional Logic of Affirmative Action* (Duke University Press, Durham, 1992). See Nicholas Smith 'Affirmative Action under the New Constitution' (1995) 11 (1) *SAJHR* 84, 95–101, where the argument is summarised in terms similar to the following paragraphs.

The idea, then, is that if American society is 80 per cent white and 20 per cent black we should expect that blacks would receive 20 per cent of all jobs, promotions, university acceptances, professional appointments and so on. If whites have more than 80 per cent of these then they have more than their fair share. If some of their opportunities are redistributed until they only have 80 per cent they cannot be heard to complain that anything has been taken from them unfairly or that they have been discriminated against. Even whites who have not discriminated against blacks could not complain about the redistribution because they had no more right to the unequal distribution than one has a right to stolen property. And if some whites lose more than others that also does not matter, for the same reason. And, furthermore, one cannot attack affirmative action programmes on the ground that they do not take from the group of whites who can afford it most. Regardless of inequalities in the white community, if it has more than its 80 per cent it has more than the percentage to which it is entitled.

Conversely if whites in this hypothetical community are entitled to 80 per cent then they should not be made to do with less and affirmative action programmes that required this would be unjustified. A suggestion, therefore, that no whites should receive university acceptances at top universities for the next 15 years to make up for past discrimination, should be rejected. Acceptance of this motivation for affirmative action does not necessarily also mean endorsement of a rigid quota system. It might, for example, be counter-productive in the scenario outlined above to set aside 20 per cent of university places at the best universities for blacks. That might be so because the effects of discrimination might mean that not enough blacks have had adequate preparation for university life at that level.

I think this argument, or something like it, plays a central role in the case for affirmative action for African Americans. It has strong intuitive appeal but it clashes, as affirmative action does in general, with other widely held moral intuitions. Criticisms of the argument may be dealt with under three headings. It may first be doubted whether discrimination is the only possible cause of group disparities in a situation like our hypothetical. In other words the moral motivation for affirmative action may be questioned if we can show that the present disproportionate success of whites as compared to blacks in America is not necessarily the result of discrimination. The motivation for affirmative action, in terms of an argument based on past discrimination, would then lack a foundation. At the very least the question of how much redistribution is due would become difficult to answer.

Even if we agree that discrimination is an adequate explanation of black disadvantage today we may wonder whether affirmative action is the right solution. Part of that question is about exactly who should benefit from affirmative action and who should pay the cost. I will respond to that question after introducing another rationale for affirmative action – a forward looking rationale which focuses on disadvantage caused by the *present* circumstances of black people in America. The third aspect of evaluating affirmative action, whether in terms of its past discrimination or present discrimination rationales, is about its effectiveness, in the narrow sense. Whether one thinks affirmative action is a form of compensation, a way of dealing with present discrimination, or (I will consider this only briefly despite its prominent role in US affirmative action jurisprudence) a means to exploit the diversity of a nation in a way which benefits everyone, one still has to be convinced that it works. If all affirmative action ever achieved was to transfer opportunity from poor and lower middle class whites to middle class blacks its efficacy as a tool to achieve social justice would be difficult to demonstrate. If affirmative action can only do that, while its direct beneficiaries may suffer self doubt, while confirming white racist suspicions that blacks cannot make it on their own, then it is not justified. Good motivation is not enough to justify it.

The Effects of Past Discrimination

Turning to the first issue then, while few people would argue that discrimination is not *a* cause of black disadvantage in America some would argue there are other possible causes. It has been argued, for example, that because studies suggest both a strong link between IQ and life opportunities and a gap between black and white test scores, that there is at least one explanation for black disadvantage which does not need to rely solely on discrimination.[11] Basic equality should not be applied in a way that just ignores a particular factual inequality. We are committed to it despite real differences.

One can refuse to engage with this particular argument (or any argument which tries to show that the gap between black and white success in America is not entirely caused by discrimination) on the ground that it is offensive, even racist, and so not one to which it is worth responding. Few arguments could be less politically correct of course, as the strong response to the publication of *The Bell Curve*[12] in 1995 showed, than those which suggest a genetic link between IQ and race.[13] If there was no real possibility that the premises of anti-affirmative action arguments based on IQ scores were right it would be pointless to consider these arguments.

But believing that IQ exists and that there is evidence for the claim that there are at least some different results for different race or ethnic groups is not like believing something obviously absurd, such as that there never was any discrimination against blacks in America. The charge of racism (a clear rejection of basic equality) is too quick anyway because different group IQ scores do not establish that some groups are fundamentally different to others. We need to ask what causes the differences and we need to consider the significance of the

---

11   See, for example, Nicholas Capaldi *Out Of Order: Affirmative Action and the Crisis of Doctrinaire Liberalism* (Prometheus Books, New York, 1985) 131.

12   Richard J. Herrnstein and Charles Murray *The Bell Curve* (The Free Press, New York, 1994).

13   See, for example, Steven Fraser 'Introduction' in Steven Fraser (ed.) *The Bell Curve Wars* (Basic Books, New York, 1995) 1.

differences however they may be caused. It is not at all likely that the answers to these questions will shake our belief in basic equality but they are relevant to the justification of affirmative action.

There are 'mental tests', as they are referred to in the literature, and they do show clear group differences. Moreover, while not everyone thinks they are worth the paper they are printed on there is no plausible reason to think that everyone who takes IQ and other forms of mental testing seriously is racist or ethnocentric or obviously wrong. A full evaluation of the IQ argument (that the cause of different group scores is partly genetic and so some group disadvantage was no one's fault) can only be completed by the relevant experts over time. In the meantime there is serious doubt, shared by some who believe in the hardness of IQ science, that the argument is sound. The key premise, that ethnic, or racial, IQ differences are partly genetic, is doubted. But because, as Glenn Loury says,[14] no one is going to 'put the genie back in the bottle', we might as well survey the evidence briefly.

The concept of IQ has connotations of innateness and as Steven Pinker notes, there are many intellectuals who do deny that talent, and intelligence in particular, can be inborn, because they fear that this would lead to the characterising of some groups as inferior.[15] But there are a lot of different though interconnected issues here. First, there is the question of whether talk about IQ (and test scores for it and other sorts of cognitive tests such as university entrance tests or science competitions and so forth) is at all meaningful. Does it tell us something important about human potential and ability? If we answer that in the affirmative we then also have to ask what the cause of the apparent differences between *groups* in this regard is. Only then can we think about the relevance of what we know for the affirmative action debate.

It might seem difficult to deny that there is such a thing as intelligence. And that some people are more intelligent than others. Pinker notes, *ad hominem*:

> People who say that IQ is meaningless will quickly invoke it when the discussion turns to executing a murderer with an IQ of 64, removing lead paint that lowers a child's IQ by five points, or the presidential qualifications of George W. Bush.[16]

As a scientist he claims:

> In any case, there is now ample evidence that intelligence is a stable property of an individual, that it can be linked to features in the brain (including overall size, amount of gray matter in the frontal lobes, speed of neural conduction, and metabolism of cerebral glucose), that it is partly heritable among individuals,

---

14   Glenn C. Loury *The Anatomy of Racial Inequality* (Harvard University Press, Cambridge, 2002) 89.

15   Pinker *The Blank Slate*, above n. 1, 149.

16   Ibid. 150. It is one of life's little ironies that Bush's successor, Barack Obama, is criticised by some as being too intellectual.

and that it predicts some of the variation in life outcomes such as income and social status.[17]

It is, as he also says, again *ad hominem*, odd that academics would deny this because they are, as a class, obsessed with intelligence and are discussing it all the time in terms of student admissions and hiring decisions.[18]

It is clear that tests for intelligence, whatever their worth, do show not only individual but group differences as well, though the group differences are not permanent and the data about them is devilishly difficult to interpret. Group assessment of intelligence is not a purely modern preoccupation. In his world-wide survey of racial and cultural matters Thomas Sowell gives us an historical example and his interpretation of it:

> Cicero warned his fellow Romans not to buy British slaves, for he found them unusually difficult to teach. While some would consider such an assessment as mere evidence of bias or racism, there is no a priori reason to dismiss Cicero's first hand observations, on the strength of general presumptions among those 20 centuries removed from the facts. Indeed, much of what is known of the cultural and technological gulf between the tribal Britons of that era and the more advanced civilization existing on the continent of Europe would tend to support Cicero's conclusion of differences in mental performance, at that time. Whether these differences were genetic is another question entirely.[19]

The Britons have improved, though their fourteen year olds lag behind the Australians in science test scores.[20] (Since neither group, as a group, is currently disadvantaged, the nationals of these countries probably care much less about this, if they are aware of it, than they do about sports results.) Dr Sowell's large study shows clear ethnic/racial differences in a whole range of tests. In America it is (East) Asian American students who, for example, come out top in mathematics and they do that even when they come from poorer families than other students who sat the test.[21]

So while wealthier countries are faring better in IQ, science, maths and other such tests in general, the correlation of wealth and mental performance is not shown to be a causal relationship. Sowell also refers to studies of adults in India, the results of which showed differential ethnic group results and, as all the

---

17   Ibid.

18   Ibid.

19   Thomas Sowell *Race and Culture* (Basic Books, NewYork, 1994) 156–7.

20   Ibid. 158. Here, and in what follows, I am a little guilty of conflating discussion of IQ scores with other sorts of tests. IQ tests can be more 'culture-free' than maths or science tests. But the whole discussion is about cognitive, as opposed to (for example) athletic, ability.

21   Ibid. 159.

participants were illiterate, could not be explained away as the result of differential access to education. In fact the variations found were larger than the troublesome differences between blacks and whites in America, where there has of course been an inequality of educational opportunity.[22]

The differences are also not just overall differences. There are also group differences in particular areas, such as spatial conceptualising.[23] In his work on race and intelligence that I have been referring to, Sowell reports all sorts of group differences on the results of cognitive tests; both internationally and within countries. One of his main points is that the fact that there are different scores on cognitive tests for various groups in present day America is to be expected. Internationally and intra-nationally, throughout the whole history of such testing, such group differences are evident.

If IQ exists (as a reliable description of cognitive ability) and group IQ differences exist, and black American scores are lower, on these and other tests, than white American scores then the past discrimination argument for affirmative action for blacks in the United States might seem to be weakened. Particularly because the different results in these tests do not under predict success in higher education, in the case of American blacks.[24] And there is a black/white divide not only in terms of IQ scores but also in terms of more real world tests such as aptitude tests, and academic achievement. Sowell claims the latter also do not under predict black educational or job achievement.[25]

But the refutation of the past discrimination argument by this means depends, at least partly, on what causes low scores on cognitive tests. Most directly it is caused by ability of course. But is the lack of ability 'permanent'? The authors of *The Bell Curve*, Herrnstein and Murray, report that: controlling for socio-economic status, which is difficult, might reduce the black/white difference by a third;[26] the difference in black and white test scores is diminishing;[27] and it might, under the right conditions, disappear altogether at some stage.[28] Thomas Sowell also cites evidence that black scores are improving relative to those of whites.[29] The *Bell Curve* authors list and discuss various arguments for and against thinking that genetic differences might be involved in the explanation of the Black/White gap. They reach no conclusion themselves on whether the cause is

---

22   Ibid.

23   Ibid. 162. This does raise the question of whether intelligence is necessarily a single phenomenon. See Howard Gardener 'Cracking Open the IQ Box' in Steven Fraser (ed.) *The Bell Curve Wars*, above n. 13, 23.

24   Sowell *Race and Culture*, above n. 19, 173.

25   Ibid. But see Brian Barry *Culture and Equality* (Harvard University Press, Cambridge, 2001) 101 who cites studies which suggest a low correlation between black scores on cognitive tests and job performance.

26   Herrnstein and Murray *The Bell Curve*, above n. 12, 286.

27   Ibid. 289.

28   Ibid. 293.

29   Sowell *Race and Culture*, above n. 19, 168.

partly genetic although they read the data as 'tipping toward a mixture of genetic and environmental influences'.[30] According to Richard Nisbet, Herrnstein and Murray's conclusions underestimate the strength of the environmental thesis.[31] But despite the strength of feeling engendered by the publication of *The Bell Curve*, it is important to remember that even it is ultimately agnostic on this point.

Sowell, too, notes the evidence for environmental causes of group IQ scores. Studies of children born and raised in Germany whose mothers were German and whose fathers were part of the occupation forces after World War II showed no differences in IQ between the children whose American fathers were white and those who were black.[32] Other studies have shown that the IQ scores of immigrant groups in America have gone up over time, in the absence of much genetic change caused by inter-marrying.[33] Some studies suggest that women are less susceptible to environmental influences than men. If that is the case the predominance of high IQ black women compared to black men, which is not found in the case of black orphans raised by whites, also suggests an environmental explanation.[34]

There is also the so called 'Flynn effect' which refers to the fact, noted by James Flynn and others, that IQ scores are rising in general. In studied examples each generation of the same genetic stock has done better on some tests than the previous generation, which would suggest an environmental cause for group differences.[35] Sowell has argued that the authors of *The Bell Curve* do not take the Flynn effect seriously enough:

> While *The Bell Curve* cites the work of James R. Flynn, who found substantial increases in mental test performances from one generation to the next in a number of countries around the world, they seem not to acknowledge the devastating implications of that finding for the genetic theory of inter-group differences or for their own reiteration of long-standing claims that the higher fertility of low-IQ groups implies a declining national IQ.[36]

If there was good evidence that the black/white test scores were genetically caused you would expect an evolutionary psychologist like Steven Pinker to know about it. He, however, is content to rely on Sowell's findings that ethnic

---

30   Herrnstein and Murray *The Bell Curve*, above n. 12, 131.

31   Richard Nisbet, 'Race, IQ and Scientism' in Steven Fraser (ed.) *The Bell Curve Wars*, above n. 13, 36, 48–53. See also 'Curveball' by Stephen Jay Gould in Steven Fraser (ed.) *The Bell Curve Wars*, above n. 13, 11, for a scholarly attack on the idea that IQ tests measure our 'intelligence', and their relevance for social policy.

32   Sowell *Race and Culture*, above n. 19, 170.

33   Ibid. 170–71.

34   Ibid. 170.

35   Thomas Sowell 'Ethnicity and IQ' in Steven Fraser (ed.) *The Bell Curve Wars*, above n. 13, 70.

36   Ibid. 74.

group differences in IQ have been common throughout the twentieth century, with groups not in the cultural mainstream, for whatever reason, often having scores lower than the population average. These included immigrant European groups who in some cases scored below the average to the same extent as blacks have done, as a group, in recent times. Though Pinker notes the gap disappeared after a few generations he argues that, as the experience of black people under slavery and segregation is not comparable with other immigrant groups' assimilation into mainstream society, 'their transition to mainstream cultural patterns could easily take longer'.[37] Given our history of assenting to invalid arguments about racial differences it would appear wise to ask that any suggestion of inheritable socially significant differences be comprehensively established.

So critics of the past discrimination argument for affirmative action do not have a good case based on permanent group differences in cognitive ability. Everyone agrees that environmental factors play a role in IQ scores, and it is not proven that these factors alone cannot explain group differences in these and other tests. But the critics of the past discrimination argument do not have to rely on genetics. If the difference in black/white scores is entirely the result of environmental causes, and we have reason enough to think it is, it still has to be shown that black disadvantage was entirely caused by discrimination against blacks after their arrival in America, rather than by other social causes.

This is the basis for the most common mode of objection that affirmative action for recent immigrants to America cannot be justified. They obviously were not enslaved or discriminated against, in America, so how can affirmative action for them be based on the past discrimination rationale?[38] For black people who are descendants of those who suffered slavery and discrimination the critic would seem to have to find environmental factors that predate arrival in America. This may seem fanciful to us. But Thomas Sowell says that is because we have not read the history of race and culture.

Cultural Destiny

In his book *Race and Culture* Sowell tracks the persistence of various characteristics of ethnic/racial groups in various historical contexts and different places.[39] The first chapter of this book provides many examples of this. The generalisations found there are not the unsubtle caricatures of ethnocentric thought. He does not talk about ethnic groups in broad undifferentiated terms. He notes that the differences between subgroups are often as large as differences between larger groupings.[40] He tells us, for example:

---

37 Pinker *The Blank Slate*, above n. 1, 144.
38 See Terry Eastland *Ending Affirmative Action* (Basic Books, New York, 1996) Ch. 7.
39 Sowell *Race and Culture*, above n. 19, Ch. 1.
40 Ibid. 3.

> People of Scottish ancestry have long been among the more prosperous groups
> in the United States, but people of the same ancestry in the Appalachian region
> have also constituted one of the most enduring pockets of poverty among white
> Americans.[41]

The reason he advances for this variance in Scottish immigrant success is an
application of Sowell's core thesis in *Race and Culture*:

> As long as our view is confined to American society, it is plausible to believe
> that 'objective conditions' in Appalachia, or the way people were 'treated' there,
> accounts for the anomaly. Indeed, prevailing social doctrines all but require that
> approach.[42]

The 'prevailing social doctrines' he refers to are the set of ideas which suggest
we are entirely the creatures of our present and recent environments. This theory
claims that as long as group A has been in society X for a reasonable amount
of time any relative disadvantage of group A in society X must be a result of
relative deprivation and discrimination suffered, and not remedied, by group A
in society X.

Perhaps no one believes that in such stark terms but it is a familiar idea and it
often plays a role in the past discrimination argument for affirmative action. That
argument seems weakened if the disadvantaged group is already disadvantaged
compared to other groups already in the society, when it first enters that society.
According to Sowell the fortunes of the Scottish group that is not doing well need
not have been produced by the effects of discrimination against them in America
because: 'if the history of the Scots is viewed internationally, then it becomes clear
that the subgroup which settled in Appalachia differed culturally from other Scots
before either boarded the ships to cross the Atlantic'.[43]

Detailing the uniform successes in various fields of various groups or
subgroups in vastly different circumstances, Sowell argues that it is not plausible
to think that the fate of these groups depended on the circumstances in which
they found themselves. In Russia the Russians might explain away the farming
prowess of the Germans in terms of special favours granted by the government to
German immigrants. But when German farmers are also remarkably successful in
Australia, Mexico, Brazil, Honduras, the United States, Chile and Paraguay then it
is more difficult to argue that the success is not the product of cultural traits which
persist over much time and in many different environments.[44]

It is not true, Sowell argues, that societies simply assign roles to various groups
which they in turn are obliged to accept. One can, contrary to this idea, attribute a

---

41   Ibid.
42   Ibid.
43   Ibid. 3.
44   Ibid. 11.

group's position to its own cultural characteristics. One may think this is simply resorting to prejudiced stereotypes. But how else, he asks, can one explain that in Argentina, Australia, the United States, Poland, Jamaica, Brazil, England, Curacao and Russia (amongst even more countries) Jews predominantly filled the role of middleman minority.[45] There are and have been other middleman minorities of course and Sowell argues they share the cultural traits that make them succeed, and persist in them across a wide range of environments.

What makes people do well? What is a successful culture, or how does an unsuccessful culture become successful. Sowell argues that, for one thing, a culture that is lagging behind will do a better job at catching up if it is receptive to new learning. He discusses the fate of some which were not. By comparison he mentions the Japanese who have more than once learned from others and then overtaken them.[46] Education by itself has not proved to be the panacea social reformers have thought it to be, because people might be culturally inclined to think of it as an escape from the difficult and sometimes indelicate tasks which must be undertaken in a modern economy.[47] He describes cultural change or acquisition but more in terms of how it happened in fact rather than how to make it happen. This is, I suppose, because Sowell is against 'social engineering' in general. The thing he stresses most, in any event, is that people need to acquire the right 'cultural capital'.[48] A reticence about requiring such capital can hold people back, as can an unwarranted pride in and commitment to outmoded ways.

What does all this strident modernism have to do with blacks in America at the beginning of the twenty-first century? Sowell's reminder that it is not the case that our fate is entirely sealed by our present and recent experience is something to note; but slavery and discriminatory legislation were real in America. His own data can be used as a partial critique of his rejection of the past discrimination argument. I am not convinced that what he says about deficits in cultural capital and the persistence of cultural traits explains the present plight of black America.

African Americans, as a group, are better off than black South Africans. The different present condition of blacks in South Africa and blacks in America results mostly from the relative longevity of racial oppression in South Africa.[49] Sowell tells us the gradual ending of state enforced discrimination in the United States coincided with, in the 20 years preceding the introduction of the Civil Rights Act of 1964, a two-fold increase in the number of black Americans attending college. This was accompanied by an increase in the number of black professionals and occupational improvement for blacks generally.[50] But if taking away most

---

45   Ibid. 11–12.

46   Ibid. 18–22.

47   Ibid. 22–8.

48   Thomas Sowell *Conquests and Cultures* (Basic Books, New York, 1998) 334.

49   Sowell *Race and Culture*, above n. 19, 99. Apartheid was just starting in earnest when state sanctioned discrimination in the United States was coming to an end.

50   Sowell *Affirmative Action Around the World*, above 4, 20.

of the discrimination makes things get better that would seem to suggest it was discrimination, not some aspect of group culture, which was holding people back. That improvement of average African American prospects might be evidence supporting an argument that affirmative action is not necessary, but not one which suggests that discrimination is not the key causal factor to historical black American disadvantage.

Moreover black slaves were very clearly consigned, in America, to certain roles. That must have had some effect on their 'culture'. And the New World slave owner practice, described in another of Sowell's books, of separating black slaves from their fellow tribe members meant that it would be more difficult for them to perpetuate cultural practices than it would be for voluntary immigrants.[51] As he says, about black slaves brought to the Western Hemisphere to work in plantations as unskilled field hands:

> They entered Western civilisation at the bottom, acquiring only the rudiments of that culture, such as the spoken language and familiarity with the simplest technology. To varying degrees they lost the culture they brought over from Africa, without acquiring the full range of European culture.[52]

And because the African population in the US increased naturally it did not need, in terms of the requirements of the slave owners, to be replenished by new arrivals. This also meant that traditional African culture disappeared at a faster rate than, for example, in Brazil where African languages were still being spoken at the end of the eighteenth century.[53] This would all seem to lead to the conclusion, about cultural influences on black achievement in America, reached by Glenn Loury:

> Some conservative writers attribute black American disadvantage entirely or in part to purported patterns of 'social pathology' said to be characteristic of 'black culture'. Yet even were that to be so – and the point is eminently arguable – such 'pathology' could not be rightly understood as an alien cultural blemish imposed on an otherwise pristine Euro-American canvas. Rather, it could only be seen as a domestic product, made over the generations wholly in the good old USA, for which the entire nation bears a responsibility. Clearly, this would not be the case – at least, not to the same degree – were there to be found any comparable, adverse cultural patterns among (say) Dominican or Korean immigrants. [54]

The unhelpful culture that is part of the way of life in impoverished black ghettos is of course the culture of those people, and they are, in a sense, responsible for it. The fact that it was 'made in America' does not absolve those who live it from all

---

51 Sowell *Conquests and Cultures*, above n. 48, 158–9.
52 Ibid.
53 Ibid.
54 Loury *The Anatomy of Racial Inequality*, above n. 14, 12.

responsibility for it. But that culture, like all culture in that sense of the word, is a response to challenges posed by the broader society. It is bad sociology to think it sprung from nowhere or was hiding in some African collective unconsciousness.

Sowell's evidence can thus be interpreted to support a conclusion he would not accept. The forces that caused black disadvantage in America are all American. But he does not accept the first part of the past-discrimination argument – that absent discrimination blacks would now be on a par with whites. In *Affirmative Action Around the World* he addresses this issue in his chapter on the United States.[55] His analysis of this point is scattered throughout his thoughts on whether affirmative action works, whether it is actually beneficial for blacks. He has other (free market) fish to fry and he punctuates his treatment of the past discrimination argument with his other main argument about affirmative action – that it harms African Americans. He does not say much about the black culture that could have held black Americans back even if they had not been discriminated against.

Sowell also argues that we cannot say discrimination has been the only cause of black disadvantage because, for one thing, in other countries where there was less racial oppression of blacks they were less well off than blacks in America according to comparisons made at various times. This was because, Sowell explains, they were relatively recent arrivals in those countries, and so relatively less acculturated.[56] But group disparities can have different causes. Discrimination can be *the* cause in one situation without it being the only cause in every situation. In any event the group disparities in the other situations he is talking about, other Western Hemisphere destinations for black slaves, still have to be explained. Might we not say the 'racial oppression' there is, as it was in the United States to begin with, forcing Africans to be there in the first place and not equipping them with whatever they needed to live there, as equals.

The past discrimination argument, in America, is of course one about domestic justice in America. It cannot be weakened by asking whether things would have been better for them if African Americans had stayed in Africa.[57] The argument is about the proper response to what took place in America seeing they did end up there in the way that they did – as slaves. We do know that all other things being equal immigrant groups would have come to America with different sets of skills and types of historical achievements and strategies for dealing with life's difficulties. And that would give us reason to think that even if they had been treated equally they might have fared differently. But blacks in America had their culture disrupted and interrupted and were then forced to fit into the slave owner's culture at a pace determined by their masters. It is hard to deny responsibility when you have assumed that level of control.

---

55   Sowell *Affirmative Action Around the World*, above n. 4, Ch. 6. This book is a fascinating study of the ubiquity of this kind of preferential policy.

56   Sowell *Conquests and Cultures*, above n. 48, 168.

57   See Andrew Valls 'The Libertarian Case for Affirmative Action' (1999) 25 (2) *Social Theory and Practice* 299, 309.

Groups that have been allowed to maintain much more cultural continuity, whatever other injustices and indignities they have suffered in America, have not had comparable experiences in that respect. It is not enough to say: 'well, look at the P's, they have suffered more throughout history than the Q's and yet they have done better'. Even more context is required than the copious detail Sowell provides. Even if the different fates of white and other (not black) groups was not determined only by what happened to them in America it remains true that their experience in America was very different from the black experience. And it can quite plausibly be argued that the history which did happen made it far more difficult for blacks to succeed.[58]

Sowell does offer a sympathetic analysis of why sub-Saharan Africa has lagged behind in general. He explains this in terms of isolation, mainly. The lack of navigable waterways, a dearth of natural harbours and shallow coastal waters together with long distances between the hinterland and coastal areas all made maritime trade difficult, thus also diminishing the opportunities for cultural exchange.[59] Sowell lists many other geographical challenges the continent presents to its inhabitants and discusses how these worked together to impede development in this region:

> Like other places relatively isolated from broader cultural developments – the Scottish highlands, parts of the Balkans, or the South Sea islands, for example – much of sub-Saharan Africa tended to lag behind the technological, organizational, and economic progress in other parts of the world. [60]

And while these geographical factors affected relatively small areas in Europe or Asia or other parts of the world, their effects in Africa were widespread and constrained many peoples.[61]

The cultural responses people make to live with these sorts of difficulties might not be helpful in different contexts but if any of this disadvantage is supposed to have survived the American experience of American blacks that fact would need to be explained. Sowell says, approvingly, that the Japanese first imitated the West and then competed on equal terms with them but that is precisely what African Americans were not allowed to do. Past discrimination will not have determined every aspect of black American destiny of course, but it might at least explain a great deal of the present.

We cannot say, by comparison, that justice would have required affirmative action for disadvantaged groups on their voluntary arrival in America to make up for deficits caused by prior events. At least that cannot be, as it cannot now be

---

58   See Gertrude Ezorsky *Racism and Justice* (Cornell University Press, New York, 1991) 57–60.

59   Sowell *Conquests and Cultures*, above n. 48, 101–9.

60   Ibid. 107.

61   Ibid.

for recent arrivals, justified by application of the past discrimination argument. This is because the past discrimination argument is about unfair treatment people have received in the United States at the hands of other Americans. If the Africans who were enslaved had come voluntarily, as immigrants, with cultural traits that adversely affected their success in America, the past discrimination argument would not be available to them; but they did not come voluntarily. The plausibility of the initial motivation for affirmative action, for black Americans, seems intact. The discrimination of the past was a breach of basic equality. It seems reasonable to think our commitment to basic equality requires us to do something about that discrimination. But — here is the next hurdle for the past discrimination argument — we cannot be sure what would have happened without slavery and Jim Crow laws, so we cannot presume to know how to put African Americans in the position they would have been in absent discrimination.

Counterfactual Puzzles

Sowell is concerned about the certainty of some, that all would be well absent discrimination. In terms of income, he thinks that:

> It cannot simply be assumed that blacks would have had the same incomes as whites in the absence of racial discrimination, given that various groups of American whites have had very different incomes from one another at various periods of history.[62]

That point is worth careful consideration, as it illustrates a more general point: it is always difficult to work out what would have happened if the particular injustices of the past had never been committed.[63]

Perhaps the best way to make a past discrimination argument is not by asking precisely how things might have been. Can we not simply say that absent any sort of discrimination against blacks by whites their position would at least be much better today? And that that is enough to at least justify *some compensation*? The counterfactual past discrimination argument requires that all of the difference between the success of white and black America be explained by discrimination. Perhaps that is a tall order. But the experience of slavery and discrimination would harm any group of people even if only while they were being oppressed. While we cannot be sure that the effects of discrimination would be the same on any group that is partly because the circumstances of discrimination always differ to some extent.

It should be noted that the fact that the experience of other groups (not blacks) was different in America does not mean that they should be excluded from any assessment of past injustices. Particularly they should not be if these assessments

---

62   Ibid. 118.
63   See Jeremy Waldron 'Superseding Historic Injustice' (1992) 103 *Ethics* 4.

are intended as part of a project designed to bring about a distribution that would have prevailed had the injustices of the past (all of them) not taken place. As Jeremy Waldron has argued, in an argument dealing with the specific injustice of land dispossession, the legitimacy of this type of counterfactual exercise is weakened if, in undertaking it, we do not attempt to achieve what backward looking justice requires *in general*.[64]

That would require us to assess the effects of all prior injustice in America. I have argued that blacks are not to be blamed for their relatively bleak group situation simply because other groups have had their own hardships and some have survived them better. If blacks had had another group's history their fate might have been more like the fate of that group. The fate they did embody was that of slavery and discrimination and it is not morally implausible to ask that something be done about that, something more than just bringing discrimination to an end. But that does not mean the position of other groups should not be considered. If we tried, working from some general theory of justice, to put all racial/ethnic groups in the position they would have been in now if things had been just that, would mean some adjustment amongst non-black groups as well. That is not fatal to the past discrimination argument. It simply means it must be applied to everyone. But that does make it extremely complicated.

Extending the principle to all groups raises at least one awkward question too. People got to where they are now as the result of all sorts of factors. This, you will remember, is one of Thomas Sowell's main themes. All sorts of injustices, heroic effort, inaction and plain circumstance like physical environment, brought us to our present situations. It would be very difficult to work out where every group in America would be if it had been treated perfectly since it, or its members over the years, arrived in America. And even if we could it is not clear that all groups other than blacks would be equally well off now because their pre-American histories would differ. If that is right I am not even sure how to ask where blacks should be relative to the rest. Should they share the average fortune of other groups perhaps?

Because discrimination based on race is perhaps, with sex discrimination, the clearest breach of basic equality and because basic equality is such an important value in modern political philosophy we feel motivated to think about how we can make up for past racist discrimination. This worthy motivation, however, should not make us overlook the difficulties of achieving this in more than a token way. Apart from the fact that we cannot be sure where everyone would have ended up if there had been no discrimination, the situation of our present inequality is in some ways not advisably alterable. We should not, for example, artificially change the prison population in America now just because we know that blacks are overrepresented in the prisons and that that is largely the result of circumstances that many blacks are unjustly born into.

There is, in any event, something odd about focussing on the past in our efforts to do justice now. We see this, for example, when we ask the question: what

---

64   Ibid. 12–13.

should we do about the discrimination suffered by some groups in the past who, for various reasons which need not lead us to think they are somehow superior to black people, have, as a group, done well despite that history? (By 'done well' I mean they are not unfavourably disproportionately represented in the good and bad things in life that most of us care about.) Should we compensate those groups anyway? If we think we should then we seem to be thinking about historical group injustice in terms of a model of justice which makes more intuitive sense when dealing with recent injustices against individuals.

We think it is important to restore John's car, which was stolen last year, to him even if he does not need it because he has a new one (or two other cars). Sometimes this model of justice seems to be implicit in past discrimination arguments justifying affirmative action. The level of prosperity and success we think the victims of discrimination would have enjoyed if they had not been unjustly dealt with is something that was *stolen* from them, and it should, accordingly, be given back. We do give John his recovered car back, regardless of whether he needs it, because justice demands that but that idea of justice has a consequential aspect which should not be overlooked. If we do not restore John's car to him simply because he does not need it we, at the very least, encourage theft from anyone who has anything more than she needs. What is the counterpart of the moral hazard in the case of historical group injustice? We might say: 'If we do not compensate for historical discrimination then, if people discriminate now and get away with it justice might never be done'. But that problem is partly solved by making sure they do not get away with it now. And it, the problem of the unpunished wrongdoer, applies to all wrongdoing anyway.

There is another reason for restoring John's car to him of course. It is *his* car and we believe in property rights in one form or another. Should we not compensate groups who were discriminated against in the past regardless of whether they are relatively deprived now? They had a right not to be discriminated against just as John had a right not to be involuntarily dispossessed of his car. The idea seems counterintuitive though. Perhaps most importantly because we live in a world where other things seem more pressing than the need to compensate groups that are not relatively deprived.[65]

Perhaps the problem is larger still. We might think that absent discrimination we would all be, as groups, at the same level now. There are, however, groups that have done better, for some complicated reason again not attributable to original superiority, in the face of discrimination, than they would have done if they had been spared the injustice. Should they now be taken down a peg or two? Our intuition is probably that groups that have been discriminated against but that

---

65   See Waldron 'Superseding Historic Injustice', above n. 63, generally, for a discussion of the problems that arise when we try to transfer our intuitions about contemporary injustices to the case of historical wrongs. My comments here are inspired by his remarkable contribution, which I hope I have more or less understood, to this kind of problem in general.

have done well nevertheless would be awkward recipients of affirmative action and we would be particularly hard pressed to think of a plausible justification for *restraining* their development now.

The past discrimination argument, which seems to survive arguments to the effect that past discrimination does not at least partly explain the present condition of some groups does run into these counterfactual puzzles. It also has difficulty explaining exactly which individuals should benefit from affirmative action and who should suffer the disbenefit. I will return to those questions after introducing another type of argument – the forward looking argument premised on the fact of present discrimination and segregation. I will now consider that argument for affirmative action (for African Americans) and the question of its fairness to those directly affected by it. I will then turn to the issue of whether, even if it is otherwise justifiable in principle, affirmative action is an effective tool.

The Forward Looking (Present Discrimination) Argument

Although a lot of the plain prejudice inspired behaviour of the past may really be a thing of the past in America, its effects linger in different ways. Blacks might need resources and opportunities they do not have to help them catch up but their catching up might also be impeded in another way. They might be facing a new set of problems. Their very (group) disadvantage might now be counted against them when they look for work, or investment opportunities, or accommodation, or a quiet life free from harassment. Whether the profiling they are subjected to by the police, employers, landlords or bankers is 'rational' or bigoted, its effect is the same as plain old-fashioned discrimination.[66]

Elisabeth Anderson, in her defence of forward looking affirmative action, cites statistics to show that there is much, in some cases increasing, *de facto* racial segregation in the United States. This segregation is residential, educational and, to a lesser but significant extent, occupational.[67] In terms of occupational segregation she cites studies which also show segregation within firms: 'One survey of jobs found that half of all job titles were occupied by whites only, and one-quarter of blacks worked in jobs to which only blacks were assigned'.[68] Anderson argues that this *de facto* segregation results in inequality of opportunity for blacks.

---

66   See Richard Thompson Ford *The Race Card* (Farrar, Straus and Giroux, New York, 2008) for a thoughtful discussion of the decline, and persistence, of the old-fashioned type of bigoted discrimination.

67   Elisabeth S. Anderson 'Integration, Affirmative Action, and Strict Scrutiny' (2002) 77 *N Y U L Rev* 1195, 1199–204. See also Ezorsky *Racism and Justice*, above n. 58, 14–18.

68   Anderson 'Integration, Affirmative Action, and Strict Scrutiny', above n. 67, 1200.

De facto segregation means lack of access to social networks. Because many job opportunities are communicated by word of mouth and many whites who hear about them do not know many blacks, at work or in their neighbourhoods, many blacks will not get to hear about such opportunities.[69] Job growth has also not been taking place in the areas that blacks mostly live in. It therefore costs blacks significantly more to get to work. Residential segregation also leads to unfavourable property values in predominantly black areas which leads to reduced opportunities for capital growth and access to credit – which in turn leads to fewer business opportunities.[70] Professional services are also harder to come by in segregated economically deprived areas as professionals are less likely to set up shop there.[71] Access to services is thus affected by this segregation and the conditions for fair competition generally are not in place.

Racial segregation, Anderson argues, does not only cause inequality of economic opportunity. It also harms democracy as the discussion about and reflection on our various interests does not go well in segregated societies and segregation encourages discriminatory policing by emphasising the idea that people have, according to skin colour, a place where they should be and should not be.[72]

Might affirmative action not be a good response to this present 'institutional discrimination'? The discrimination caused by the 'racial stigma', as Glenn Loury calls it, that blacks have to live with. They have to live with it because people generalise about them on the basis of their group's disproportionate representation amongst, for example, the ranks of the imprisoned and the impecunious.[73] A group response to deprivation might be justified, not as an act of compensation for past discrimination then, but as an antidote for present structural discrimination.

James Flynn also argues that the disadvantage of being black in America now will persist until group differences change. He focuses mainly on the issue of racial profiling, not just by the police, but generally, and states the matter plainly: 'No one expects police to search white matrons in suburban neighbourhoods for drugs as they do young black males'.[74] Flynn recognises that some whites may unreflectively think that being black in America is, because of measures already taken to compensate them, to be privileged.[75] He suggests a thought experiment that should show this to be at least counterintuitive. Assuming that parents want the best for their children, how many whites would, he asks, in the event of their death, want their children to be adopted by black parents. He allows, for the

---

69   Ibid. 1202.

70   Ibid. 1203.

71   Ibid. 1204.

72   Ibid. 1205–6.

73   Loury *The Anatomy of Racial Inequality*, above n. 14, Ch. 3.

74   James R. Flynn 'Group Differences: Is the Good Society Possible?' (1996) 28 *Journal of Biosocial Science* 573, 577.

75   Ibid. 578. See also Thompson *The Race Card*, above n. 66 Ch. 3 and 4.

purposes of the experiment, that their children could magically change skin colour so they would not experience any alienation due to their appearance. If few white parents would choose the black adoption option then most do not really believe that blacks in America are not currently disadvantaged.[76]

The argument then is that affirmative action is justified as a countermeasure, to set off, in part, the effects of *ongoing* barriers to black advancement. If there are present obstacles to black advancement and these operate to bring about the same effect as plain prejudice – because they mean that blacks are negatively profiled on the basis of social statistics about their average fortunes – then affirmative action can be used to redress this situation. It can be used to achieve 'integration' in Anderson's terms or, in Loury's terms again, to overcome the 'stigma' of being black.

Why exactly should we be concerned about the racial profiling of blacks today in America, if it is not produced by the behaviour of prejudiced individuals? Apart from the wrong of discrimination against individuals on the basis of group characteristics, I think the fact that the profiling was caused indirectly by a failure to treat members of those groups, previously, as equals might be part of our reason for being concerned about it. The past is not irrelevant here, as it will not be in matters of discrimination based on sex. The past discrimination helps to distinguish such a group from one which has chosen its present fate in a way that blacks could not. A religious sect that diminished its secular material prospects over generations for theological reasons, for example, would not have the same sort of claim to preferential treatment now.

But this forward looking approach, based on present structural difficulties, spawned by an oppressive past, though it does not ignore history, does not try to create a hypothetical present which we would be living in if the past had been morally better. It tries to respond to an existing condition which is harmful to blacks, to individual persons, now. The future oriented justification for affirmative action also offers an answer to another large question that often exercises the minds of the opponents of affirmative action. Why, in any event, are we concerned about justice for groups rather than individuals?

One might not be convinced by the rejection of the idea that we are, after all, individuals. It might be conceded that we are inextricably (but not unalterably) culturally situated in one context or another. But we might nevertheless insist that there are, fundamentally, less well off *people* rather than groups. In this vein one might ask why we should worry about how many blacks are poor rather than just about how many poor people (or well off people, doctors, lawyers etc.), *per se*, there are. It is often pointed out that having affirmative action programmes in university selection in America on the basis of poverty would not help as many blacks as affirmative action based on race. But if there are enough poor white people to make that true does this not show that race is not the issue? If our commitment to basic equality means we should be worried about equality of welfare, or at least about extreme, undeserved inequality of welfare, surely we

---

76   Ibid.

would not be happy just as long as there were equal numbers of white and black poor. Would that really be a more just society?

Racism is an important injustice of course but these critics are not necessarily ignoring that: they would presumably not be happy if every white person was adequately well off and every black person was not, due to discrimination against them. But critics of affirmative action might wonder whether poverty or ignorance, or deprivation of any sort even is the primary concern of the supporters of preferential policies. Perhaps they are, these detractors might think, simply concerned with proportionality *per se*.

Supporters of affirmative action might like to think that critics of preferential policies are all right wing free market fundamentalists whose commitment to the 'individual' is simplistic because the individuals whose freedom they want to protect are too isolated from each other. It might seem that critics of group rights are concerned about subjects that are too rational and independent to be the real world individuals who are dependent on each other and their social circumstances in a myriad of ways. Some detractors of affirmative action may err in that way. But affirmative action can itself be seen as the product of an uncritical acceptance of the economic status quo. Supporters of affirmative action can seem to hold the view that the poor deserve their lot unless it is the result of racist or sexist discrimination. All will be well if the socio-economic classes, from extremely poor to very rich, are populated proportionately by all the groups which are currently the focus of the supporters of preferential policies.

There may be truth, in terms of the motives of some unscrupulous or unthinking individuals, behind these latter suspicions – any good idea or tool can, after all, be misused. But it is not necessary to think that group equality is an end in itself in order to support group conscious policies as a way of dealing with *present* discrimination. This is true whether that discrimination is prejudiced or 'rational', because it is *individuals* who are being discriminated against when people are dealt with harshly according to correct or incorrect beliefs about one of the groups to which they belong. The motivation for forward looking affirmative action for blacks in America does not rely on vague notions of uniform group destiny. There is, here, no attempt to create a world that might have been as if that were an end in itself; and no quest to achieve group proportionality for its own sake. This last point distinguishes the forward looking argument for affirmative action from one based on the supposed inherent value of *diversity*. A digression is warranted.

The Diversity Rationale

In terms of higher education, one would expect some diversity of views and experiences amongst those who would gain access to elite institutions. If there is not enough, one reason might be that the successful applicants are mostly from the same race/socio-economic group. That would not mean they would all think the same of course. Certainly not in America – home to as many world views as any country — although a broadly capitalist, modernist view would be the dominant one. It would be very patronising and plainly wrong to think that any group of a hundred white Harvard law school students would all have the same views on important matters. And while most of the students who attend university in California may be Californians they will also not be intellectual clones.

It is also trite to say that most of the learning that takes place at university is by means of reading books and discussing the contents of those works rather than just by meeting new people and sharing their existing ideas: if that were not the case parents would expect their children to emerge from holiday camps in a more erudite condition than when they entered them. It is also true that, as Elisabeth Anderson puts it:

> If the true educational interest is to ensure that a diversity of opinions be heard
> in the classroom, schools should select students directly for the ideological
> diversity they can be expected to bring to the classroom, rather than use race as
> a crude proxy for this.[77]

Viewing diversity as a self-standing reason to practise affirmative action makes one ask, she says, why race is more important than, say, blood type.[78]

It is true, though, that even if students of other races will not necessarily have different ideas about the origins of the universe or the nature of democracy, they might have some quite different experiences to share and different perspectives on how well American democracy is treating its citizens. Middle class blacks are also amongst the victims of racial profiling: they may not share the poverty of people who live in largely black ghettos but they do look like them. The point of wanting racially mixed classes is perhaps not so much about enriching education with a wide range of 'views' – that is what books are for – but about representation of an oppressed class that needs a voice. The voice is needed to express the interests of an oppressed group, not to make the experience of white students a more exotic one. As Anderson, who makes this point, stresses, however, one black student can achieve the latter purpose, in the same way one jazz player can.[79]

Diversity on its own will not justify substantial affirmative action. Proportionality exercises will look like middle class musical chairs if they are not explained as a means of achieving justice, at least in the long run, for those who most need it. It is hard to imagine how affirmative action could be consistent with basic equality if it required people to lose opportunities because of their membership of a racial group if the only benefit to others was the chance of a more interesting environment in which to study or work. A far better reason for having a substantial number of black students in elite institutions is that some could benefit from the networking opportunities that scholarly comradeship has always provided in the white community.

---

77 Anderson 'Integration, Affirmative Action, and Strict Scrutiny', above n. 67, 1221, citing O'Connor J.'s dissent in *Metro Broad., Inc.* v *FCC* 497 US 547, 621 (1990).

78 Anderson 'Integration, Affirmative Action, and Strict Scrutiny', above n. 67, 1222.

79 Ibid. 1222.

Thus distinguished from other current rationales for affirmative action for African Americans the forward looking argument looks promising. It must, however, like all forms of affirmative action, also survive interrogation about its fairness and its effectiveness. Whether we want to employ affirmative action as a remedy for past discrimination or as a means to ameliorate present discrimination we have to ask: does employing affirmative action take into account the interests and concerns of those affected by it, and does it work? I will tackle those questions, in that order, shortly. But first I want to briefly address another question the forward looking argument raises. Is there not already a remedy for present discrimination?

Why is the Prohibition of Discrimination not Enough?

If the fact, in the case of the forward looking motivation for affirmative action, of present discrimination is the problem, why is ordinary anti-discrimination law not sufficient to deal with it? That law need not only be directed at 'irrational' discrimination; it can also be used to prohibit discrimination based on statistical profiling (unless that could, in certain circumstances, be justified as reasonable differentiation on the grounds that it benefited everyone, including blacks).[80] It seems like a vote of no confidence in ordinary anti–discrimination law to say that we need affirmative action to deal with *present* discrimination. It might be argued, though, that anti-discrimination law that focuses on discrete acts of discrimination by employers or service providers might not prevent the wider harm caused by an act of discrimination.

Anderson suggests that the knock-on effects of discrimination are particularly prevalent in the case of American blacks because their segregated situation means that when one person is discriminated against, the effects of that discrimination spread to other members of the community and are long lasting:

> If a firm denies one's neighbor a job due to discrimination, one loses a potential role model, a source of information about job openings at the firm, and a connection who could provide a credible job reference to the firm's owner. This loss is negligible for one who has plenty of other neighbors with connections to mainstream opportunities. But if segregation means one's social network is limited to mostly disadvantaged people like one's neighbor, their disadvantages become one's own. Once these disadvantages become shared, one's community becomes a site of concentrated and self reinforcing disadvantage, perpetuating the effects of discrimination over time.[81]

---

80   For an interesting attempt to justify racial profiling by the police in America see Mathias Risse and Richard Zeckhauser 'Racial Profiling' (2004) 32 (2) *Philosophy and Public Affairs* 131.

81   Anderson 'Integration, Affirmative Action, and Strict Scrutiny', above n. 67, 1207. Anderson is not comparing, in this article, ordinary anti-discrimination law's ability to

If this is true, though, is it the case that only affirmative action, and not ordinary discrimination law, can solve the problem? It does suggest the solution to the problem of present discrimination against blacks should be one that responds to the wider effects of discrimination. But note that this is not because ordinary discrimination law, which prohibits A from discriminating against B in situation X, cannot, at least in theory, deal with the problem. If we think only affirmative action can remedy the discrimination blacks now face in America then we must be assuming that plain discrimination law does not work. If it was working, the neighbour in Anderson's example just cited would have had a remedy and most firms would not discriminate for fear of the consequences. The 'site of concentrated and self reinforcing disadvantage' would not exist.[82]

So the present discrimination argument implies that ordinary discrimination law does not solve the problem of current discrimination. But the proponents of the present discrimination argument would not advocate its repeal, as detractors of all equality legislation, like Thomas Sowell and Richard Epstein, would.[83] They, the supporters of forward looking affirmative action, seem to think of affirmative action as an *additional* weapon in the fight against present discrimination, one which is needed to deal with the effects of discrete acts of discrimination to which the ordinary law fails to respond. If that is how they see things it does not follow that they should seek the repeal of ordinary anti-discrimination law, although their scepticism about it may give succour to those who would repeal it. Assuming though, as seems reasonable, that ordinary discrimination law, like most other laws, will not prevent all the mischief it was aimed at, it is not unreasonable to think about measures that may help to fill the gaps. Most obviously because discrimination law is not applicable to events that did not take place. If A never gets to know about job opportunities that are informally announced he cannot sue. The next hurdle facing the present discrimination argument is the question of its fairness in relation to those affected by preferential policies.

Does Affirmative Action Treat Affected Individuals Fairly?

How is affirmative action supposed to play the supporting role, to fill the gaps left by the uneven application and success of discrimination law? And how, in doing this, does it serve basic equality? The law which forbids discrete acts of discrimination requires the state, in all contexts, and private moral agents in some contexts, to treat people as equals. Acts of discrimination deny basic equality. By failing to respond to acts of discrimination and by allowing their results to fester,

---

solve the problem, with using the affirmative action solution. I am raising the issue myself in order to ask whether affirmative action is necessary here.

82   Ibid.

83   See Richard A. Epstein, *Forbidden Grounds: The Case Against Employment Discrimination Laws* (Harvard University Press, Cambridge, 1992).

basic equality is denied even further. Can affirmative action for African Americans help prevent this by reversing some of the effects of 'untreated discrimination'? Perhaps it can if it will help to repair the damaged social network described by Anderson.[84] And because it is intended to solve a social problem, in this sense of 'social', forward looking affirmative action may not need to worry about exactly who the individual beneficiaries of affirmative action are.

One of the most common criticisms of affirmative action is the one that complains about many of the beneficiaries of affirmative action being too well off to need preferential treatment.[85] Of course one can, generally, be entitled to compensation even if one does not need it. And if (ordinary, prejudiced) discrimination persists in America today, as it does of course to some extent, there is the ongoing injury caused to all blacks by the knowledge that some are harmed just because they are black. Full blown widespread racism in America is arguably too recent for us to be able to shrug off that harm as something suffered by all groups from time to time. But the focus on need is not arbitrary. Affirmative action has a price tag, however judiciously it might be applied, and sceptics are not likely to consider using it to improve the situation of a group that is already doing well, however badly they may have been treated in the past. So why allow the black middle class to benefit from it?

The forward looking argument notes that the blacks who fill affirmative action places, and who are typically middle class,[86] are only the *direct* beneficiaries of affirmative action. If the middle class black beneficiaries of affirmative action in America can be what Professor Anderson calls 'agents of integration'[87] who are 'partners with the practitioners of affirmative action in breaking down the barriers that block black access to mainstream opportunities and benefits' then the objection that affirmative action benefits the wrong people loses much of its force.[88] Anderson cites studies which show that the black middle class is more likely, than its white counterpart, to maintain links with impoverished communities, because, as most of them are first generation, they are more likely to be linked to them by residential and family ties.

Black students at elite colleges, who may have been the direct beneficiaries of affirmative action, are also more likely to hold leadership positions in community organisations than whites with the same level of education.[89] This is not just a

---

84 Anderson 'Integration, Affirmative Action, and Strict Scrutiny', above n. 67, 1195–207.

85 See Eastland *Ending Affirmative Action*, above n. 38.

86 But see Ezorsky *Racism and Justice*, above n. 58, 63–4. Professor Ezorsky notes that affirmative action is not only used at the level of high paid professions or for gaining the education required for such positions.

87 Anderson 'Integration, Affirmative Action, And Strict Scrutiny', above n. 67, 1212.

88 Ibid.

89 Ibid. 1213.

question of providing role models, although that is part of it. The idea is that the direct beneficiaries of affirmative action can provide a link, in different ways, to networks of opportunity. As Anderson sums up, 'the targets of affirmative action's benefits are those who are best able to perform a role as agents of integration'.[90]

That does not mean that the individual beneficiaries of affirmative action do not get something that a young person in a black ghetto, whose life chances are relatively ruined, does not get. But the forward looking rationale for affirmative action gives that asymmetry a purpose. Affirmative action is intended to help repair the social fabric that produces a disproportionate number of people who do not have the opportunities of the black middle class affirmative action beneficiary.

With the forward looking argument we can explain the role of the direct beneficiary in a way that does not make him seem doubly undeserving. It might be thought unfair that those who have managed, as African Americans, to gain some qualifications now receive even more while the blighted victims of discrimination remain two steps behind. But if the direct beneficiaries play a role in helping others they do not seem needlessly privileged. It is not pointless then to choose black people who do not make up the 'underclass of blacks'. The forward looking argument explains why 'some advocates of affirmative action continue to point to the underclass as though it was an argument for policies aimed at those positioned *above* the underclass'.[91] It is. The forward looking approach argues that affirmative action helps the underclass by helping the middle class.

The past discrimination argument for affirmative action seems to find it more difficult to explain why less disadvantaged blacks should gain most from affirmative action. Even if we can know exactly what should be transferred from whites to blacks, as between groups, because of past discrimination, we still need to ask why only some blacks should get it and some whites should give it. It is not enough to say that the blacks who benefit are only getting what blacks as a group deserve and whites who suffer the disbenefit are only losing what they did not deserve. By allowing the redistribution of opportunity to affect only some in each group we could be creating a new unfairness. It is not enough to say that the nature of affirmative action makes this inevitable because only blacks with at least some qualifications are good candidates for it and only whites with similar or slightly higher qualifications are suitable donees of opportunities they would otherwise have had.

Affirmative action may, though, be seen as a way of compensating all blacks. If the benefit given to those Anderson calls 'agents of integration' can be seen as a means of uplifting the whole community then the development potential of affirmative action can be seen, perhaps, as a form of compensation and not just integration. Efforts to integrate disadvantaged blacks into mainstream society by means of affirmative action might just as well be called compensation. It is not

---

90   Ibid. 1212.
91   Eastland *Ending Affirmative Action*, above n. 38, 155. That is to say, Eastland may be missing the point.

denied that the *need* for it arose because of the way blacks were treated in the past. The extent of *de facto* segregation in America today and the phenomenon of racial profiling did not arise out of nowhere. But the forward looking argument responds more directly to a current problem and does not rely on a complicated calculus of what might have been, which is particularly difficult when we have to start factoring in the effect of new arrivals to America, black or white.

But what about the whites who lose opportunities because of affirmative action? The 'innocent white victim' looms large in any evaluation of affirmative action.[92] The whites who do lose an opportunity for training or employment because of affirmative action are not necessarily the least well off members of that group, although they might include some of those, because they will be people who have almost made the cut and who would have made it but for affirmative action. This means they may well have a good high school education or its equivalent – they will not usually be literally poor whites (except in the case of affirmative action applied to less well paid jobs; of which, as noted, there are instances). But they are also usually not the most well off. If a sacrifice has to be made so that blacks may achieve integration why should the sacrifice not be made by the whites who can afford it most? If the answer is 'well affirmative action does not work like that' then why not use something else that will do the job without causing that hardship?

Black beneficiaries are allowed to benefit, even though as individuals they may not be the best candidates for compensation or advancement if they are already relatively advantaged in relation to other blacks. But that is at least a case of someone *gaining* something extra because they are in a position to advance the interests of the least well off blacks. If that is the only way the situation of less well off blacks can be improved then, perhaps, so be it. One must not forget the burden of being a role model[93] and perhaps the 'extra' can be seen as compensation for that. The whites who lose out because of affirmative action do *lose* something, however, and they are not compensated for that.

The point about the 'white victim' is not only a concern about merit or efficiency, although these are important issues because these ideas are important for the community as a whole: it matters to all of us that we have the best surgeons. The problem is also about who should pay the price and why – it is an issue of basic equality. If all whites (or everyone) paid equally through the tax system, for some project designed to uplift depressed black communities, they would all lose some of the money they had earned, perhaps by their own meritorious efforts. But they would pay equally, at least as between the members of their income tax band. With affirmative action some whites are singled out and only they pay.

The past discrimination argument says 'no matter, they are only losing what was not theirs in the first place' – the return of stolen property idea. But surely

---

92   See Eastland *Ending Affirmative Action*, above n. 38, Ch. 1.

93   See Richard Delgado 'Affirmative Action as a Majoritarian Device: Or, Do You Really Want To Be A Role Model' (1991) 89 *Mich L Rev* 1224.

if a group owes a debt it should be paid by the group? The past discrimination argument does give us a reason to think in abstract groups up to a point. But to say if things had been different whites as a group would have X and blacks as a group would have Y, tells us little about who, specifically, should pay compensation to make that so now. If anyone should then we only know it is whites, as opposed to blacks, who should be paying. Any unjustified assumption about exactly who should be paying is an *ignoratio elenchi*. The issue might not be as salient if the groups were small and their proprietary interests were essentially communal, but in the context of modern affirmative action debates this is not the case.

It is not enough to say, as the past discrimination argument does, to the white applicant who loses an opportunity due to affirmative action that those places or opportunities are not really theirs because their (white group) has too many already. It is the majority which ultimately decides to implement affirmative action, in America. So even if whites, as per the past discrimination argument, have more than their fair share they should pay their dues, as a group, in such a way that all affected by the payment are treated fairly.

The forward looking argument too faces this challenge. According to it African Americans have to be the agents of integration, or of black advancement generally, but in doing so they achieve something for themselves. If they can survive the pressures of being a role model and awkward questions about their 'real ability' they can be the heroes of the piece, and achieve something for themselves. The white 'agents of integration' simply have to fall on their swords. It is not that sacrificing some of the interests of some people for the good of all is never consistent with basic equality. We have, however, to distinguish between ways of denying the interests of some in a certain context which are consistent with basic equality, from those which are not.

If a country, for example, has a greater objective need for some industries than others the government may favour those which are needed more because that is in everyone's interests, even the interests ultimately of those who would prefer to work in the disfavoured industries. Denying blacks who would be lawyers in Texas in the 1950s entrance to law school because the white majority had no (subjective, we might say) need for black lawyers was, on the other hand, not justified. Black people's concerns were simply ignored and that is precisely what constitutes the denial of basic equality.[94] Ronald Dworkin thinks the position of the whites who are not appointed or selected due to affirmative action is like that of those who would have liked to work in a disfavoured industry and not like that of the blacks who wanted to attend law school in Texas in the 1950s. The latter were excluded because of prejudice against them whereas the former are not.[95] It is true that affirmative action, unlike racist discrimination against blacks, is not

---

94 See the discussion in Ronald Dworkin *Taking Rights Seriously* (Duckworth, London, 1977) 223; for a more recent treatment of the topic see Ronald Dworkin *Sovereign Virtue* (Harvard University Press, Cambridge, 2000) 410.

95 Dworkin *Sovereign Virtue*, above n. 94, 411.

motivated by prejudice. But the absence of bad motives and the presence of good intentions are not enough to make a policy just. People are still being intentionally excluded. Why are these whites not unjustly treated when they lose opportunities because they are white?

Writing in the context of higher education in America, Dworkin argues that there is no injustice if blacks are given preferential access to selective institutions. He notes there is no right, in America, to university education as such.[96] Usually intelligence, as displayed on entrance tests, is the requirement for entrance to selective institutions. No one is not treated as an equal simply because she fails to score highly enough on those tests, he says. Intelligence is the principal criterion (there are others of course) we use for admission to institutions like law school, or medical school, because we think it is better to have intelligent lawyers and doctors. But if we have few black doctors, because of past and present discrimination, then we have a greater need for black doctors than white doctors now. Taking race into account is just the same, now, as taking intelligence into account has always been.[97]

Dworkin does not mean, of course, that there is something about being black, *per se*, that makes one a better lawyer or doctor. It's just black lawyers might serve the black community better, or more willingly, for now. Because blacks and whites in America to some extent have different experiences it may be the case that some black lawyers will have a better understanding of some black litigants needs and concerns than the average white lawyer would, and socially segregated societies need services in each community. The point should not be over stressed. Class differences still make their own barriers of ignorance and no lawyer entirely shares the world view of her poor and lower middle class clients.

There is moreover no single 'black culture' in America to which all black professionals will have instant epistemic access.[98] Like gay and straight people, blacks and whites share a culture.[99] They may play different roles in that culture at times but they do not live in different worlds with entirely different frames of reference. I should, on the other hand, not press that point too far. When people live in partly segregated circumstances they do develop some cultural differences; but the work of some lawyers and doctors from relatively privileged backgrounds, and various racial backgrounds, who make it their business to understand the circumstances others live in, should also not be underestimated.

The case may be somewhat different in some kinds of work such as that of police officers. Police personnel usually have to work in situations that are at least potentially conflictual. To say that given the level of racial tension in some American cities, as in many other parts of the world, a multiracial police force

96 Dworkin *Taking Rights Seriously*, above n. 94, 227.

97 Ibid. 225.

98 See Kwame Anthony Appiah and Amy Gutmann *Color Conscious* (Princeton University Press, Princeton, 1996) 88–9.

99 Ibid. 88–9.

will be more effective than one whose members are all, or very disproportionately, white seems like common sense. There may even be aspects of police work where race (or gender) is a prerequisite; undercover work for example. [100] Even in the case of things like police work, and perhaps social work generally, race based staffing decisions are race based and being black (or white in some suburbs?) is only a qualification because the world is racially disfigured. But we must take the world as we find it. Subjective needs are important too. Where race or sex is as clearly a requirement as, say, the ability to shoot straight, it might be that we are not even talking about affirmative action anymore. But even in the case of institutions like the police force, not all preferential treatment based on race will fall outside of what we call affirmative action.

In the case of the professions one typically studies for at selective institutions of higher education, it can only be the tentative belief that greater black representation in the professions will help to ameliorate the effects of *de facto* segregation that justifies affirmative action for African Americans. Black doctors and lawyers may be thought more likely to service under serviced black communities. Having more blacks in class may improve everyone's educational experiences and more blacks might be encouraged to aspire to these professions. The black community as a whole may benefit from its increased integration into the wider society. All Americans may benefit in terms of racial harmony. These results are valuable and confidence in them certainly is a reason to think affirmative action worthwhile.

But while the positive results of affirmative action may be real, that still does not explain why the whites who lose opportunities due to affirmative action have not been unfairly treated. 'We do not need you in this role because we have a racial imbalance which you may not have caused, and may not have benefited from, but which must be fixed in the interests of other people' does not sound quite like the more traditional 'we do not need you in this role because you do not seem to have the potential to fulfil the requirements of it'.[101] It is not quite enough to say no one is entitled to a place at university. No one is 'entitled' to a particular job either but we take into account restraints imposed by considerations of fairness when we allocate these things. Distinctions on grounds like race are arbitrary unless justified.

Those who bear the brunt of affirmative action have lost something, the right to compete for offices and other opportunities in terms of the usual rules. Do we

---

100   Louis P. Pojman 'The Case Against Affirmative Action'. Available at: http://www.dean.usma.edu./english/pojman/PublishedWorks/AffirmativeAction.html [accessed: 31 August 2005] 5. See also Michael Walzer *Spheres of Justice* (Martin Robertson & Company Ltd, Oxford, 1983) 148.

101   See Michael Sandel *Justice* (Penguin Books, London, 2009) 180 where he notes, in relation to the diversity argument, that universities can seem a bit confused about their mission in this way. Professor Sandel's brief treatment, in this book, deftly shows how and why affirmative action is, still, such a difficult moral issue.

really want to say those rules are no longer the default position and that ignoring them does not impose a cost on those who lose opportunities under substitute rules which are now being used as a measure to help a disadvantaged group? The forward looking argument for affirmative action, like ordinary anti-discrimination measures, is trying to deal with the fact of present discrimination. But unlike the latter, affirmative action does not directly address the discrimination, it compensates for it by changing the rules. If we do not want to reform the 'usual way we decide these things' then we have to justify depriving these whites of what they would have had if the usual principles had been applied. This conundrum cannot be easily dismissed; unless we think the rules themselves are arbitrary or discriminatory. The proviso warrants another digression.

Is Merit a Myth?

One way to respond to the accusation that affirmative action 'lowers standards' is to ask questions about the validity of the standards. If the standards are meaningless then the whites who lose their places due to affirmative action have not been excluded despite 'deserving' their places – because the idea of merit is now questioned. If no one deserves any position on merit then, given severe racial imbalances, we can apply affirmative action to uplift disadvantaged communities without being unfair to anyone. Even if we think standards are important we should reconsider their suitability from time to time anyway.

There might be many reasons for changing the way we evaluate applicants for jobs and places in selective training or educational opportunities. Some of the criteria we use may, at times, be crude and not particularly helpful for selecting the best applicants. Medical schools, for example, realise that high test scores may not always pick the best doctor, but interrogating the motives of 20 year-olds in interviews or reading their essays on why they want to be doctors might not help much either.

Still, we can only continue the search for what we think are relevant criteria. One objection, however, is that we cannot find objective criteria, only alternatives from different cultural perspectives.[102] Are the criteria we use to allocate positions and opportunities necessarily 'cultural'? I think they are, but only trivially. The intelligence – intellectual, emotional and practical – that makes for a good doctor is a culturally bound intelligence, but not in the sense that it is likely to produce a good doctor in only some sorts of contemporary societies. We expect even the white male English speaking graduates of Harvard Medical School to doctor well anywhere in the world today, though language and local customs may often have to be interpreted for them and they will have to respect the latter to do their job well.

---

102   I have already suggested the pitfalls that accompany this type of argument. See Ch. 7.

Medical knowledge is universally applicable, even if its, you might say, public relations[103] may differ according to context. And knowledge barriers between medical practitioners and their patients exist in the so-called western world; whose inhabitants, like other people, are not blessed with innate knowledge about the latest developments in medical science. The difference between a white American doctor and a white American lawyer, who has not read a great deal about medicine, is large and it is a 'cultural' difference too, even if the lawyer has a basically scientific worldview. This is because culture is about more than large worldviews. It is also about how we communicate, achieve tasks, and solve problems in our immediate environment. The medically illiterate lawyer shares the doctor's culture in the larger sense but she is not part of the *subculture* of medically knowledgeable people (doctors and nurses etc.) and sometimes will know as little about what one does in a situation requiring in-depth medical knowledge as she does about the worldview of an ancient culture she has never studied.

This is not to deny that there are sometimes different routes to the same knowledge. Some pre-modern cultures may have been be able to cure an ailment in ways not known to the Harvard graduate. But the modern doctor and the traditional healer are both bound by the facts of the matter. And these facts, including why both sorts of remedies work on occasion, can, in principle, be explained in the terms of modern medical science. It is true some people have no faith in modern medical science, and some people think all older forms of medical practice are useless. But that, as I have suggested, is a public relations challenge; not a reason to think we can really know nothing about healing which is of universal value.

Even if affirmative action debates are not always perfectly informed by all the fields of knowledge relevant to the topic, they are, of course, conducted in an intellectual context. And the present one is more than a little sceptical about claims to accurate knowledge and the merit we attach to that. But unless we share that scepticism, and it is by no means universally agreed that we should,[104] there is no reason to doubt the idea that some individuals are more suited for advanced medical training than others.

It would be particularly difficult to sustain an argument that blacks in America were kept out of medical school for the kind of cultural differences I am talking about here. American blacks are as 'western' as white Americans. As the history I took from Thomas Sowell shows, the only difference is that blacks were for a long time denied many of the fruits of that cultural heritage.[105] But the general

---

103   I do not mean that in any trivial sense. In providing medical advice one has to take into account people's existing views of the matter and convincing people, respectfully, to cooperate with medical advice, can be a tricky matter.

104   See Simon Blackburn *Truth* (Allen Lane, London, 2005) for a helpful recent discussion of various kinds of epistemological relativism. The point is made more directly in Ophelia Benson and Jeremy Stangroom *Why Truth Matters* (Continuum, London, 2006).

105   Ibid.

argument is worth mentioning as it is part of the contemporary discussion of affirmative action.

Apart from the larger group culture argument there is also an argument that qualifications are arbitrary in our modern technological culture generally. Affirmative action may be applied at all levels of commerce and industry, not just in the professions taken up by the graduates of elite universities. The qualifications for and best methods of appraising some roles may be difficult to pin down. But we would, however, probably find, with Brian Barry that 'even the most strenuously post-modern academics tend to agree that some departmental secretaries are a lot better than others at the job'.[106]

Barry disagrees with Iris Marion Young, who talks about the 'myth of merit',[107] on the question of assessing applicants for positions or promotions. He thinks that, although, as Professor Young argues, some jobs may seem to include so many different tasks that it is impossible to assess performance in them, we are able to distinguish between a good worker and a bad one. Here the point, that Professor Young is trying to make, is not one about the relativity of knowledge. The argument is that the notion of being 'qualified' for certain positions is too vague to be relied on in an argument against preferential treatment for some groups.[108]

Referring to an example of Young's, Barry does not think this means we cannot tell a good travel agent from a bad one.[109] I think Professor Barry is right to stress that however closely we look at the ways in which people are excluded from certain roles we will still think some criteria are relevant and that selecting some people rather than others may always be sensible and justifiable. Barry does not share Thomas Sowell's confidence in cognitive test scores but still believes some people are qualified for certain positions and others not.[110]

The relevant criteria may be difficult to measure and committees will make mistakes in their application. But that does not mean we should abandon all criteria, other than group proportionality, for filling positions. Young thinks some of the criteria we use are cultural in the sense of not being part of the narrow set of technical skills needed for the job.[111] But not all the skills of a good practitioner in any profession or trade need to be 'technical' in order to be amenable to fair evaluation.

Some behavioural traits that employers do require can be relevant although not 'technical' skills in the sense Young seems to intend. As Barry says: 'there is

---

106   Barry *Culture and Equality*, above n. 25, 99.

107   Iris Marion Young *Justice and the Politics of Difference* (Princeton University Press, Princeton, 1990) 192–222.

108   Ibid.

109   Barry *Culture and Equality*, above n. 25, 99. See Young *Justice and the Politics of Difference*, above n. 107, 202.

110   Barry *Culture and Equality*, above n. 25, 98–103.

111   Young *Justice and the Politics of Difference*, above n. 107, 200–202.

nothing mythical about a conception of merit that includes characteristics such as diligence, conscientiousness, reliability and cooperativeness'.[112] This does not mean, he stresses, that one must be insensitive to differences in expression which really are irrelevant to work performance. I think some employers do expect their employees to recast themselves in the employer's image and that can certainly constitute discrimination, or 'oppression' as Professor Young prefers to call it. It is also true, as Barry says, that there will be some grey areas and tribunals will have to weigh factors from time to time.[113] But some legitimate ways of 'fitting in' will always be required, although they may change, because simple cooperation always requires that.

As skills based on knowledge and cooperative endeavour are possible to acquire, and necessary, we cannot conclude that affirmative action merely alters an arbitrary order in the direction of better group representation. The redistribution of opportunities on racial (or gender based) lines must be justified and distinguished from discrimination. It is a denial of basic equality if it cannot be. We cannot plausibly suggest, in the debate about affirmative action for black Americans, that there is no unfairness in denying whites places and opportunities required for affirmative action candidates because all such places and opportunities are actually randomly allocated.

Can Rejecting Better Qualified White Candidates be Justified?

Is the position of better qualified white candidates really like those who want to work in an industry that has lost its state subsidy, as Dworkin suggests? In any decision it makes about the fate of its citizens a state must consider the plight of those affected by it. Even a policy which benefits everyone, eventually, might not be justified if it harms one group disproportionately. We might not think affirmative action is justified if we consider exactly who the people are that it harms. Affirmative action picks 'the next most disadvantaged group'.[114] And it has to, because, as Michael Walzer argues: '[u]nless one is prepared to give up the very idea of qualification, the costs cannot be distributed any further'.[115] Walzer thinks that we cannot just say 'oh well, the situation of blacks is dire and something has to be done', because he thinks affirmative action was the first resort, not the last.[116]

Walzer thinks that race based affirmative action in America is a way of avoiding the substantial redistribution that would be required to really repair the damage done by discrimination against blacks.[117] He is right to say that affirmative

---

112 Barry *Culture and Equality*, above n. 25, 99–100.
113 Ibid. 103.
114 Walzer *Spheres of Justice*, above n. 100, 154.
115 Ibid.
116 Ibid.
117 Ibid. 153–4.

action does not involve a radical redistribution. Now, almost 30 years after he wrote that, it is even clearer that hardly anyone with any influence wants a *radical* redistribution. But the point, in the forward looking argument, about the role of the beneficiaries of affirmative action remains. Affirmative action for blacks in America may achieve more than just a change in the skin colour of the upper middle class. It may also help those trapped in segregated communities, even if Walzer is right to think that something else could do the job more comprehensively.

Perhaps affirmative action does offer the prospect of a more secure future for all, including the whites who are now disadvantaged by it, if it produces the greater social stability its advocates think it has and will. This does distinguish affirmative action from racial classifications which ignore the interests of some group entirely. And it is also true that if it is not a case of 'Yale or jail'[118] for the direct, black, beneficiaries of affirmative action, that applies to the whites who lose opportunities too. And they are less likely to find prejudice against them as an obstacle to finding good employment than their black peers.

It can seem that all these considerations are pretty evenly balanced. Affirmative action policies will typically not be motivated by any hostile intent and they do promise all a share in the general benefits which should come with improved social integration. But they do sacrifice the more immediate interests of some, and only some, to achieve those benefits.

Is Affirmative Action Effective?

To justify sacrificing such significant interests on the alter of racial justice, though, one must at least be sure that affirmative action achieves what it promises, without too many bad side effects. Much, though not all, of the current debate about affirmative action in America is about its effectiveness. I do not try to summarise that debate or the research underlying it here. I will refer only to a recent episode in the ongoing project to show the efficacy of affirmative action for African Americans in higher education. I do hope to illustrate with that example how incomplete the project of demonstrating affirmative action's value is – even in that intuitively plausible context.

The publication, in 1998, of *The Shape of the River* by two past presidents of prestigious American universities, Derek Bok and William Bowen, was seen by supporters of affirmative action as a very good indication that the policy has good results, at least in higher education.[119] Ronald Dworkin, who previously had defended affirmative action against attacks that it was unprincipled, and had adopted a wait and see approach to the question of the effects of affirmative action, thinks that, while we should be open to new findings, *The Shape of the River* gives

---

118   Sowell *Affirmative Action Around the World*, above n. 4, 158.

119   Derek Bok and William G. Bowen *The Shape of the River* (Princeton University Press, Princeton, 1998).

us reason to think affirmative action works.[120] He notes first its central finding that blacks perform better at the more selective universities, which were the subjects of the Bok and Bowen study. This would seem to refute the notion that affirmative action for blacks in America mismatches blacks by placing them in the wrong institutions, where they are likely to fail.

This was Thomas Sowell's chief complaint about affirmative action in higher education before *The Shape of the River* and it still is. Sowell is unmoved by Bok and Bowen's findings in this regard. He argues, and cites statistics in favour of his conclusion, that the key factor determining the relative success of black students is not how selective the institution is, but how large the difference is between white and black entrance test scores in the pool of applicants for places in a university.[121] Bowen and Bok themselves note the decreasing gap between black and white scores among those applying to the elite colleges as compared to other tertiary institutions.[122]

The elite universities also have better staff student ratios and this, Sowell says, may benefit those black students who need more tutoring.[123] He compares the percentage of black students failing to graduate at Stanford (13 per cent in six years) with the percentage for the University of California at Berkeley (42 per cent for the same period), noting that the staff student ratio at Berkeley was more than double that at Stanford and notes similar statistics for a comparison of Yale with the University of Michigan at Ann Arbour.[124]

One may wonder what the point of Sowell's criticism is here. If there is no significant mismatch in the case of black students attending elite institutions and if extra tutoring helps to deal with the relatively impoverished backgrounds those students come from, then what is the problem with them being there? It cannot be the fact that they do not succeed there, if they do. Sowell's larger point here is that Bok and Bowen's sample is too limited to tell us anything about affirmative action in higher education in general. Perhaps it is, but if the study shows that affirmative action in this special case of top tier universities is not putting blacks into programmes in which they are unlikely to succeed, that is significant although it does not, as he says, show 'mismatching [in general] does not hurt black student's prospects of graduating, after all'.[125] But it was not trying to show that, the study was trying to show there was no mismatch in the institutions covered by the study.

Sowell's point seems to be that this has only been shown to be the case at universities, top tier or otherwise, where there is a lesser difference between black and white scores in entrance tests. That would make sense of course, if the tests

---

120 Dworkin *Sovereign Virtue*, above n. 94, 388.
121 Sowell *Affirmative Action Around the World*, above n. 4, 154.
122 Ibid.
123 Ibid. 157.
124 Ibid.
125 Ibid. 154.

are worth anything, but if there is no serious mismatch at some elite institutions then affirmative action at these does not set blacks up to fail. If Bok and Bowen have shown that, they have, as I suggested, told us something useful. Even if it is a bit odd, affirmative action might work better at some more selective universities than at some institutions to which it is, in general, easier to gain access. But Sowell does show that being a selective institution is not the key issue. There is a big difference in the black/white test score gap between some of the institutions studied by Bowen and Bok, between Harvard and Rice University for example, although all the institutions in their sample are selective.[126]

Another of Sowell's criticisms is relevant to this key *Shape of the River* finding. The study produced statistics about the achievement of blacks at the institutions studied, not about the achievement of blacks *admitted in terms of an affirmative action programme.*[127] Sowell's complaint, that the data used in *The Shape of the River* were not made available generally, is also important.[128] The matter of the effectiveness of affirmative action is not cut and dried and needs to be researched more thoroughly, and openly, than it has been.

It is also surely true, as Sowell argues, that it is not a case of 'Yale or jail'.[129] If the students who get into Yale on an affirmative action basis could have studied law or medicine at a slightly less prestigious institution without affirmative action we do have to explain why only Yale would do. We might be able to make an argument that their being at Yale makes the Yale experience a better one, but why do black students have to risk possible negative effects of affirmative action to make Yale a more rounded experience for others? Perhaps because Yale graduates would then be more likely to understand the constraints faced by other blacks – if the blacks who get into Yale are able and likely to convey this knowledge. But blacks obviously do not need to go to Yale to be better represented in the professions in general.

They might, though, as Dworkin stresses, relying on Bok and Bowen,[130] do better later in life simply because they have attended a more elite institution. Whether that helps blacks in general again depends on the truth of the trickle-down theory developed by Anderson. Dworkin also thinks it is clear that the study shows that there is 'some reason to doubt whether there is any general and deep-seated antagonism to affirmative action specifically in university admissions'.[131] Most impressively, perhaps, in this regard, *The Shape of the River* provides data which suggest that the whites who one would think are most likely to object to affirmative

---

126   Ibid. 155, the gap at Rice has been nearly three times that at Harvard.

127   But see Elizabeth S. Anderson 'From Normative to Empirical Sociology in the Affirmative Action Debate: Bowen and Bok's *The Shape of the River*' (2000) 50 (2) *J Legal Educ* 286, 295.

128   Sowell *Affirmative Action Around the World*, above n. 4, 156.

129   Ibid. 158.

130   Dworkin *Sovereign Virtue*, above n. 94, 394.

131   Ibid. 398.

action, those with lower entrance test scores who were more likely not to get their first choice of university or programme, are *not* more likely to object to it.[132]

Dworkin also notes that most blacks surveyed in the study thought that affirmative action had been good for them, all things considered, and had improved their life chances. He does concede that it is not a good thing if any black person feels stigmatised because of affirmative action. But any harm caused by such feelings can be outweighed by the good that affirmative action might do, and the students surveyed were saying the good results do outweigh the bad.[133]

Dworkin stresses, citing the Bowen and Bok study and others, what he thinks would happen to black enrolment at selective institutions if affirmative action were abandoned. It would plummet and far fewer blacks would enter the professions.[134] There would of course be fewer blacks at the elite institutions. It is not clear, though, that fewer blacks would enter higher education *per se*. Sowell cites figures to show the latter has not happened in California and Texas where affirmative action (in Texas only for a time) has been restricted recently.[135] And some less selective institutions in the United States also train people for the professions. Still, it obviously is the case that fewer blacks would get into some, more elite, institutions but for affirmative action. This would be true unless those institutions suddenly became more competent in the matter of recruiting suitably qualified, hitherto unnoticed, black students. But as an argument for affirmative action this is somewhat question begging. We need to show that affirmative action is the best response to the under representation of certain groups in higher education – not just that better representation can be achieved with it.

Does affirmative action in higher education work in a deeper sense? In terms of the diversity rationale it might be thought that it obviously will. If people study separately they will clearly have less chance to get to know and understand each other. As Dworkin notes, the Bowen and Bok study concludes that black and white students did interact to a significant extent and that support for diversity programmes has been growing.[136] While diversity is not an absolute good, and is sometimes quite meaningless, if better race relations can be achieved by racially diverse classes that is a point in their favour. But, as Stanley Rothman, Seymour Lipset and Neil Nevitte caution, studies on these issues rely on 'the reported attitudes, perceptions, and memories of students, faculty, and administrators'[137] and the positive attitude of the respondents:

---

132 Ibid. 397–8.

133 Ibid. 399.

134 Ibid. 399.

135 Sowell *Affirmative Action Around the World*, above n. 4, 159–61.

136 Dworkin *Sovereign Virtue*, above n. 94, 397.

137 Stanley Rothman, Seymour Martin Lipset and Neil Nevitte 'Racial Diversity Reconsidered'. Available at: http://www.thepublicintetrest.com/archives/2003spring/article2.html [accessed: 4 December 2005], 3.

could just as easily reflect an increase in conscious or unconscious efforts to give socially appropriate answers, a result of the growing emphasis on these programmes at elite schools, where they are frequently presented as highly important moral imperatives.[138]

Students are taught diversity is a good thing and when you ask them if it is a good thing, they say it is. The authors note that when they asked students, as part of their own study, which included a 140 institutions of higher learning, whether students agreed with the statement 'No one should be given special preference in jobs or college admissions on the basis of their gender or race' two thirds of the students strongly agreed.[139] They did find support for inclusion of courses, as a voluntary option, intended to encourage cross-cultural understanding. Rothman et al. suggest that what is happening here is that people are almost universally in favour of racial inclusion and diversity in general, but when they are asked to reflect on the necessary sacrifices affirmative action demands they might well report negative attitudes towards preferential treatment. The authors give more examples of this.[140]

Bok and Bowen accept that the question of whites who lose their place due to affirmative action is a large one but feel they cannot be indifferent to the race of students admitted because, amongst others, government officials, CEOs, bar associations, medical associations have 'repeatedly stressed the importance of attracting more minority members into their fields'.[141] They feel that: '[i]n view of these needs, we are not indifferent to which student gets the graduate fellowship'.[142] This frankness is welcome but the value of *The Shape of the River* can be recognised while noting that where its findings take the form: 'so many people think this is a good idea that it really must be', it will not convince everyone. The value of the study is that it does show that affirmative action in higher education in America is not thoroughly discredited. Its weakness is that it cannot completely explain why it should be practised.

Those who value basic equality would naturally like American employers to have all the black applicants they would like to have. We want this because we think the reason the black candidates are not available in America, or in countries like South Africa which share a similar history of discrimination and exploitation, is because they have not had equal opportunities in the past. But we should want greater understanding of how affirmative action works and why, seeing it is divisive to some extent at least wherever it is practiced,[143] it is the best way to solve the problem.

---

138   Ibid.

139   Ibid. 4.

140   Ibid. 4–5.

141   Bowen and Bok *The Shape of the River*, above n. 119, 283.

142   Ibid. 283.

143   In New Zealand, if my adopted country's people will forgive me, silence about affirmative action and some other issues, to do with race or culture, is frequently misinterpreted to mean enthusiasm.

At the moment, 45 years or so after its implementation in America, it is not clear, one way or the other, it seems to me, whether affirmative action for African Americans is worth having. In terms of affirmative action's results in higher education in America, Dworkin says, of *The Shape of the River*, that it has raised the standard of debate and that that standard must be maintained in any project that tries to show Bok and Bowen are wrong.[144] That is not much by way of convincing justification; so long after the introduction of affirmative action in the United States. Elizabeth Anderson notes that Bok and Bowen's study does not say much about the benefits of university affirmative action for other blacks who are not the direct beneficiaries of affirmative action.[145]

In her review of *The Shape of the River* she argues that Bok and Bowen's focus on the involvement of blacks in community work after graduation is not the right test for affirmative action's effectiveness. She thinks the most important question is whether affirmative action benefits the black community by providing professional services and employment which would be lost if affirmative action were scrapped.[146] That, with respect, is right on the money. I will return to this point in a moment.

Recently retired United States Supreme Court Justice Sandra Day O'Connor, whose vote in split decisions has been pivotal in keeping affirmative action alive in the United States, has suggested, in the latest affirmative action case to reach the US Supreme Court, that race based affirmative action might be needed, in America, for another 25 years.[147] Hopefully during that time, if it is allowed to continue for that long, some clearer means of assessing it will become apparent. That assessment is sorely needed because affirmative action can only be justified, in light of the potential disadvantage it can cause to black and white candidates for various opportunities and positions, if it really can deliver long-term racial justice and if it is the best way to do it, in terms of results and side effects. All that is, at least, necessary.

If African Americans are facing (prejudiced and 'statistical') discrimination, then something should be done about it. If anti-discrimination law is not enough and if something else will help, it should, all else being equal, be tried. The ideal solution would be one that was contributed to by every American taxpayer. Considerations of fairness, of basic equality itself, suggest this; but so does the idea that blacks and whites would then be solving the problem together. If affirmative action is being used because vast programmes of urban renewal will tax wealthy Americans too much, it is less justified.

My final point about affirmative action's effectiveness: good consequences have to be weighed against bad. I have not discussed all the complaints that critics

---

144   Dworkin *Sovereign Virtue*, above n. 94, 390.

145   Anderson 'From Normative to Empirical Sociology in the Affirmative Action Debate: Bowen and Bok's *The Shape of the River*', above n. 127, 284–305.

146   Ibid. 290–97.

147   *Grutter* v *Bollinger* 539 US 306, 343.

of affirmative action have about its alleged bad effects.[148] If affirmative action really does cause racial divisiveness, if it does discourage hard work in some contexts or if it just adds to the stigmatised status of its direct beneficiaries, then the good that it does will have to outweigh all of this too. Not every negative effect need be seen as a new social evil which would not exist if affirmative action was not practised. If affirmative action inflames the prejudices of already prejudiced whites one could argue, as Elisabeth Anderson does, that these whites would always find something to justify their racist attitudes.[149] It is also true, on the other hand, that we should be wary of providing excuses for continued bigotry.

Different Contexts and Groups

I hope I have at least made it clear how complex and inchoate the task of justifying affirmative action is, even in the context of one debate. I restricted my discussion to one case because the question of whether affirmative action is consistent with basic equality cannot just be asked once. It must be asked separately in every situation which is materially different from some other situations. Not every argument for affirmative action will have the same features.

In particular an argument for affirmative action for women in America, or in a country where women have achieved a similar level of liberation, would be similar to the one made for African Americans only in some respects. Women are not a segregated community in America, or anywhere else, in the sense that blacks are, to a certain extent, in that country. But they were discriminated against, and even in countries where that discrimination is now prohibited we cannot be confident that they are not still discriminated against at times. The effects of the historical discrimination linger as they do in the case of racial discrimination. It is true, however, that because women can be oppressed without being poor, normal access to education can bring about rapid change, comparatively speaking.

There are important complications in the debate about affirmative action for women to do with family 'responsibilities' and child bearing itself. Is affirmative action an appropriate response to the fact that a woman's career development may be made difficult by her role as the bearer of children and her disproportionate role as care giver? I do not address this question here, though it is important. It can only arise in the context of gender because only women can give birth, but it is related to one of the questions that is asked in the race context. Superficially, the case of child bearing gives us a counter-example if we thought that all disadvantage must be caused by discrimination. It is not anyone's fault that childbearing must interfere with the development of at least some careers to at least some extent.

---

148   See, for example, Stephan Thernstrom and Abigail Thernstrom *America in Black and White* (Simon and Schuster, New York, 1997).

149   Anderson 'From Normative to Empirical Sociology in the Affirmative Action Debate: Bowen and Bok's *The Shape of the River*', above n. 127, 297.

Here there is a real group difference which, unlike theories about average innate group intelligence, cannot be doubted. But how to respond to the difference is another matter. Women do not have to bear children. If we want them to it does not seem much to ask that we make some sort of adjustments to the structure of paid work to accommodate their needs.

In general it may be noted that some of the hard questions posed by race based affirmative action are relevant in the gender context too. Some women, like some African Americans, would prefer not to have their colleagues wondering if their success was due, in part, to preferential treatment. And some men, like some American whites, may feel they have done nothing to deserve being overlooked because of their (male) group membership. There are also factual issues and, as with race, they are very controversial. Here I just want to note one difficulty that will remain until we are in possession of a lot more facts.

I have referred to the modern debate about sex differences.[150] There is agreement at least that our (fairly recent) common sense notion that men and women are on average equally intelligent, insofar as we can measure such things, is correct.[151] But I have referred above to authorities who suggest this does not mean that men and women, as groups, always have the same *interests* and that where their interests do, in general, differ this is not necessarily due to oppressive environmental factors. This factual issue is relevant because, if these authorities are right, it cannot be argued that if women are disproportionately represented in some positions valued by our society that is necessarily *entirely* due to discrimination.

There is no point in worrying about the fact that fewer women enter a particular sort of career – say certain types of engineering – if it really is the case that fewer women are interested in that career and no environmental improvement would produce a greater number who were. It is true that the more we do come to know, as a matter of generally accepted science, if our knowledge in this area does indeed advance and if it does inform us of interesting differences between the sexes, the greater the temptation will be to indulge in invidious profiling of individuals. But that is, strictly speaking, a separate, though important, issue.

Strategic suppression of facts is seldom a good idea. There is no point in pursuing a social policy as potentially divisive as affirmative action in contexts which are the results of unforced choices. Matters will seldom be as simple as I might seem to be suggesting. Even if fewer women than men would choose to work on oil rigs that does not mean those who do will not be discriminated against. But to say the under representation of women, or men, in some occupations might not be entirely the result of sex discrimination is not to say that discrimination plays no part; or that it has not been endemic in other contexts.

These are fairly sensitive matters I suppose – but that does not mean that we cannot be expected to remain objective and avoid substituting vitriol for good argument. The emotional outbursts and episodes of academic vindictiveness that

---

150   See Ch. 6.
151   Pinker *The Blank Slate*, above n. 1, 344.

sometimes accompany the discussion of sex (and race, or ethnic) differences are extremely silly and only encourage the perception that there are no good arguments to counter truly sexist or racist views. Sex has always been a more interesting difference than race. Understanding the difference it makes is a difficult task, but then so is understanding the nature of the atom. We would not be impressed by a physicist who encouraged the suppression of theories which contradicted her own.

Although less famously, affirmative action thrives outside of America. As Thomas Sowell patiently points out, affirmative action, or something like it, is ubiquitous in the modern world.[152] The complex set of arguments about affirmative action for American blacks cannot be relevant, certainly not in every respect, to the justification of every sort of preferential policy. I chose to focus my discussion mainly on the American race example partly because the problem of racial justice in America makes the case for affirmative action for blacks and some other groups in that country at least plausible. I only partly mean to suggest that if it is not justified in that case it will be hard to justify in any situation. That is partly true but there are some situations where it might seem even easier to justify preferential treatment; for women in Afghanistan for example. Sowell is right to note, in the affirmative action context, though it is true generally, that people are fond of thinking their situation is unique.[153] But there is always the possibility that situations might be at least partly different.

America and South Africa, for example, though they share a history of racial oppression which is similar in many ways, differ greatly in terms of the political environment in which affirmative action operates. The ruling party in South Africa fully supports preferential policies and these are specifically protected in the Constitution.[154] But it is quite likely that implicit and explicit political and social pressure alone would have brought about a vast transformation in that country, after its democratisation in 1994, in terms of job and educational opportunities, at least in terms of lower and middle level opportunities. Because blacks automatically had political power, after democratisation, as most South Africans are black, there was no need to use affirmative action to ensure that issues that affect black people were kept in the public eye. (It is true, though, that much of the 'voluntary' integration in recent years in South Africa has taken the form of affirmative action.)[155]

Because blacks do form such a large majority in South Africa, a grossly disproportionate distribution of desirable places and opportunities was, after democratisation, more obvious, more embarrassing and more vulnerable to immediate political pressure than in the United States today. Because of the more recent repealing of discriminatory laws and the highly systematic segregation

---

152   Sowell *Affirmative Action Around the World*, above n. 4, 1–2.

153   Ibid. 1.

154   Constitution of the Republic of South Africa, Act 108 of 1996 s 9(2).

155   See Kanya Adam 'The Politics of Redress: South African Style Affirmative Action' (1997) 35 (2) *The Journal of Modern African Studies* 231, 234.

and repression of different racial and ethnic groups in South Africa by the white minority regime, there is, in that country, a greater danger of unqualified people being promoted too quickly than there is in America. The danger here is in benefiting individuals who cannot really advance the economic integration of other black people and whose deployment may harm the prospects of all South Africans. These are just some of the more plainly visible differences between situations which intuitively have a lot in common.

Some instances of affirmative action are found in quite different contexts. Affirmative action in Malaysia, where, like South Africa, the beneficiaries are members of a majority group but, unlike South Africa, have not been systematically discriminated against by other groups in that country, would seem much more difficult to justify than American or South African preferential policies. This is particularly true as the motive for preferential practices in Malaysia seems to be infected by cronyism.[156] 'Affirmative action' there, as in the case of preferential treatment for Afrikaans speaking whites in apartheid South Africa after 1948, seems to be more about political accommodation than about social justice.[157]

In order to even partially morally justify a preferential group policy, does there always have to be a group that has been discriminated against? I think it is much harder to justify affirmative action in other circumstances. The kind of affirmative action that Elizabeth Anderson supports – affirmative action as integration – is a response to a type of present discrimination but the segregated circumstances of some American blacks today is related to earlier systematic discrimination. Affirmative action for new waves of immigrants to America seems more difficult to justify, even if these immigrants do find it hard to integrate, though it might depend on why the integration is difficult.[158]

We cannot place under the rubric of 'discrimination' just any cause of a group's current relative disadvantage. Even if a group of newcomers had suffered discrimination elsewhere, it would be difficult to argue, as a matter of justice, that they should be the beneficiaries of affirmative action, if they are not being discriminated against in their new country (of course sometimes they will be).

A country might reasonably provide special assistance for refugees, or for groups of immigrants it wants to attract, in order to help them settle into new circumstances. But the cost for that will normally be spread amongst all its taxpayers and will not fall on one group of citizens only, as it would if affirmative action is used to integrate new settlers. The unfairly chosen victim problem looms much larger in this situation. Even if, as is surely the case, not every white American disbenefited by affirmative action caused or benefits from current black disadvantage, there is still a plausible sense in which they can be exhorted to gracefully accept their lot for the sake of the greater good of American racial

---

156   Sowell *Affirmative Action Around the World*, above n. 4, Ch. 3.

157   See Leonard Thompson *A History of South Africa* (Yale University Press, New Haven, 1995) 187–9.

158   See Eastland *Ending Affirmative Action*, above n. 38, 149–51.

justice. Their consolation is the fact that at least they do not face the difficulties faced by many blacks due to racial profiling. But to ask them to make that sacrifice, alone, in the service of a progressive immigration policy seems too much.[159] Even where a group of newcomers suffers from employers' reluctance to hire them, for whatever reason, asking one segment of one group within the nation to remedy this seems a lot to ask. In the case of affirmative action for African Americans, the whites who are excluded may not themselves have discriminated against black people but they can still be said to be in some sense taking care of their, American, problem, *as Americans*. That, communitarian perhaps, argument just has no force when it comes to new arrivals.[160]

There may also be groups of people, within a society, which lag behind others for reasons which need not have much to do with discrimination. Take the case, which I have mentioned, of a group which has disengaged from modernisation for religious or 'cultural' reasons. What if such a group decided to abandon its other-worldly path and embrace modernity? In a social democracy they would of course be entitled to basic welfare but, as a group, they would lag behind others and be under-represented in the sorts of positions valued in modern society. Would that be a reason to treat them preferentially with regard to their applications for such positions? It might seem kind to do so but the kindness consists once again in dispensing someone else's opportunities.

What is to Be Done?

All in all there certainly is a danger in thinking that every group variation, in terms of the benefits and burdens experienced in any given society, is the result of some injustice that group has experienced, and is experiencing, at the hands of that society, but where it is there is at least some reason to think affirmative action is defensible. Even in the most deserving cases affirmative action may, however, be both an unfair imposition on members of other groups and a remedy of uncertain efficacy. Those questions are linked by our uncertainty about particular facts. Apart from not knowing, with enough certainty, yet if affirmative action will work and will complete its work in a reasonable time, we probably cannot be sure as yet there is no better way to get the job done, no other more direct way to solve the problem of group injustice which would not involve distorting the idea of merit in contexts where merit is important.

The question of whether there is an alternative to affirmative action is not just about whether we should rather have class based solutions. Poverty can be a culture

---

159   Perhaps this point could be used, *reductio ad absurdum*, to argue against affirmative action in general. The question of immigrants raises issues about inter-state justice. I do not discuss these here. For a discussion of some of the issues see John Rawls *The Law of Peoples* (Harvard University Press, Cambridge, 2001).

160   See Michael Sandel *Justice* above, n. 101, Ch. 9.

that is hard to escape and educational institutions in many countries have for a long time sought to assist poorer members of the community with scholarships. To suggest that is all we need is, however, to deny the existence of, for example, racial injustice. Affirmative action is premised on the fact of the denial of opportunity caused by group membership. Getting a university education may be difficult if you are poor. But you might be poor because your mother is black and suffers discrimination in the workplace, when she needs a loan, or by not being connected to a network of information about opportunities to apply for jobs. People are disadvantaged for different reasons; some of those are to do with prejudice which causes discrimination which leads to disadvantage, which in turn leads to a dearth of opportunities because of the shunning of the disadvantaged group which allows the cycle to continue. It would seem the solution must do something about the status of the group, mostly for the sake of its more vulnerable members, although successful members of the group will also suffer from prejudice at times. As I have said, whether that something should be affirmative action depends on whether it works and has fewer bad effects than other solutions. The blatancy of that point has unfortunately not led to research which unequivocally decides the matter one way or the other.

There have been other efforts to improve the lot of disadvantaged groups. Efforts to uplift impoverished communities by providing community based education and training have been tried in America.[161] Barbara Bergmann notes these programmes have also been going for 30 years and their job is not done.[162] She thinks that if part of the problem in gaining access to the world of success is to do with present discrimination, whether of the prejudiced or rational-statistical variety, then education and training alone will not do the job.[163] Here the broader social context is important: not all countries which have relatively disadvantaged groups are as racially polarised as America is. Where there is more good will between the disadvantaged and other groups, education and training may translate more easily into opportunity.

What should we do while waiting for more perfect knowledge? If we decide to continue or go ahead with affirmative action programmes in situations where the justification for doing so seems plausible, we should do so in ways most likely to achieve its most morally plausible goals. This is not just a matter of efficiency. Affirmative action comes in many forms. Each type requires justification, just as different types of taxes do. If we think we can justify a particular affirmative action programme on the grounds that it will benefit a disadvantaged community generally, by integrating it with the more successful sector of society, that will only be reason to practise affirmative action which has that aim in mind. And it will only provide reason to practise it in a way most likely to achieve that goal.

---

161   See Barbara R. Bergmann *In Defense of Affirmative Action* (Basic Books, New York, 1996) 177.

162   Ibid.

163   Ibid.

It will not, for example, justify practices that pay no attention to those goals by ignoring the idea of capability altogether and which aim only to achieve greater 'representation' in general.

We should, therefore, ensure that the direct beneficiaries of affirmative action are well qualified enough to play their roles. If we lower standards too much we might increase the level of diversity in workplaces and universities but that would only be a useful result if diversity was in itself an end worth achieving. If it was we would feel obliged to think that favouring candidates from groups that were *not* disadvantaged was appropriate in situations where those groups were under represented or not represented. This use of affirmative action, which has had some supporters,[164] would in my view be bizarre. But if we do not feel that diversity in itself would justify such a remedy then we may argue, *reductio absurdum*, that affirmative action for *disadvantaged* groups is also not sensibly thought of as a means to diversity as an end in itself.

In education and employment, our commitment to basic equality inspires attempts to achieve improved equality of opportunity for unfairly disadvantaged groups. That disadvantage will only be removed when those groups are able to compete with others without special assistance in areas that count. This is important to bear in mind in affirmative action in higher education and in business. In business, black managers, for example, may be disproportionately expected to play 'soft' roles in industry.[165] In higher education the danger is that measures taken to include and support students from disadvantaged groups may not direct them to areas where their participation may be most helpful to the integration of their group. Real integration is achieved by ensuring there are enough doctors and lawyers and other professionals to serve, in various ways, disadvantaged communities, not by producing a surplus of graduates who have studied the sociological reasons for the dearth of professionals from disadvantaged groups.

My only other suggestion is that affirmative action should remain contentious. Where government, including the public tertiary education sector, practises affirmative action it should expect and welcome scrutiny and there should be a clearer idea about the expected duration of such initiatives than there seems to be in at least many cases.[166] The greatest danger posed by not having at least tentative timetables for preferential policies, is their becoming normal. The danger is that if this way of allocating places and opportunities becomes standard we will lapse into thinking that proportionality is an end in itself. Perhaps some do think this, but it is surely not something to encourage. Affirmative action should be seen as a temporary (even if fairly long term) measure; an honest attempt to *solve* a problem rather than just a way of *living with it*. State funded practitioners of affirmative action should also put, and be required to put, more effort into the study of the

---

164   Eastland *Ending Affirmative Action*, above n. 38, 114.

165   See Duncan Innes et al. (eds) *Power and Profit* (Oxford University Press, Cape Town, 1992) 131.

166   Sowell *Affirmative Action Around the World*, above n. 4, 3.

effects, positive and negative, of their programmes. But if this is taken seriously the study of affirmative action needs to be more than a propaganda exercise.

It is better, therefore, to think of affirmative action as a political issue rather than an established moral right. Our duty, in the service of basic equality, not to discriminate against others, issues in a moral right not to be discriminated against. We have reason to feel certain of that. Our views about affirmative action, however, should be tentative. Because the different concerns for different groups of people seem to be too equally weighted for us to have much confidence about which path to take. The issue should therefore be subject to ongoing political scrutiny. Americans may feel that the debate over affirmative action is divisive and never ending but there are other nations which have little or no rigorous debate on the issue, and that is worse. Perhaps the debate in the US is too political, but it is at least a debate.

My remarks about affirmative action thus conclude with the same sense of incompleteness as my treatment of indirect discrimination did. The core concerns of basic egalitarians, in the human rights law context need much more careful attention. Legal ideas and schemes far outstrip our understanding of the relevant moral concerns. In the last few paragraphs I became as 'practical' as I have been in this book but I will end this chapter on affirmative action by returning to more obviously theoretical matters.

The link between the idea of basic equality and affirmative action seems obvious but what it means to apply the value in this context is not. The uncertainty present when we first consider the matter survives, I have argued, a good few decades of debate in America and elsewhere. The difficulty is, in part, about assessing the facts; a difficulty which I have argued can be partly overcome, in some contexts, by *trying* to assess the facts. But there may be more conceptual work to do as well. It is not that we do not know what basic equality demands, in general, but the way it applies to this issue may need to be conceived more broadly than it typically is. Because basic equality is denied by discrimination we think it requires us to respond to the effects of discrimination. It does, all things being equal. We also need to consider the effects on other people of our attempts to right the wrongs of discrimination. This balancing is hard to get right – partly because we do not understand all the relevant causes and effects[167] – hence our difficulty with this topic.

The argument takes place, however, in the context of other assumptions about what basic equality (amongst other considerations) requires. Affirmative action is a political response, made in certain specific political settings. Its appropriateness may be related to assumptions made in those contexts but not others. That is partly a question of political sociology rather than political philosophy. Some societies have wounds they think need healing.

---

167 Anderson 'From Normative to Empirical Sociology in the Affirmative Action Debate: Bowen and Bok's *The Shape of the River*', above n. 127, 284, 304–5.

But affirmative action is also debated against the backdrop of political theory. Unless, which seems unlikely, its practice in certain situations is required by every theory of justice, it must be an entailment of one or some theories of justice, or of none. If Will Kymlicka is even partly right to suggest that modern theories of justice are principally theories about what basic equality requires[168] then it is in this broader theoretical context that we must ultimately determine whether affirmative action is consistent with that value.

Affirmative action might seem most compatible with Robert Nozick's theory[169] which focuses, in its theory of the just distribution of property, more on the question of *historical* entitlement than other contemporary theories do. But affirmative action may also be thought to be an entailment of John Rawls's support of 'fair equality of opportunity'.[170] That idea, as Rawls argues, can mean more than just meritocracy.[171] Merit is only respected, in Rawls's scheme, if it benefits the least fortunate – those who would lose out altogether in a pure meritocracy.[172] The instrumental nature of the value of respecting merit means that it will have to be shown to be a good thing in any particular situation. Perhaps it is not absolutely required when there is a pressing need to overcome the effects of discrimination.

Another theory of justice might question the basic way we distribute goods in liberal democracies. I referred to Iris Marion Young's critique of the idea of merit.[173] Her approach seems to dismiss the idea of merit altogether. I disagreed with that conclusion but it illustrates how challenges to any of the background assumptions we may make when discussing affirmative action, some of which are assumptions about what basic equality requires, can threaten to complicate the debate in unexpected ways. There is nothing peculiar about affirmative action in this regard of course. Any social thesis can be upset by the introduction of novel considerations. But awareness of this can serve to remind us that broader explorations of the role of basic equality in political theory may have implications, which we have not thought of, for specific problems like affirmative action.

Affirmative action is typically an intervention which is aimed at increasing the share of economic benefits that certain groups receive. Further progress in the vexed debate about the implications for a theory of distributive equality of a commitment to basic equality would seem to hold the promise of some insights which would help us to think about affirmative action. That debate, about distributional equality, also seems intractable for the moment[174] but it will continue of course and I think

---

168   See Ch. 1.

169   Robert Nozick *Anarchy, State and Utopia* (Blackwell, Oxford, 1975).

170   John Rawls *A Theory of Justice* (Oxford University Press, Oxford, 1971) 83.

171   Ibid.

172   Ibid. 84.

173   Young *Justice and the Politics of Difference*, above n. 107.

174   See Ronald Dworkin *Sovereign Virtue*, above n. 94 Ch. 2; Samuel Scheffler 'What is Egalitarianism?' (2003) 31 *Philosophy and Public Affairs* 5, criticising Dworkin's approach to the issue of distributional equality; Elizabeth Anderson 'What is the Point

our understanding of the moral quandaries the idea of affirmative action produces could be improved by looking more closely for connections between what basic equality means for distributive equality and what it might mean for affirmative action, and discrimination generally, although as I said at the outset, I do think these are separate issues to a certain extent.

of Equality?' (1999) 109 *Ethics* 287, in similar vein to Scheffler, but also developing an alternative theory.

Conclusion

The task of understanding what basic equality demands from us in our social policy is enormous. It is also very important because it seems so obviously right to most of us that there can be no justification for a distinction between persons as such. That widely shared intuition is justified because we are equal in important ways which make sense of the idea of basic equality. That moral principle has substance. 'Equality' is not an empty notion, though it is an abstract one. The idea has determinate content in a plethora of contexts.

Almost all (of what we agree are) denials of basic equality in practice are now accompanied by at least a pretence of devotion to that value. The idea of equality has ancient roots, which I have said almost nothing about in this book, but the widespread belief that we are all each other's equals and that we can infer from this that all should be free from discrimination and enjoy equal human liberties, and which provides us with a common principle with which to engage in what are some of the most urgent moral debates of our age, is quite modern.

To be sure, the full theoretical basis of popular claims to equality is not always well understood. Religious people sometimes find it difficult to comprehend the need to respect the rights of those who do not share their doctrines. Many, religious or otherwise, find it hard to support equal rights for gays and lesbians, and there are still many pockets of resistance to the idea that women should have a full and public role in a just society. But the incipient idea, of basic equality, is there in public debate about our most pressing concerns whether they be about oppression by foreign powers, the suppression of some groups within a nation or what we should do about the relative disadvantage of some groups in society. These and many other debates are now often framed in terms of the need to consider the interests and concerns of all affected parties and typically include claims that this is not being done. There is no reason to think that this is an unhelpful way to frame these issues.

It is important, though, to remember the justification for our commitment to basic equality: our sameness. This will help us to be aware that we will always need more or less what other people need. Grandiose claims about difference are what gave rise to the need to talk about equality. The way out of our discriminatory patterns of relating to each other involves recognising that basic sameness that makes us a human community; a community of moral personalities. Appeals to 'cultural' diversity have to be tempered by that understanding lest we spin new fantasies of uniqueness. Cultural relativism is likely to be incompatible with basic equality because it demands that we take people's beliefs and customs as axiomatic regardless of whether they facilitate harmonious existence and personal fulfilment in a modern cosmopolitan setting. Taking equality seriously requires refinement and reform of our value systems. If preserving the integrity of all cultures is anyone's prime commitment then, because that will involve preserving discrimination and other forms of denying basic equality, they obviously will have a higher value than equality.

It is disquieting, perhaps, that debates about discrimination, the paradigm human rights denial of basic equality, have become so convoluted and uninformative. But as I have argued, we, rather than the idea of equality itself, are to blame for this. Partly because we have strayed, in jurisprudential discourse, from the broad core idea of the equality of persons, into an endless array of conceptions of equality, much equality talk is confusing and there is also not enough agreement about who has or has not been wronged as there could be. This is because we have laws that raise questions as much as they offer solutions. What basic equality means in terms of how we should live together is a question we have only just begun to answer. That our task has just begun is clear from our attempts to resolve conundrums that stand at the centre of contemporary discussions of equality law.

The two most well-known issues in 'equality law', the problem of indirect (in its various senses) discrimination and the practice of affirmative action, are difficult to resolve precisely because considerations of (basic) equality itself are in tension. Alternative conceptions of equality which are not implications of basic equality will only succeed in ignoring the interests of some, and that will be a denial of basic equality, not an application of it.

The first thing to do is to work out what basic equality dictates in the matter of the just treatment of historically disadvantaged groups and then to fashion rules, or abandon rules, in an attempt to implement our understanding of what is required. Whether a better execution of that task will lead to a simpler set of equality law or allow us to do away with the law's vagueness altogether is hard to say. Perhaps, at least in part, we would have come to know how to adapt the rest of our law to conform with our improved understanding of what equality requires.

There are many other important issues in legal and political philosophy which are 'equality issues' in the sense that the requirement to treat people as equals plays an important role in any competent treatment of them. As I suggested at the end of the last chapter, further developments in our understanding of what basic equality requires in terms of distributional equality may also improve our prospects for moral clarity on the vexed subject of remedial action and discrimination in general. But distributive justice is in some ways a separate topic. Its issues will not be resolved by simply making 'discrimination' the cause of every unequal result in welfare or happiness, or success.

Despite lack of clear agreement about what it is, equality's puzzles will continue to be debated in courts and parliaments. But the most helpful contributions, I think, will come from discussions which stand back a little from the practice of equality law and engage painstakingly, issue by issue, in a careful moral analysis which weighs up the competing demands of all our social values while insisting that there must be no distinctions which treat some as intrinsically more important than others.

Bibliography

Books

Albertyn, Cathi and Goldblatt, Beth 'Equality' in Stu Woolman et al. (eds) *Constitutional Law of South Africa* (2nd edn, Juta and Co Ltd, Cape Town, 2002) Ch. 35.

Anscombe, G.E.M. *Intention* (2nd edn, Basil Blackwell, Oxford, 1963).

Appiah, Kwame Anthony *The Ethics of Identity* (Princeton University Press, Princeton 2005).

Appiah, Kwame Anthony *Cosmopolitanism* (W.W. Norton and Co. Inc, New York, 2007).

Appiah, Kwame Anthony and Gutmann, Amy *Color Consciousness* (Princeton University Press, Princeton, 1996).

Aristotle, *The Politics* (Ernest Barker, rev R.F. Stalley, Oxford World Classics, Oxford, 1995).

Ayer, A.J. *Language Truth and Logic* (Pelican Books, Harmondsworth, 1971).

Ayer, A.J. *The Central Questions of Philosophy* (Penguin Books, Harmondsworth, 1976).

Barclay, Linda 'Liberalism and Diversity' in *The Oxford Handbook of Contemporary Philosophy* (Oxford, London, 2005) 155, 159.

Barry, Brian *Culture and Equality* (Harvard University Press, Cambridge, 2001).

Benn, Stanley 'Egalitarianism and the Equal Consideration of Interests' in J. Roland Pennock and John Chapman (eds) *Nomos* IX *Equality* (Atherton Press, New York, 1967).

Benson, Ophelia and Stangroom, Jeremy *Why Truth Matters* (Continuum, London, 2006).

Bergmann, Barbara R. *In Defense of Affirmative Action* (Basic Books, New York, 1996).

Berlin, Isaiah *Four Essays on Liberty* (Oxford University Press, Oxford, 1969).

Blackburn, Simon *Ruling Passions* (Oxford University Press, Oxford, 1998).

Blackburn, Simon *Spreading the Word* (Oxford University Press, Oxford, 1984).

Blackburn, Simon *Truth* (Allen Lane, London, 2005).

Bok, Derek and Bowen, William G. *The Shape of the River* (Princeton University Press, Princeton, 1998).

Capaldi, Nicholas *Out of Order: Affirmative Action and the Crisis of Doctrinaire Liberalism* (Prometheus Books, New York, 1985).

Carrithers, Michael *Why Humans Have Cultures* (Oxford University Press, New York, 1992).

Chemerinsky, Erwin *Constitutional Law* (3rd edn, Aspen Publishers, New York, 2006).

Devins, Neal and Davison, Douglas M. 'Introduction' in Neal Devins and Douglas M. Davison (eds) *Redefining Equality* (Oxford University Press, New York, 1998).

Diamond, Jarod *Guns, Germs and Steel* (Vintage, London, 1998).

Dworkin, Ronald *Taking Rights Seriously* (Duckworth, London, 1977).

Dworkin, Ronald *A Matter of Principle* (Harvard University Press, Cambridge, 1985).

Dworkin, Ronald *Law's Empire* (Fontana Press, London, 1986).

Dworkin, Ronald *Life's Dominion* (Vintage Books, New York, 1994).

Dworkin, Ronald *Freedom's Law* (Oxford University Press, Oxford, 1996).

Dworkin, Ronald 'Do Liberty and Equality Conflict?' in Paul Barker (ed.) *Living as Equals* (Oxford University Press, Oxford, 1996).

Dworkin, Ronald *Sovereign Virtue* (Harvard University Press, Cambridge, 2000).

Eastland, Terry *Ending Affirmative Action* (Basic Books, New York, 1996).

Epstein, Richard A. *Forbidden Grounds: The Case Against Employment Discrimination Laws* (Harvard University Press, Cambridge, 1992).

Eisgruber, Christopher and Sager, Lawrence *Religious Freedom and the Constitution* (Harvard University Press, Cambridge, 2007).

Ezorsky, Gertrude *Racism and Justice* (Cornell University Press, New York, 1991).

Faundez, Julio *Affirmative Action* (International Labour Organisation, Geneva, 1994).

Fiscus, Ronald *The Constitutional Logic of Affirmative Action* (Duke University Press, Durham, 1992).

Flew, Anthony *The Politics of Procrustes* (Temple Smith, London, 1981).

France, Anatole *Le Lys rouge* (Calman-Levy, 1927).

Frankena, William 'The Concept of Social Justice' in R. Brandt (ed.) *Social Justice* 17 (Prentice-Hall, Englewood Cliffs, 1962) 1.

Fraser, Steven 'Introduction' in Steven Fraser (ed.) *The Bell Curve Wars* (Basic Books, New York, 1995) 1.

Fredman, Sandra *Discrimination Law* (Oxford University Press, Oxford, 2002).

Gardener, Howard 'Cracking Open the IQ Box' in Steven Fraser (ed.) *The Bell Curve Wars* (Basic Books, New York, 1995) 23.

Girvin, S.D. 'Race and Race Classification' in A.J. Rycroft (ed.) *Race and the Law in South Africa* (Juta and Co Ltd, Johannesburg, 1987) 1.

Gould, Stephen Jay 'Curveball' in Steven Fraser (ed.) *The Bell Curve Wars* (Basic Books, New York, 1995) 11.

Grayling, Anthony *What is Good?* (Weidenfeld and Nicolson, London, 2003).

Gutmann, Amy *Identity in Democracy* (Princeton University Press, Princeton, 2003) 38.

Hare, R.M. *Moral Thinking* (Clarendon Press, Oxford, 1981).

Herrnstein, Richard J. and Murray, Charles *The Bell Curve* (The Free Press, New York, 1994).

Hogg, Peter W. *Constitutional Law of Canada* (4th edn, Thompsons Carswell, Scarborough, 1997).

Hume, David *A Treatise of Human Nature* (L.A. Selby Bigge (ed.) Oxford University Press, Oxford, 1888).

Huscroft, Grant 'Freedom from Discrimination' in Paul Rishworth et al. (eds) *The New Zealand Bill of Rights* (Oxford University Press, Melbourne, 2003) 366.

Huscroft Grant 'Freedom of Expression' in Paul Rishworth et al. (eds) *The New Zealand Bill of Rights* (Oxford University Press, Melbourne, 1993) 308.

Innes, Duncan et al. (eds) *Power and Profit* (Oxford University Press, Cape Town, 1992).

Kentridge, Janet 'Equality' in Chaskalson et al. (eds) *Constitutional Law of South Africa* (Juta and Co Ltd, Cape Town, 1996) Ch. 14.

Kohn, Marek *The Race Gallery* (Jonathan Cape, London, 1995).

Kymlicka, Will *Contemporary Political Philosophy* (Oxford University Press, Oxford, 1990).

Kymlicka, Will *Multicultural Citizenship* (Oxford, Oxford University Press, 1995).

Kymlicka, Will *Contemporary Political Philosophy* (2nd edn, Oxford University Press, Oxford, 2002).

Leibowitz, David and Spitz, Derek 'Human Dignity' in Chaskalson et al. (eds) *Constitutional Law of South Africa* (Juta and Co Ltd, Cape Town, 1996).

Levy, Jacob T. 'Classifying Cultural Rights' in Ian Shapiro and Will Kymlicka *Ethnicity and Group Rights* (New York University Press, New York, 1997).

Lilla, Mark et al. *The Legacy of Isaiah Berlin* (The New York Review of Books, New York, 2001).

Loury, Glenn C. *The Anatomy of Racial Inequality* (Harvard University Press, Cambridge, 2002).

Mackie, J.L. *Ethics: Inventing Right and Wrong* (Penguin Books, Harmondsworth, 1977).

MacKinnon, Catherine *Only Words* (Harper Collins, London, 1994).

McDonald, Margaret 'Natural Rights' (1947) reprinted in Jeremy Waldron (ed.) *Theories of Rights* (Oxford University Press, Oxford, 1984).

McCrudden, Christopher 'Changing Notions of Discrimination' in Stephen Guest and Alan Milne (eds) *Equality and Discrimination* (Franz Steiner Verlag Wiesbaden GMBH, Stuttgart, 1985) 83.

Meyerson, Denise *Rights Limited* (Juta and Co Ltd, Cape Town, 1997).

Mills, Nicolaus (ed.) *Debating Affirmative Action* (Dell Publishing, New York, 1994).

Moore, George Edward *Principia Ethica* (Cambridge University Press, Cambridge, 1959).

Nisbet, Richard 'Race, IQ and Scientism' in Steven Fraser (ed.) *The Bell Curve Wars* 36.

Nozick, Robert *Anarchy, State and Utopia* (Blackwell, Oxford, 1975).

Nussbaum, Martha *Liberty of Culture* (Basic Books, New York, 2008).

Parfit, Derek 'Equality or Priority' in Matthew Clayton and Andrew Williams (eds) *The Ideal of Equality* (Macmillan Press, Basingstoke, 2000).

Pennock, J. Roland 'Introduction' in J. Roland Pennock and John W. Chapman (eds) *Nomos* IX *Equality* (Atherton Press, New York, 1967).

Pinker, Steven *The Blank Slate* (Penguin Books, New York, 2002).

Pojman, Louis P. and Westmoreland, Robert (eds) *Equality* (Oxford University Press, New York, 1997).

Post, Robert and Rogin, Michael (eds) *Race and Representation* (Zone Books, New York, 1998).

Rashdall, Hastings *The Theory of Good and Evil* (2nd edn, vol. 1, Oxford University Press, Oxford, 1924).

Rawls, John *A Theory of Justice* (Oxford University Press, Oxford, 1971).

Rawls, John *The Law of Peoples* (Harvard University Press, Cambridge, 2001).

Raz, Joseph *The Morality of Freedom* (Clarendon Press, Oxford, 1986).

Rishworth, Paul et al. *The New Zealand Bill of Rights* (Oxford University Press, Melbourne, 2003).

Sandel, Michael *Justice* (Penguin Books, London, 2009).

Scruton, Roger *A Dictionary of Political Thought* (Macmillan Press, London, 1996).

Scruton Roger *Animal Rights and Wrongs* (Metro Books, London, 2000)

Searle, John R. *The Construction of Social Reality* (Penguin Books, London, 1995).

Sen, Amartya *Identity and Violence* (Penguin Books, London, 2007).

Sen, Amartya *The Idea of Justice* (Harvard University Press, Cambridge, 2009).

Singer, Peter *Animal Liberation* (3rd edn, Jonathan Cape, London, 2002).

Singer, Peter *Practical Ethics* (2nd edn, Cambridge University Press, Cambridge, 1993).

Sowell, Thomas *Race and Culture* (Basic Books, New York, 1994).

Sowell, Thomas *Conquests and Cultures* (Basic Books, New York, 1998).

Sowell, Thomas *Affirmative Action Around the World* (Yale University Press, New Haven, 2004).

Thernstrom, Stephan and Thernstrom, Abigail *America in Black and White* (Simon and Schuster, New York, 1997).

Thompson, Leonard *A History of South Africa* (Yale University Press, New Haven, 1995).

Vlastos, Gregory 'Justice and Equality' in R. Brandt (ed.) *Social Justice* 17 (Prentice-Hall, Englewood Cliffs, 1962) 31.

Waldron, Jeremy *God Locke and Equality* (Cambridge University Press, Cambridge, 2002).

Waldron, Jeremy 'Indirect Discrimination' in Stephen Guest and Alan Milne (eds) *Equality and Discrimination* (Franz Steiner Verlag Wiesbaden GMBH, Stuttgart, 1985) 93.

Walzer, Michael *Spheres of Justice* (Martin Robertson & Company Ltd, Oxford, 1983).

Warnke, Georgia *After Indentity* (Cambridge University Press, Cambridge, 2007).

Weinstein, James 'An American's View of the Canadian Hate Speech Decisions' in W.J. Waluchow (ed.) *Free Expression* (Clarendon Press, Oxford, 1994) 175.

West, Robin *Re-Imagining Justice* (Ashgate Publishing Limited, Aldershot, 2003).

Westen, Peter *Speaking of Equality* (Princeton University Press, Princeton, 1990).

Williams, Bernard 'The Idea of Equality' in Peter Laslett and W.G. Runciman (eds) *Philosophy Politics and Society* (Basil Blackwell, Oxford, 1972).

Williams, Bernard *Ethics and the Limits of Philosophy* (Fontana Press, London, 1985).

Wong, David 'Relativism' in Peter Singer (ed.) *A Companion to Ethics* (Blackwell, Oxford, 1993) 442.

Woolman, Stu 'Dignity', in Woolman, Roux, Klaaren, Stein and Chaskalson, *Constitutional Law of South Africa* (2nd edn, Jutas, Cape Town, 2002) Ch. 36.

Young, Iris Marion *Justice and the Politics of Difference* (Princeton University Press, Princeton, 1990).

Journal Articles

Adam, Kanya 'The Politics of Redress: South African Style Affirmative Action', (1997) 35 (2) *The Journal of Modern African Studies* 231.

Alexander, Larry 'What Makes Wrongful Discrimination Wrong? Biases, Preferences, Stereotypes, and Proxies' (1992) 141 *U Pa L Rev* 149.

Anderson, Elizabeth S. 'Integration, Affirmative Action, and Strict Scrutiny' (2002) 77 *N Y U L Rev* 1195.

Anderson, Elizabeth S. 'From Normative to Empirical Sociology in the Affirmative Action Debate: Bowen and Bok's *The Shape of the River*' (2000) 50 (2) *J Legal Educ* 286.

Anderson, Elizabeth S. 'What is the Point of Equality?' (1999) 109 *Ethics* 287.

Barnard, Catherine and Hepple, Bob 'Substantive Equality' (2000) 59 *Cambridge L J* 562.

Collins, Hugh 'Discrimination, Equality and Social Inclusion' (2003) 66 *M L R*, 16.

Delgado, R. 'Affirmative Action as a Majoritarian Device: Or, Do You Really Want to be a Role Model?' (1991) 89 *Mich L Rev* 1224.

Dworkin, Ronald 'Is There a Right to Pornography?', (1981), 1 (2), *Oxford Journal of Legal Studies* 177.

Dworkin, Ronald 'Women and Pornography' (1993) 40 (17) *New York Review of Books* 38.

Fabre, Cecile 'Book Review of *God Locke and Equality*' *M L R* May 2003 470.

Fagan, Anton 'Dignity and Unfair Discrimination: A Value Misplaced and a Right Misunderstood' (1998) 14 *SAJHR* 220.

Feldman, David 'Human Dignity as a Legal Value, Part 1' (1999) *Winter Pub L* 682.

Feldman, David 'Human Dignity as a Legal Value Part 2' (2000) *Spring Pub L* 61.

Flynn, James R. 'Group Differences: Is the Good Society Possible?' (1996) 28 *Journal of Biosocial Science* 573.

Frug, Mary Joe 'Sexual Equality and Sexual Difference in American Law' (1992) 26 *New Eng L Rev* 665.

Grabham, Emily 'Law v Canada: New Directions for Equality Under the Canadian Charter' (2002) 22 *Oxford J. Legal Stud.* 641, 653.

Greenawalt, Kent '"Prescriptive Equality": Two Steps Forward' (1997) 110 *Harv L Rev* 1265.

Hart, H.L.A. 'Between Utility and Rights' (1979) 79 *Colum Law Rev* 828.

Huscroft, Grant 'Discrimination, Dignity, and the Limits of Equality' (2000) 9 *Otago Law Review* 697.

Kitcher, Philip 'Does Race have a Future?' (2007) (35) *Philosophy and Public Affairs* 293.

Levy, Jacob T. 'Liberal Jacobinism' (2004) 114 *Ethics* 318.

Littleton, Christina A. 'Restructuring Sexual Equality' (1987) 75 *CLR* 1279.

Lye, Linda 'Title VII'S Tangled Tale: The Erosion and Confusion of Disparate Impact and the Business Necessity Defense' (1998) 19 *Berkeley J Emp & Lab L* 315.

O'Connell, Rory 'Cinderella Comes to the Ball: Art 14 and the Right to Non-discrimination in the ECHR' *Legal Studies* 29 (2) June 2009 211.

Peters, Christopher J. 'Equality Revisited' (1997) 110 *Harv L Rev* 1211.

Pojman, Louis P. 'Are Human Rights Based on Equal Human Worth?' (1992) 53 *Philosophy and Phenomenological Research* 605.

Réaume, Denise G. 'Discrimination and Dignity' (2003) 63 *La L Rev* 645.

Risse, Mathias and Zeckhauser, Richard 'Racial Profiling' (2004) 32 (2) *Philosophy and Public Affairs* 131.

Scheffler, Samuel 'What is Egalitarianism?' (2003) 31 *Philosophy and Public Affairs* 5.

Smith, Nicholas 'Affirmative Action under the New Constitution' (1995) 11 (1) *SAJHR* 84.

Stevenson, C.L. 'Persuasive Definitions' (1938) *XLVII Mind* 331.

Sunstein, C. 'The Anticaste Principle' (1994) 92 *Mich L Rev* 2410.

Waldron, Jeremy 'The Substance of Equality' (1991) 89 *Mich L Rev* 1350.

Waldron, Jeremy 'Superseding Historic Injustice' (1992) 103 *Ethics* 4.

Waldron, Jeremy 'Whose Nuremburg Laws?' review of Patricia Williams, *Seeing a Colourblind Future*, London Review of Books, 19 March 1998, 12.

Waldron, Jeremy 'How to Argue For a Universal Claim' (1999) 30 *Colum Hum Rts L Rev* 305, at 307.

Waldron, Jeremy 'The Logic of Cultural Accommodation' (2002) 59 *Washington and Lee Law Review* 3.

Westen, Peter 'The Empty Idea of Equality' (1982) 95 *Harv L Rev* 537.

Williams, Bernard 'From Freedom to Liberty: The Construction of a Political Value' (2001) 30 *Philosophy and Public Affairs* 3.

Williams, Joan C. 'Dissolving the Sameness Difference Debate: A Post-Modern Path Beyond Essentialism in Feminist and Critical Race Theory' (1991) *Duke L J* 296.
Valls, Andrew 'The Libertarian Case for Affirmative Action' (1999) 25 (2) *Social Theory and Practice* 299.

Cases

United States

Albemarle Paper Co. v *Moody* 422 US 405 (1975).
Brown v *Topeka Board of Education* 347 US 483 (1954).
Employment Division v *Smith* 494 US 872 (1990).
Griggs v *Duke Power Co.* 401 US 424 (1971).
Grutter v *Bollinger* 539 US 306, 343 (2003).
Metro Broad., Inc. v *FCC* 497 US 547 (1990).
Regents of the University of California v *Bakke* 438 US 265 (1978).
Sherbert v *Werner* 374 US 398 (1963).
United States v *Seeger* 380 US 163 1965.
Wards Cove Packing Co. v *Antonio* 490 US 642 (1989).

Canada

Law v *Canada (Minister of Employment and Immigration)* [1999] 1 SCR 497

South Africa

City Council of Pretoria v *Walker* 1998 (2) SA 363 (CC), 1998(3) BCLR 257 (CC).
President of the Republic of South Africa and Another v *Hugo* 1997 (6) BCLR 759 (CC); 1997 (4) SA 1 (CC).
Prinsloo v *van der Linde* 1997 (3) SA 300 (CC); 1997 (6) BCLR 759 (CC).

Other

Ackermann, L.W.H. 'Equality and the South African Constitution: The Role of Dignity' Bram Fischer lecture delivered at Rhodes House, Oxford, on 26 May, 2000.
Blackburn, Simon 'Universalizability' in *The Oxford Dictionary of Philosophy* (Oxford University Press, Oxford, 1996). Available at: http://www.oxfordreference.com/views/ENTRY.html?subview=Maientry=t98.e2435 [accessed: 20 March 2005].

Fredman, Sandra 'A Critical Review of the Concept of Equality in UK Anti-Discrimination Legislation' Working Paper No. 3, Cambridge Centre for Public Law and Judge Institute of Management Studies, November 1999.

Pojman, Louis P. 'The Case Against Affirmative Action'. Available at: http://www.dean.usma.edu./english/pojman/PublishedWorks/AffirmativeAction.html [accessed: 31 August 2005].

Rothman, Stanley, Lipset, Seymour Martin and Nevitte, Neil 'Racial Diversity Reconsidered'. Available at: http://www.thepublicintetrest.com/archives/2003spring/article2.html [accessed: 4 December 2005].

Waldron, Jeremy 'Basic Equality' (2008). New York University Public Law and Legal Theory Working Papers. Paper 107.

Index